Haim Gerber

Oppression and Salvation

STUDIEN ZUR SPRACHE, GESCHICHTE UND KULTUR DER TÜRKVÖLKER

Begründet von
György Hazai

Herausgegeben von
Pál Fodor, Barbara Kellner-Heinkele,
Simone-Christiane Raschmann

STUDIEN ZUR SPRACHE, GESCHICHTE UND KULTUR DER TÜRKVÖLKER

Band 27

Haim Gerber

Oppression and Salvation

Annotated Legal Documents from the Ottoman Book of Complaints of 1675

KLAUS SCHWARZ VERLAG • BERLIN

Bibliographic information published by the Deutsche Nationalbibliothek
The Deutsche Nationalbibliothek lists this publication
in the Deutsche Nationalbibliografie; detailed bibliographic data
are available in the internet at *http://dnb.dnb.de*

www.klaus-schwarz-verlag.com

First edition
Layout & Production: J2P Berlin
Printed in Hungary
ISBN 978-3-87997-472-6

Table of Contents

Acknowledgement

I thank Gerd Winkelhane, Klaus Schwarz Verlag's Managing Director and an Ottomanist, for supporting and encouraging this project, as well as for helping with the editing.

A note on transliteration

This study is heavily based on Turkish and Arabic terms, so that total consistency was impossible. I have opted to give "special status" to the term Shari'a (the Muslim sacred law). All other terms are transcribed according to the current rules in Modern Turkish.

Introduction

This book sets out to translate and edit a selection of Ottoman historical documents from the original old Ottoman language into English. The reference is to the documents of the Vienna Book of Complaints (*Şikayet Defteri*), a large volume of documents published by the Austrian Academy in 1984 in a facsimile form.[1] The volume contains some 2,800 summaries of documents that are for the most part orders about complaints from citizens (and citizen groups) about wrongs done to them by various state officials during the previous year, as well as the orders from the center (formally the Sultan, but in reality the *Divan*, which included the Grand Vizier and the chief dignitaries of the state, in effect the Ottoman government) relating to the means of addressing the problems raised. The story of how this volume found its way into the Austrian archive is, of course, fascinating in itself. Briefly (since the full story has been told by Professor Hans Georg Majer, the editor of the original German volume),[2] this volume accompanied the Ottoman Grand Vizier while on campaign in the Austrian front in 1675. As the campaign did not go well for the Ottomans, they eventually abandoned camp and withdrew, leaving behind many items, including this volume.

There is evidence that there was an intention to issue a translation of the volume (like calling it "volume 1"). It is understandable why this never materialized: the different handwritings in it are exceedingly difficult to decipher.[3] This is unfortunate, as it has caused the volume to be extremely under-researched, even though this is no doubt one of the most fascinating sources for information on Ottoman life and politics in the seventeenth century. That this volume deserves a full-length monograph to analyze its varied contents goes without saying. This study tries to partially fill this need by publishing a selection of 145 complaints, which are intended to be more or less a representative sample of the contents of the book. It must be emphasized that since the book has already been "published", my part here can only be the translation of chosen documents, rather than an editing in the full sense. In addition to providing a strong taste of the central issues covered in the book, brigandage and tax and related forms of oppression, I concentrate on some important aspects of the Ottoman legal system that inadvertently came to light in this volume.

1 Hans G. Majer, ed., *Das Osmanische Registerbuch der Beschwerden (Şikayet Defteri), vom Jahre 1675*, Verlag der Osterreichischen Akademie der Wissenschaften, Vienna, 1984.

2 Majer, *Şikayet Defteri*, Introduction.

3 Majer was aided in his work by a group of well-known Ottomanists, who together made a major contribution to the value of the book by deciphering all of the place names and indexing them. This in itself is a job of herculean proportions, which greatly facilitated my own work.

The phenomenon of complaints was a central tenet in the ideology of the Ottoman Empire, an obsession it inherited from former Middle Eastern empires, Islamic and pre-Islamic. Attention was directed in particular to the tendency of state officials to overstep the bounds of their authority, exploiting vast areas of the countryside and the extremely poor communication to enrich themselves at the expense of the poor citizens and, in the process, to undermine the legitimacy of the ruler himself. Halil Inalcık pointed out many years ago the centrality of the concept of justice (*adalet*) to the Ottoman state,[4] and recently, Linda Darling published a massive book showing that much of this ideology was succinctly summarized by the concept of "Circle of Justice", pointing out that the poor peasants were producing the wealth of the state, but if they were fleeced too much, everybody would be impoverished, the elite included; the ruler weakened; and in due course his legitimacy was undermined and his length of rule considerably shortened.[5] The practical problem was that those who taxed the people were officials, and the ability of the ruler to control them was problematic in the extreme. This is no doubt the key issue in this collection of documents, and in my view, it was also the key issue in Ottoman political life at the time.

I need to say a few things on the process of selection of the documents before proceeding. It is naïve to think that one can simply pick up any chance document and translate it. Although, with experience, many Ottomanists could understand the contents of most of the documents in the Book, scientific translation means deciphering every word of the document—no mean task at all. This, however, was the task to be performed if this book was to be published.

It is important for me to emphasize that strictly speaking the complaints themselves are not the focus of my interest, but rather the general idea that the complaints convey about the Ottoman Empire in the seventeenth century—its life problems, the relations between the small citizens and the government, and the like. To achieve this, I read the entire volume, minus the perhaps twenty percent that proved impossible to decipher. The sample that I chose to translate is meant to convey the unique flavor of the documents, many of the documents having a unique flavor in the form of one or two first person narrative sentences (so rare in the Ottoman archives) that seem authentic and are often sharp and edgy.

As I have said in the last paragraph, as I was reading the Book of Complaints (a very long process in any case), in time I became interested in something bigger than the complaints alone. It is true that it is difficult to think of something bigger than the contents of the complaints. One can read in the volume of terrible tax extortions committed by state officials against peasants that forced the

4 Halil Inalcık, *The Ottoman Empire*, London: Weidenfeld and Nicolson, 1973, pp. 65 ff.

5 Linda Darling, *A History of Social Justice and Political Power in the Middle East: The Circle of Justice from Mesopotamia to Globalization*, New York: Routledge, 2013.

victims to cry out that their ability to carry on is at an end and that they are facing dispersal and sure death in the near future again and again. It has been pointed out, and I entirely agree, that these cries may have been somewhat exaggerated, but my strong feeling is that they are not invented, but rather convey harsh realities. Abusers in the Book of Complaints never put it on record that their "good name" was being smeared by the peasants.

On the other hand, so many complaints of harsh abuses might give the impression that the Ottoman Empire in its entirety should have collapsed as a consequence. That this did not happen, should give us reason to ask, "Why not?" In fact, in the book of complaints itself, there is evidence of processes and people that worked against that abuse and deprivation of rights. Maybe the right image here is the Dutch boy who put his finger in a crack in the dam and saved the city. In our case, the elements that may have saved the day for the Ottoman Empire were the top bureaucrats, the officials of the *Divan* and their aids, and the top *ulema*, mainly Kadis (the Muslim judge). For these two elements, it was personal—the survival of the state was their chief social and political interest, and they did what it took to achieve its survival. The record shows that the Kadis were the chief tool the system used to stem the tide of deteriorating standards of government—ninety-nine percent of the complaints were sent back to the Kadi with an order to take care of the situation. Some critical scholars, particularly under the influence of American Realism, take other scholars to task for not providing a good explanation of the personal agendas of Kadis while practicing Ottoman-Islamic law. These scholars probably do not realize that supplying fair justice was a personal, material interest of the Kadi as much as of the Sultan, in as much as popular legitimacy was necessary for the survival of the state.[6] In addition, a large number of complaints were created in the Shari'a court because of a complaint to the kadi, and a large section of different complaints demanding that the kadi be the one to take care of things. The outcome of all this is that the Book of Complaints cannot really be understood without delving deeply into the role of the Kadis in it, and without recognizing that this is in fact a document that is above all a legal document. Rather than shunning legal issues as has been done by most scholars, I decided to make the extra effort and adopt this point of view, which in any case really means looking at politics of law rather than the law proper.

In the first place, the *Şikayet Defteri* is a legal document because many of the complaints stem from the point of departure that a certain Shari'a law has been broken, violating the natural rights of certain groups of citizens. More important

6 See Kristen Stilt, "Price Setting and Hoarding in Mamluk Egypt: The Lessons of Legal Realism for Islamic Legal Studies", in Peri Bearman et al., eds., *The Law Applied*, London: Tauris, 2008, pp. 57-77.

than this, however, the *Şikayet* is a legal document from an additional, methodological perspective: the document provides a perspective on the Kadi, his court, and his position in the state, which are unlikely to be obtained from any other source. Particularly, such information cannot be had from the Kadi record (*sicill*) itself, as this source only looks at itself from the inside, solving day-to-day problems. We do not know what the common people really thought of the kadi court and of the Kadi himself. We also do not know much about how the central government perceived the role of the Kadi. Inadvertently, the *Şikayet* supplies plenty of insights on these issues. It was for these reasons that I decided to look at the complaints with a broader view than that confined to the narrative of abuses.

In addition to shining a light on the kadi court, the Book of Complaints also supplies us with several insights on important issues in Ottoman-Islamic law, insights that neither the *Divan* secretaries nor the complainants intended, but that are nevertheless there. It would be a shame not to elucidate them. Ironically, the research of all these seemingly side issues does not create a distance from our main concern, which is how the Ottoman system dealt with the problem of abuses and corruption, but rather attacks the same problem from different angels to finally converge on the main point, which is the position of the Kadi in the Ottoman legal and political world.

Former Studies of the Complaints Literature

Suraiya Faroqhi is the main scholar who has grappled with a source similar to the complaints literature to date.[7] In her important article, Faroqhi points out that presenting the ruler with complaints about wrongs done to them was one of the most basic rights of citizens. This idea stood in opposition to a basic idea in Ottoman society: that society was naturally divided into two parts, each occupied by a different class—at the apex stood the *askers*, or members of the administrative-military elite, and at the bottom stood the citizens, or *reaya*, who were actually devoid of any rights. The *askers* filled all the administrative posts and collected all the taxes that were to be collected, and in all probability, most of them thought that they were allowed to do anything. As far as they were concerned, the simple citizens had no rights at all, and a peasant not respecting their position and striving to climb the social ladder to become an *asker* was the worst type of social mayhem possible. The common people knew that this was actually far from being the case, however. The common people had a set of rights vouchsafed by the Shari'a, Islamic law that no one, not even the Sultan, had the right to violate without specific legal justification. A man (and a woman)

7 Suraiya Faroqhi, "Political Activity among Ottoman Taxpayers and the Problem of Sultanic Legitimation, (1570–1650)", *Journal of the Economic and Social History of the Orient*, 35 (1992), pp. 1-39.

were innocent unless a proper charge was brought against them in a Shari'a law case and properly proven. If *reaya* were wronged in this regard, they were quick to launch complaints and send them to the Sultan.

Though Faroqhi uses another source than the one used in this study (her source is the *Mühimme Defteri*), a register of the "Important Things" going on between the center and the provinces, there is a far reaching resemblance between her complaints and mine. In both cases the main abuses were tax extortions imposed mainly on the peasantry, pocketed mainly by provincial governors and their aids. It seems that in 1675, however, the situation worsened, as in company with tax extortion there came a whole set of other serious abuses. The main tool of tax abuses seems to have been the same, the tour (*devir*), conducted by an army unit of mounted, armed soldiers extorting money and provisions, often even living in the peasants' houses. In both cases, there was a threat of emigration made to the center in case the extortion continued. However, again in 1675, there was the additional threat of death to the taxpayers, with an obvious added moral blemish on the central power, which knew what was going on and did not stop it. In 1675, there was also evidence that these were not just threats, but that these things had already taken place. In 1675, as in the late sixteenth century, one senses that an element of exaggeration is involved, especially in regards to the last point.

Another publication that tackled the subject of complaints is Michael Ursinus' collection of documents from the Rumeli province in the later part of the eighteenth century.[8] The structure of the institution in this case is quite different from that of the Vienna Book of Complaints, but we nevertheless deal with complaints, and in that sense, it deserves a brief comment. The complaints found by Ursinus were not sent to the central government but to the provincial governor of the Rumeli Province in the Balkans. At the beginning of his study, Ursinus suggests that this would indicate that the Ottoman government in fact expected governors to adjudicate. Later, however, he seems to have second thoughts on this, taking a cue from an earlier phase in the history of the same province, where evidence shows that when a complaint came to the province that required a trial, a Kadi would be invited to conduct an ordinary shar'i trial, rather than the governor being the judge himself. In any case, the complaints in Ursinus's collection do not bear a close connection to the complaints in the Vienna Book of Complaints because most of the complaints in the Rumeli province collection are of minor importance and for the most part, consist of complaints against private individuals, state authority being absent altogether. This means that the *Divan* would probably not even consider dealing with these documents,

8 Michael Ursinus, *Grievance Administration (Şikayet) in an Ottoman Province*, London: Royal Asiatic Society Books, 2005

which makes them a different phenomenon from the ones dealt with in this work.

Halil Inalcık has published two studies that touch on the topic of complaints. Inalcık has published an important collection of what may be called "Justice Rescripts" (*Adaletnameler*), that is, general orders sent out to the provinces that notified everybody of widespread abuses recently detected throughout the state and warned all provincial governors of the dire consequences of not attending to the problem with the utmost diligence. Many of the abuses mentioned in the Justice Rescripts are mentioned in the complaints analyzed by Faroqhi and by the collection translated here. Faroqhi is right to point out that there is no doubt that the people who handled the complaints in the sixteenth century (and in 1675) were probably aware of the earlier rescripts.[9] Inalcık also published a useful study that analyzes a sample of complaints from a diplomatic point of view.[10]

The Book's Structure and Contents

The Introductory Chapters

Several preliminary chapters seemed necessary to write in order to facilitate understanding of the documents of the Book of Complaints. In chapter 1, I deal with the structure of the Ottoman-Islamic legal institutions as I see them today. As already noted above, the complaints are in the first place legal documents, since they narrate the violation of legal rights and seek their restoration. However, they become even "more legal" in nature (if this is possible) with the legal twist I have chosen to add to the reading of the documents. This reading is in the documents; but possibly most readers would ignore these points as maybe too tedious. I think they are extremely important and also fascinating. In any case, in these introductory notes I explain how and why the chapter on law is important to further the understanding of the *Şikayet* documents.

Let me start by reiterating that the *Şikayet* is a legal document of importance because its distinct hero is the Kadi, the Islamic judge. From the point of view of both the central government and the common people, the Kadi was the supertanker of solving the abuses created by state officials, both in terms of ability and trust placed in him, particularly by the common people—a highly sensitive and reliable barometer in my view. Why did the common people feel such positive feeling towards the Kadi? It must have had something to do with the impression created by the Kadi in his handling of the court and the legal system. An appreciation of the daily quality of justice supplied by the Kadi is an absolute

9 Halil Inalcık, "Adaletnameler", *Belgeler*, 2 (1965), pp. 49-145.

10 Halil Inalcık, "Şikayet Hakkı: Arz-ı Hal ve Arz-ı Mahzarlar", *Osmanlı Araştırmaları*, 7-8 (1988), pp. 33-54.

necessity here. I do this by addressing the quality of the Kadi's work as analyzed in some studies, and more statistically, by checking the class basis of trial outcomes to find out whether the Kadi was biased in this sense at all.

I also deal with the question of current procedure in the Shari'a court in this chapter. This again is made necessary by various themes appearing in the Book of Complaints. In countless documents in the book the complaining people say, though nothing has been proven against us by means of just witnesses (*şuhud udul*), we were victims of such and such an act. It is not just a statement in the sense that one is assumed innocent unless proven guilty, but there is a specific procedure to prove guilt. That procedure was by formal trial before the Kadi, not the unformed and personal intuition of the Kadi, but via exact witnessing of objective witnesses carefully screened by the Kadi for reliability. This sounds like a plea for a formal application of the law, nothing less. This is enhanced by another topic in the Book of Complaints: Complaints against deputy judges (*naibs*), specifically the local judges or those hired locally. Many of these judges managed to serve for many years, ingratiating themselves with state officials, and we have seen that the *Divan* itself related to those as "trouble". The reference is obviously to the middling echelons of the provincial bureaucracy. To return to the *naibs*, their closeness to officials led to the loss of money for the poor citizens in all sorts of ways. Thus, close personal ties were again a source of corruption and frowned upon by the center. If we also remember that the quick transfer of officials and judges from one place to another was always one of the cornerstones of the Ottoman administration and governance (expressly explained by the dangers of close acquaintances and resulting friendships), then we must realize that for the Ottomans, to say that their law was based on a tendency towards formalism, was not a denigration at all; strict application of the law was for them a virtue, not a fault. Any personal approach would be tantamount to opening the floodgates of corruption. If you, as Kadi, wanted to develop personal relations with your poor subalterns, the price was that you also had to develop relations with members of the upper class. Thus, one of "our" complaints—hailing ironically, though entirely by chance, from Ayntab—shows a man who complained that an Ayntab strong man (*zi kudret*) killed his brother, and demanded that the *Divan* transfer the case to Maraş, fearing an undue influence on the court. Incredibly, the wish was granted. It is in this context that I analyze a register of the Bursa Kadi *sicill* that has been published in its entirety recently, down to the names of the court witnesses, a most useful additional element for the present study. As far as can be assessed, the procedure was indeed formal and exact, with very little room for the personal touch of a judge, if at all.

One major study that creates some waves and possible innovations in this regard is Leslie Peirce's study of sixteenth century Ayntab, which I analyze in this chapter. My conclusion is that perhaps Peirce exaggerated somewhat the extent to which Ayntab was exceptional.

In Chapter 2, I present a summary of the position of the Kadi and the *ulema* after the disappearance of the Abbasid Empire in 1258. The animosity between state and scholars that characterized the former period was no longer to be observed. While the scholars under much of classical Islam suffered from a great reduction in their authority with the rise of the *mazalim* court (most of this period their authority was in fact confined to personal status and in religious endowments), the situation changed completely under the Ottomans; no *mazalim* court was ever established, and the Imperial *Divan* did not take its place, as we shall see in this study. Not only was the authority of the Kadis not impaired by other tribunals, their authority was greatly extended to include customary areas that had nothing to do with the Shari'a; for example, for the guilds, this new area of law was not regulated by the Shari'a and behaved in alignment with its own customary law. In addition, the Ottomans allowed the rise of a new office holder called the *şeyhülislam* that became a powerful legal councilor in time that had the right to depose Sultans that crossed the legal line—in their estimation. Indeed, in the seventeenth century, about six depositions of Sultans took place, bringing the scholars' power to its all-time peak. All of this is necessary background information to understand why the Kadi's role in the book of complaints was so prominent.

In chapter 3, I present a general study of the Book of Complaints according to the topics that interest me in this book. I deal mainly with the main topics that seem to me important in the *Şikayet*, such as the question of the standing of the Kadis with the common people of the empire, and the all-important topic of the efforts made by officials to arrogate to themselves adjudicatory authorities and the efforts of Kadi and top officials to resist this tendency.

The Documents: Subjects and Chapters

Chapter 4: Tax Oppression and Brigandage

Though I have said that as far as I am concerned the main topic of the collection is Ottoman-Muslim law and politics as they are revealed in it, any such collection must devote proper attention to the two topics that are most preponderant in it: oppression via over-taxation (*zülüm* in Ottoman Turkish parlance) and brigandage (*eşkıyalık* in the same parlance). In both cases, the terms are dismal oversimplifications, since only the actual documents show the full profusion of the abusers' imagination in inventing ever new forms of extortion and molestation, all of them with a full range of pretexts inventing legal-looking cover and explanations for their use. In fact, the legal pretexts endlessly used by the abusers are another reason why a legal perspective is crucial to understand this collection of documents. The other main topic was complaints against brigands, who roamed the countryside and terrorized it, usually organized in bands of several scores, headed by a highly charismatic figure. They plundered lone travelers on the roads, marginal houses in villages, and sometimes assaulted and burned down whole villages. It goes without saying that often they killed people, thus committing the most pernicious crime on the Islamic and Ottoman law-books: highway robbery with murder. The complaints related to this topic were not against the authority of course, but certainly it was the supreme responsibility of the Muslim ruler to keep the roads safe, which means that, in a way, the complaints were pointed at the ruler and his officials. No one ever suggested that it was not the fault of the government that the Ottoman countryside in the seventeenth century was infested with brigands to an incredible degree.

It is next to impossible to assess with any exactness the harm done by brigands and tax abusers to the Ottoman economy and morale because any basis for comparison is lacking. However, it seems quite obvious that the damage was huge and long lasting. If left unchecked, it probably could have ruined the state altogether. The complaints edited here, however, show that it was addressed and quite vigorously. How vigorous exactly this intervention was, is again, impossible to say, but it certainly had some effects. It is enough to observe (in our documents) that several abusers went out of their way to intercept, capture, incarcerate, and if possible, even kill actual or potential complaint-makers. Something was done about the complaints, because, as we have seen, treating the lower classes justly was the cornerstone of the Ottoman Empire's public policy, and we can trust that this was a sincere policy because the basic idea of the "circle of justice" was well entrenched by then. Additionally, it was a reasonable and almost trivial idea that no one had any reason to question. For the top bureaucrats and top *ulema*, the idea of the "circle of justice" was by then a cornerstone of their intuitive assumption that their personal fate was tied to the fate of the Ottoman state and dynasty in an inseparable way.

Chapter 5: The Kadi and the Common People

Most of the *Şikayet* documents ended up as tasks in the hands of the Kadi, with an order to solve the problem. It must be said, however, that the Kadi was usually not the only addressee. In about half of the cases, the other addressee along with the Kadi was the civil-military governor. When one checks what was actually said in the document, however, the reference to the governor is quite rare, while the reference to the Kadi is commonplace. The Kadi should check, investigate, issue court document (*huccet*), adjudicate, and so on and so forth. However, the role of the Kadi went much further than this. In several cases the complaints started as a common plea to the Kadi launched by a village or even a greater area. The Kadi organized the transfer of the complaint to the center, sending it with his own accompanying letter that also usually included an appeal that the order to investigate the complaint be given to the Kadi. This, and several more indicators show that the common people at this time still believed in the integrity of the judges with all their hearts, despite the existence of rotten apples. This approach did not come from outer space. No one ever said, "We want the justice of the governor or the *subaşı*." The only demand was for *şuhud udul*, that is, the Shari'a court and a formal process within the Shar'. No one asked for a compromise, only for a formal process. They made it clear, that if you did not have something against them backed by "just witnesses", they should be left alone.

Chapter 6: (In)justice by State Officials

It is an old and well-known myth that provincial governors in the Ottoman Empire doubled as judges and pursued this line of activity whenever they felt like it. The complaints in the Book of Complaints seem to contradict this idea, however. To say it more carefully, these documents do not confirm that the central government approved of this activity or did not see harm in it. On the contrary, it saw it as harmful and pernicious, and would much prefer that the phenomenon did not exist. Let us say clearly that we do not really know what went on in provincial offices, so one may claim that many provincial governors implemented fair and just proceedings there. However, according to several documents in the Book of Complaints, if a governor wanted to have a fair shar'i trial in front of him, he would have invited a Kadi to be present and ordered him to conduct a shar'i trial. Nothing else seems to make sense, since none of the governors knew how to locate witnesses and how to screen them for reliability. Additionally, certainly only Kadi had the expertise to decide which of the parties should have the right to take an oath, just to cite another example. So, if the governor wanted to be fair in his conduct, the outcome would be a Shari'a court case. If, on the other hand, the governor did not care about the niceties of the Shari'a law, he invented penalties that cost his citizens a great deal of money; inventions that were the subject of severe criticism from the central government. Logically, the central government might have retorted: "Well, he is a judge; his right is to decide whatever he wishes." Quite simply, such an approach was never taken. Every such act was vehemently rejected as illegal and forbidden.

Chapter 7: Complaints Against Kadis and *Naibs* (Assistant Judges)

In a small number of cases in the Book of Complaints, the object of complaint is the Kadi himself, though more often it is the deputy judge (*naib*). Usually the reason for the complaint is that the Kadi exacted more than the legal rate from the citizens when he was issuing court documents (*huccet*), or charging more for various services performed by the court, such as the division of estates and the like. In a very small number of cases, the charge was that of perverting the course of justice in a real sense, for example, by accepting bribes in deciding cases. It is rather difficult to evaluate how this was possible, given that every case was attended by professional witnesses who had to sign at the bottom of the document, vouching for its integrity.

Chapter 8: The Shar'i Legal Process: Final?

One of the interesting questions in the legal literature on Ottoman-Muslim law is that of review: was review legal and was it practiced in reality? A related question is, without consideration for judicial review, was the trial conducted before a Kadi considered final, or could any person involved go to another court and raise the issue anew, as if no similar discussion of this issue ever took place? This last question is of course highly relevant to the position of the Kadi in this legal system, for if litigants could indeed pursue the same issue again and again, hardly anything remains of the Kadi's authority. Judicial review is also a form of limitation on the Kadi's authority, but at least in an orderly and bureaucratic fashion. It is clear then, that the question is highly important. The good news is that the Book of Complaints, inadvertently of course, contains several cases that help elucidate the approach of the system to this question.

In general, Islamic law has vague references to judicial review, and although the debate comes up from time to time, a definitive solution is still lacking. As to Ottoman law, a vague situation is currently happening as well. Recently, Rossitsa Gradeva addressed this issue by pointing out that the Kadi of Sofia had a higher degree in Islamic scholarship (*ilm*) than other local Kadis, and she assumes that this meant judicial review; but no specific case was put forward as proof. In my estimation, the documents of the Book of Complaints show that, as far as the central government was concerned, adjudication of a case a second time was strictly forbidden. Judicial review was something else—by express permission of the Sultan, the *Divan* could and would serve as the forum where this took place, though to my knowledge, no one has been able to provide a concrete example. High profile cases that for some reason were difficult to adjudicate in the provinces were brought to the *Divan*, and a top Kadi in Istanbul was brought to adjudicate them. The supremacy of the Kadi remained, and was considered indispensable.

Chapter 9: The Agent (*mübaşir*)

An additional officeholder that appears a considerable number of times in the documents is the *agent*, or *mübaşir*, a powerful person nominated by the central government to negotiate between people locked in seemingly hard conflicts. The *mübaşir* is supposed to smooth over such difficulties. How did he do that, and was it at the expense of the authorities of the Kadi? This topic was discussed by Michael Ursinus; most of the cases in the collection of complaints presented to the governor of Rumelia at the end of the eighteenth century were entrusted to a *mübaşir*, though we do not know how they were dealt with. These complaints, however, were for the most part small complaints of individuals against other individuals. The situation was entirely different in our case; quite a few cases in our complaints give concrete descriptions of the role of the agent. He was usually nominated to look after individuals who were intensely sought after, but most of the orders nominating him also clarified that his job was to additionally bring such sought after individuals to a shar'i trial. Thus, though the agent was a highly important aid to the Shari'a court in this period, he did not detract at all from the authority of the Kadi.

Chapter 10: The Role of the *Divan* in the Legal Process

In a number of documents in the Book of Complaints, we find that the order is to pass the issue to the *Divan-i Hümayun* for treatment—sometimes with, and sometimes without, the persons involved in the dispute. This raises anew the old issue of the authority of the *Divan* in legal matters. If we thought that the *Divan* was a regular, albeit supreme court, the documents at our disposal tell a different story altogether. What we see in practice, is that in many cases the *Divan* invites the parties together and organizes a perfectly ordinary shar'i trial by some of the Kadis of Istanbul. In other cases, matters that reached the *Divan* were particularly severe, though the documents do not make it clear what was done about them. My hunch is that after some clarifications, the issues were again put to Istanbul Kadis to sort out and adjudicate.

Chapter 11: Miscellaneous

Up until now, I have summarized topics that were connected with the two major issues of tax abuses and brigandage, as well as several topics that summarize aspects of the Ottoman legal system. In this last chapter in the collection, I discuss some documents that are not classifiable in these categories, and so I have labeled them "miscellaneous".

A Short Chronology of Ottoman History Until the End of the Seventeenth Century

The origin of the Ottoman Empire was as a tiny principality in Western Anatolia starting at an unknown year in the later part of the thirteenth century (the usual date given in the sources is 1290, but without evidence).[11] Since 1243, Anatolia was nominally under the control of the Mongols of Persia, who in that year defeated the Sultan of the Rum-Seljuk State that had been ruling in Anatolia. The Mongols, who for historical reasons (it must have been an influence of the later Crusades) were interested mainly in Egypt, left Western Anatolia to its own devices, only seeing to it that the Seljuks did not raise their head too defiantly again. Another regional empire, the Byzantines, also thought little of this region, particularly after 1260, when the ruling dynasty returned from exile in Nicaea, where it found refuge with the capture of Constantinople by the Fourth Crusade in 1204. The outcome was that Western Anatolia remained a no-man's land, where a series of localized principalities made an appearance, while probably making a strenuous effort to keep a low profile so as not to attract the wrath of the Mongols. Interestingly and surprisingly, the Mongols, who converted to Islam in 1295, remained focused (militarily speaking) on Egypt, and did not show any interest in Byzantium even after 1295. The Turkish principalities, on the other hand, were interested in nothing else. Is it possible that they were attracted to this direction, among other things, in order not to attract the attention of the Mongols?

The principalities, at their early stage, were apparently in between semi-nomadism and full-settlement. Their armies were still tribal in nature and expansive in character, particularly in the direction of Byzantium, the non-danger zone, as shown above. All those principalities with geographical interfaces with Byzantium were also militarily engaged against her. Of these principalities, the smallest and least well known was the Ottoman principality, centered in the area of North Western Anatolia and nearest of all of them to the now severely weakened Byzantium. This must have played a role in its expansion, as it attracted adventurist elements interested in war-booty, or elements interested in defending or expanding Islam—a one-dimensional approach here seems particularly out of place. All of these elements were folded into the Ottoman state, which, like every organization in history, was primarily interested in self-preservation and expansion.

In any case, at the beginning of the fourteenth century the Ottomans begin to expand in the direction of Byzantium, taking advantage of the relative weakness of that force in comparison to the other principalities that seemed stronger militarily. At the beginning, there was an effort to take cities within the area adjacent to them, such as Bursa in 1327 and a little later Nicaea and Nikomedia.

11 Good up-to-date accounts can be found in: Charles Melville, "Anatolia under the Mongols", and Rudi P. Lindner, "Anatolia, 1300–1450", both in Kate Fleet, ed., *The Cambridge History of Turkey*, vol. 1, Cambridge: Cambridge University Press, 2009, Chapters 3 and 4 respectively. Also central is Colin Imber's *The Ottoman Empire, 1300–1650*, Basingstoke: Pelgrave, 2009;

Around the middle of the century, they made the jump into Europe. Symbolically, this move was triggered by the Byzantines themselves, with one contending party inviting the Turks to help it against a rival party. The Ottomans had their own agenda, however, and once they established their bridgehead across the Dardanelles, they never looked back, but pushed forwards in the direction of Central Europe. At the same time, they also started to annex principalities in Anatolia.

The Taking of Constantinople

A conquest of central importance on the Ottoman road to greatness was the conquest of Constantinople/Istanbul, which was at the same time also a moment that shapes their self-perception. One is to be reminded, here, that in 1453 Constantinople was a remaining part of traditional Rome. This conquest came after several decades of minute preparations in 1453. At that time, all that remained of the once mighty Byzantium was that one city, and there was no support forthcoming from Western Europe. Byzantium was doomed against the Turkish population tide coming from Central Asia, now going on for four centuries.

Taking the Fertile Crescent

A crucial phase in the rise of the Ottoman Empire was the conquest of the Fertile Crescent, which took place in 1516–17. Apparently, provoked by the Mamluks who controlled Syria, the Ottomans invaded Northern Syria supplied with the best weapons in the world at that time, to find the Mamluks still relying on bows and arrows. In these conditions, the encounter between the two empires was not balanced, and the Ottomans defeated the Mamluks in two major encounters without further ado. As far as the Ottoman Empire was concerned, a seemingly side issue was particularly important: the Mamluk state at that time ruled the Hijaz in the Arabian Peninsula, were the two holiest shrines of Islam existed—Mecca and Medina. These shrines were then naturally annexed to the Ottoman state, providing a superb moral and ideological boost. As a non-Arab state, not even remotely connected to the tribe of Quraysh, they suffered from a real shortage of Islamic legitimation assets. Service of the two holiest shrines of Islam was a very important substitute and such service was no doubt an enormous logistical challenge, since by the early sixteenth century, large chunks of the globe had undergone conversion to Islam, particularly in South East Asia and Central Africa. This meant that the number of participants in the yearly pilgrimage to Mecca and Medina increased enormously. All of this was a supreme challenge to the organizers, who also had to contend with the threat of Bedouin attacks along the desert roads. The Ottomans assumed this enormous task without complaint, and shouldered it with enormous stamina until the end of the empire.

They also no doubt reaped the added legitimacy that this task conferred among Muslims the world over. It was a serious substitute for the title Caliph, which they could not have, and it took the form of an added title to the several the Sultan already had, that of, "servitor of the two holy Muslim shrines".

Süleyman the Magnificent and After

In the annals of the Ottoman Empire, one can differentiate quite easily between the periods of Süleyman the Magnificent (r. 1520–66), considered the Golden Age of the empire, and the period following it, considered the period of decline in the past. There is no doubt that there is something brilliant and highly attractive about the period of Süleyman, when everything seemed to go according to plan and exactly by the book, especially, to be honest, since we lack detailed archival studies on the daily life of people in this era. It is not impossible that the brilliance of the Süleymanic Era is also somewhat of a myth, created by the incessant stream of military victories. It is also possible that much of the Süleymanic aura was created by external factors, maybe even by the climatic situation, such as the extensive period of enhanced rainfall in the first part of the sixteenth century, which contributed to unprecedented demographic growth. In the later parts of the century, the rainfall declined, the population contracted, and the morale of the population may have reacted accordingly.

The Celali Revolts

An additional phenomenon to hit Ottoman society at the end of the so called golden age period, was the large scale popular revolts, called the Celali Revolts, that erupted all over the empire and lasted through the last decade of the sixteenth century and the first decade of the seventeenth century. A probable cause of these revolts was the over population that characterized the same period, with a large number of young peasants leaving their places of origin and roaming the countryside in search of targets to rob. These revolts were eventually put down with an iron fist at the end of the first decade of the seventeenth century, but the situation in Anatolia and the Balkan did not quiet for a long time. Revolts, either popular or by provincial governors, were rife throughout the century. In a way, it was an appropriate background to the picture depicted by the Book of Complaints.

The Question of Decline

As will be shown in the documents edited in this book, an intense theme in the politics of the late seventeenth century Ottoman Empire was the struggle of the Imperial Council (*Divan-i Hümayun*) and other groups within the central government (such as top *ulema*) against the debilitating effect of tax extortion by middling officials. This calls to mind the old topic of Ottoman decline, one of the most hotly debated issues in Ottoman historiography. The theory that reigned supreme in this field in the past was that after the reign of Sultan Süleyman (d. 1566), the grip of the center over the provinces and peripheries weakened considerably, and everywhere standards of good and honest administration fell, catastrophically so as time went by. This fall lasted in the empire until 1914, or at least until the early nineteenth century. The literature of the recent generation tends to view that chronology with suspicion, citing the extended longevity of the state after 1600 as a major factor speaking against it. Some researchers attack the question via empirical research, using large amounts of archival documents in the process. One distinct example is Şevket Pamuk, who studied levels of prices and personal income of workers in various areas of the empire between 1600 and the end of the empire.[12] The findings did not indicate one unrelieved period of decline; crises existed, but on the whole, the trend was one of a rise throughout the period—a finding not exactly commensurate with a general decline throughout the period. The writer himself sees his findings as relevant to the debate on decline, and suggests that these new facts indicate that the decline theorem was a past myth, borne of the fact that the Ottoman Empire did indeed suffer from severe problems in every field of life, but pointing out that several of these problems were tended to, and not without a certain measure of success.

There is, I believe, an important measure of connection between the decline theory and problem and the documents edited in this volume. Despite the relative success of the *Köprülü* Viziers, the documents of 1675 come on top of a political period of state crisis. In no other period of Ottoman history do we observe so many depositions of Sultans, and the great deal of social unrest surrounding these depositions. That the documents of the Book of Complaints then come and reveal so much oppression, tax extortion, much of it with violence and ill-treatment, can no doubt be seen as part of the crisis at the top of the system. There is hardly a doubt that the plight of the peasants was reflected in their incomes and on the general situation of the state. We should also look, however, in the Book of Complaints for the ways in which this crisis was not as catastrophic as formerly thought. The strenuous efforts of the central government to rescue a measure of good government from the jaws of deteriorating levels of government seems, on the face of it, to have borne some positive results—or else people of the lower classes would stop complaining altogether. Though it is of course an absurdity to claim that the work to stem the damage caused by abusers, discovered via the complaints, is what saved the Ottoman state in the long run, I am positive that it was part of the bigger picture.

12 Şevket Pamuk, *The Ottoman Economy and its Institutions*, Farnham: Ashgate Variorum, 2009, for example, Chapter 1.

Part I:
Background Studies

Chapter 1: Law and Order

We have seen in the Introduction that many of the documents edited here deal with law at their essence, and I have argued that this point should be pursued to the very end. I thought that it may be best to do this by writing an introductory chapter on Islamic-Ottoman law that will provide some background and trace the actual contact between Ottoman law and the Book of Complaints.

Immediately upon starting to read the Book of Complaints, we observe that the Kadi was the main hero of the book and of the phenomenon (complaining and dealing with complaints). The vast majority of the Sultanic orders issued in response to the complaints are directed at the Kadi alone, with specifications on how to act to resolve the issue at hand, although never encroaching on the Kadi's professional discretion, in as much as investigative authority and legal competence were concerned. Furthermore, when we carefully read the complaints that are also addressed to the provincial governor, the governor is almost never assigned anything to do, aside from assisting the Kadi. Moreover, many fine points hidden within the complaints show that the Kadi was quite popular with the common people of the empire, in provincial villages and towns, which meant an increased workload for them and more responsibility, and probably more legitimacy for the ruler that sent him. This is the major finding in this entire work. Obviously, it was the Kadi who was mainly expected to correct the wrong complained about, rather than, for example, provincial governors, who might be the potential source of a complaint. In fact, provincial governors were the targets of most of the complaints, and there was no happy legal pluralist scene where governors could alternate with Kadis as judges. It could not even be claimed that governors functioned as self-appointed judges who served the people with fairness and thereby avoided being detected by the historical record, because no group of citizens in our source ever asked to be judged by a provincial governor, while the Kadi was specifically asked for in a large number of cases. This is really a strong reminder that any balanced account of Ottoman law should start with the issue, not purely legal in fact, of the role of the Kadi, and the *ulema* in general, in the Ottoman legal system. Probably there took place a rise in the social role of the *ulema* in general in the Ottoman period. The rise and role of the *ulema* will be dealt with in the next chapter.

In this chapter, I marshal evidence from the legal field to try and elucidate the questions posed in this book. One such issue is the major crisis situation that bedeviled the empire in the seventeenth century (probably to some extent in the sixteenth and eighteenth centuries also), which consisted of the twin blights of large-scale tax oppression by state officials and large-scale brigandage in the countryside. Facing these two threats, the legal system of the Kadi not only shouldered much of the responsibility for dealing with the tax oppressors and the brigands, but it also kept the day to day of the law functioning. This indeed is an empirical question that this chapter seeks to explore—did the legal system deliver a bearable legal system to the people that lived under it? Put differently, it is interesting to show what the quality of justice supplied by these Kadis was, empirically speaking. If the policy of the Sultans (and their top bureaucrats) was to secure fair justice for the common people, it is interesting to see whether this really happened. This chapter will argue that the Ottoman state had an unusual interest in supplying its citizens with the maximum level of legal justice possible because, as it did not have an authentic aristocratic pedigree itself (like the Great Seljuks for example), it needed the law to provide legitimacy to enhance its reputation and prestige among its citizenry. I believe that this was indeed effective in enhancing their prestige among the people.

The rest of this chapter will deal with Ottoman law itself. I wrote a book on this topic in 1994 (based on original documentation, as well as some excellent legal studies already available, like those of Jennings, and Marcus[13]), and a summary of this book will serve as the baseline for a discussion of later criticisms, additions, and new departures by myself and others.[14]

Justifiably, I think, I started my analysis of Ottoman law with Max Weber, who provided the most fruitful historical model for studying it, even though it was deficient in empirical accuracy. Weber suggested that Islamic Law in the middle Islamic period was characterized as rational in a loose kind of way; the judge worked by weighing arguments of litigants, but in a general, cultural way, without the anchor of a specific code of law. The reason for this was that in the tenth century an event called "closure of the gates of *ictihad*" or free interpretation (whereby, Muslim jurists could freely turn to the sources of the revelation and invent new laws) took place, after which Islamic law ceased to develop, lagging increasingly behind changes in real life, until the kadi had nothing to hold on to over time, in terms of an intellectual basis for making decisions.[15]

A modern version of Weber was provided by anthropologist Lawrence Rosen, who studied the city of Sefrou in modern Morocco.[16] In his theory, the kadis did not see their function as enforcing the law in fact, but had in mind something broader, of attaining peace and harmony between litigants, reinstating them in

13 Abraham Marcus, *The Middle East on the Eve of Modernity*, New York: Columbia University Press, 1992.

14 Haim Gerber, *State, Society and Law in Islam: Ottoman Law in Comparative Perspective*, Albany: State University of New York Press, 1994.

15 Gerber, *State, Society and Law*, Chapter 1.

16 Lawrence Rosen, *The Anthropology of Justice: Law as Culture in Islamic Society*, Cambridge: Cambridge University Press, 1989.

their former social position. This finding may or may not be valid for the law in modern Morocco; it certainly does not seem valid for the Ottoman legal system. Studying mainly the kadi court record of seventeenth century Bursa (but also many other bits and pieces from other courts), I came to the conclusion that as far as Ottoman law was concerned, Weber and Rosen were fundamentally wrong. As far as Weber was concerned, while parts of the law were closed to radically new interpretation, substantial parts remained open (being called *muctahad fihi*, that is, open to *ictihad*, or free scholarly interpretation), allowing room for innovations, such as the important law regarding statute of limitations enacted by Ebu Suʿud Efendi and Süleyman in the sixteenth century, which is accepted by all jurists as part and parcel of the Shari'a.[17] More important, the old Islamic mechanisms of interpretation (*qiyas, icma*', *maslaha,* and *istihsan*) allowed new solutions to slip in without necessarily being dubbed innovations. In addition, much as real life may have changed, in reality it remained close enough to the late classical model of Islamic law to be perfectly workable. As far as Rosen was concerned, in my book on Ottoman law I found that though he may have been right about his own area of research, it was not applicable to the Ottoman legal system. The strong impression I got from reading thousands of cases was that the Kadi understood his job as being charged with enforcing the current law to the best of his ability, while keeping his objectivity as best as he could humanly do, chiefly by keeping away from the extra-judicial aspects of litigants' lives. There is a plethora of hints in the sources that there was a systematic approach in the Ottoman bureaucracy to running an empire in general. There is no sign that Kadis solved legal issues, particularly conflicts, without exact reliance on the extant law, including the extant law of procedure. For better or worse, there was no tendency to prefer the version of party without recourse to actual proof, like witnesses or admission of guilt; no extra-judicial personal intervention is ever apparent (though this generalization should probably be relaxed somewhat—see below).[18] My conclusions in this regard went hand in hand with those of Ronald Jennings, the pioneer of the study of Ottoman court records for understanding Ottoman law.

This is not to suggest at all that the Kadi and his clients were not interested in morality or the smooth working of the society in question; they simply thought that the Shari'a represented the highest form of morality, and that the Kadi's procedure represented the highest form of justice. Among other things, I can illustrate this conclusion by recalling the surprising finding, evident when reading the Book of Complaints, that many people complained to the Sultan that

17 Haim Gerber, *Islamic Law and Culture, 1600–1840,* Leiden: Brill, 1999, pp. 63-64.

18 Madeline Zilfi, "We Don't Get Along": Women and Hul Divorce in the Eighteenth Century", in Madeline Zilfi, ed., *Women in the Ottoman Empire,* Leiden: Brill, 1997, pp. 264-296.

a case of theirs had been handled illegally and unjustly, since it had not been dealt with by the Kadi, according to shar'i procedure. This was concretized by using the term upright witnesses, or *şuhud udul*, a legal creature that only a Kadi could trace and detect (a large number of documents in our collection contain this term, an obvious symbolic reference to a court proceeding before a Kadi). Also, it is important to remark that we have to be weary of the commonly held view that the ability of people to manipulate the court to suit their own interests is necessarily a good thing for the court's clients in general: if a highway robber could manipulate loopholes in the law to evade justice, it was disastrous news to most clients of the court. So, this whole argument is a slippery slope and should be handled with extreme care.

Partially against these conclusions, an important new departure in the understanding of the Ottoman legal system was suggested by Leslie Peirce in her 2003 book[19] on women and the law in the town of Ayntab in 1540–41.

The book analyzed two *sicills* from Ayntab (Southern Turkey) in 1540–1, as part of a study of gender and the law in Ayntab, but it went further than this and actually dealt with the legal culture of the Ayntab court more generally. The general argument of the book is that the role of the Kadi was not law enforcement in the narrow sense, but getting people together to solve their difficulties. In fact, the law of the book was meaningless; it was only the law on the ground, in practical life that provided an idea of the true law. This was best described in a review by Iris Agmon,[20] an enthusiastic supporter of Peirce's approach. Peirce's work here was characterized by, "the author's insistence that the law does not exist in law books, or, more accurately, not only in law books, but rather in legal practice. The underlying legal question of the book is, therefore, not which specific law was implemented in certain case [sic.] and to what extent its application followed the letter of the law. Rather, it explores *law as a process and social action*" (italics in original).[21] It is easy to see how the law, which still exists as something important at the beginning of this last sentence, loses its importance at its end, and becomes no more than a social process, that is, something that is negotiated between all the parties present at court, who all become partners in the outcome, some of them more equal than others, the Kadi is almost relegated to a secondary place: "rulers, state officials, judges, court scribes, and, most important, every man and woman requiring the court services."[22]

I tend to agree with many of these new suggestions, but not with all of them.

---

19 Leslie Peirce, *Morality Tales: Law and Gender in the Ottoman Court of Aintab*, Berkeley and Los Angeles: University of California Press, 2003, Introduction.

20 Iris Agmon, "Review" of Leslie Peirce's Morality Tales, www.h-net.org/reviews/showrev.php?id=13539.

21 Agmon, p. 2.

22 Agmon, p. 2.

My major theoretical concern with such an approach is that what it does in actuality is turn Ottoman Islamic law, a genius legal edifice that has taken centuries to build, into a sort of tribal law, where the law is really nothing more than the political maneuvering and negotiation between conflicting kin groups, without rules of procedure to speak of.[23]

Let us look into Peirce's claims with some more detail. Former *sicill* studies of Ottoman law (such as Jennings[24] and Gerber[25]) took it for granted that the Kadi was basically enforcing the law (the Shari'a mainly, but also some customary laws like guild laws, which were enforced systematically and not in an ad hoc fashion) pretty simply and accurately. Peirce, however, preferred to follow Lawrence Rosen in claiming that the Kadi was basically interested in restoring peace and harmony between litigants, rather than in enforcing the law. Peirce adds that the Kadi was also interested in returning people to their honorable state in society, even if they acted wrongfully or even criminally. The court seemed particularly bent on this when it faced women of the lower class, who had no strong kin group to back them up and support them. It cannot be emphasized strongly enough that my approach is not that the Kadi (usually that is) acted mindlessly and formally to enforce a law which he found before himself, careless of the social consequences. My approach is that Ottoman Kadis (and probably most other people in that society as well) considered the text of the Shari'a (with some additions authorized by the state) to simply be the highest form of justice possible. Any form of negotiation of this text probably meant that less justice was being done in the world. I particularly reject the suggestion that the Kadi had some secret friendly agenda for criminals, especially serious ones. Hardened criminals (that is, those with a proven record) in particular, received the full blast of the force of Ottoman law, and were condemned to death without further ado. This is hardly a reinstatement to their former social position.

At the beginning of her book, Peirce says that the focal point of her study is three stories that she unearthed in the Kadi record that go beyond the usually formulaic rendering of cases and allow more substantial discourse. These cases stretch beyond the usual one *sicill* per case, and present defendants speaking their mind freely, changing versions or wording, thus allowing the writer to penetrate into the story and unearth valuable personal details and possibly also unusual uses of the law. These stories are so central that we may take them to represent almost the entire book. For Peirce's argument to be convincing, it should be convincing in the context of these "stories".

---

23 For relevant literature see Gerber, *State, Society and Law*, Introduction.
24 Ronald Jennings, "Kadi, Court and Legal Procedure in Seventeenth Century Ottoman Kayseri", *Studia Islamica*, 48 (1978), pp. 133-172.
25 Gerber, *State, Society and Law in Islam.*

The first story is that of Ine, a child-bride who came to court and accused her father-in-law of raping her.[26] The accused flatly denied the charge. Members of the village were brought to testify, and attest that the accused is an honest man who would never do something like that. Ine could not prove her case, and her case was dismissed. Possibly the Kadi might believe her: she was just a child, not a trickster; but as I have said above, there was no proof, and the hand of the Kadi was tied. Eventually, however, the case continued and was resolved some nine month later, when Ine and her husband, Tanrıverdi, were divorced. This event took place when Tanrıverdi told the judge that Ine was unhappy in the marriage, and suggests that it should be annulled. The judge did exactly that, viz., he pronounced a *tefrik*, separation for special circumstances, exactly as the law obliged him to do in such a case. Here, Peirce comes up with what she sees as a major finding for this case: it turns out that the young couple was living in another village, not that of the Tanrıverdi's father, which was unusual sociologically. Moreover, this village was part of the endowment of the old Mamluk rulers of the area for historical reasons, and hence enjoyed a measure of autonomy vis-à-vis the Ayntab court and authorities. This move was probably connected to the wish of the young wife to get away from the village of her husband's father, for obvious reasons. Since the couple was still very young, the reasonable assumption is that this move was effected by the community, or some members of it. So, a young bride was able to move the community to do something substantial to help her in distress. Peirce's claim is that Ine, the young wife, was able to marshal some legal and social resources to help her in her plight, one outcome of which was the legal separation from her husband.

Peirce, at this point suggests that a sort of bargaining over the law is revealed by the fact that several cases came to court from this big village, which seems to have been privileged in this way, with the law seen as variable according to geographical circumstances. This is a case in which contingent circumstances created a difference in the way a certain law was applied, and this difference constituted a meeting between the law on the books and the practical circumstances in real life, the only sort of meeting that gives the law its meaning. Maybe there was a small case of privileging, though the *tefrik* could have taken place anyway. It is a rare event in Islamic law, but it is on the books. No one can say that the law did not exist before this case or after it. It can be granted that Peirce made here a contribution, but what has happened was well within the law of the book. The exceptional case was minute indeed.

The second story relates to Haciye Sabah, a teacher who ran a religious school for young women in her private home, where the actual teaching was

26 Peirce, *Morality Tales*, pp. 129-142.

done by a male "preacher" unrelated to any of the female students.[27] It is certainly a fascinating case, and an extremely rare one in Ottoman documents. It was this fact that somehow (not made clear by the documents) brought the subject to the court's attention. The offence was one of violating the rule separating women from socially unrelated males. It was minor offense, not even on the books (though extant on *fetvas*) only punishable by the discretion of the Kadi. For this violation, Sabah and the male preacher were punished by *teşhir*, ignominious exposure, and banishment from the city. At the same time, however, two of Sabah's neighbors intervened and charged Sabah with something much bigger—that she was actually teaching the students *kızılbaş* Shiism, not just Sunni religion. The period was one of intensive struggle in Anatolia between Sunnism and heretical Shiism of the type of *kızılbaş*, a popular Shii movement that supported the Safavide ruler Ismail and his successors. Being indicted for such a crime in Anatolia at the time could lead to a death verdict, because the Ottomans took the Shia at this time as an extremely dangerous and an abominable type of heresy. The Kadi of Ayntab, however, chose to look the other way and avoided prosecuting Sabah for this supposed violation, thereby, according to Peirce, manipulating and mediating the normative law in order to reinstate the accused in the social milieu as of old. Of course, the evidence for heresy was extremely dubious, as the women were seen swaying, which they could also do studying Sufism, but the refusal of the Kadi to consider prosecuting her for this is certainly telling, and constitutes a clear sort of interpretation of the law. We have to also remember, however, that the two accusers were not themselves victims of a wrong-doing. What they did was no more than defamation, itself a punishable offence at that time, though not something to be found in Shari'a manuals. So again, a slight interpretation of the law, yes, but no more than this. The attitude of the Kadi on this point is similar to his turning a blind eye to the numerous cases in Ayntab of women complaining of rape but unable to prove the accusation. Possibly, the Kadi had some sympathy for these women, since according to the book-law they were all liable to be prosecuted under the law of *kazf*, false accusation of *zina*. Here, too, there is a slight violation by the Kadi of his duty, since prosecution of a *hadd* by a Kadi was a must, not a voluntary choice. Yet, the Kadi observed here did it differently.

The third story is about Fatma, a pregnant village girl brought to court by the manager of the Sultanic domain in which the village was situated.[28] The charge was apparently *zina*, fornication, as the girl was pregnant but unmarried. The case was dealt with by the court in three entries. In the first one, Fatma claimed to have been impregnated by Ahmed, who was present in the court. Her state-

27 Peirce, *Morality Tales*, pp. 251-275.
28 Peirce, *Morality Tales*, pp. 351-374.

ment was denied by Ahmed. In the second entry, she describes in more detail how she "made *zina*" with Ahmed. In the third entry, the village imam testifies that Fatma told him that it was in fact Korkud who had illicit sex with her, and that it was a rape. He adds that Korkud's mother pressured Fatma to implicate Ahmed. When asked, Fatma reiterates that it was Ahmed, and that the Korkud story was squeezed out of her by Ahmed's mother. Peirce, in the first place analyses the language of the court, claiming it hints that the court believes Fatma. Her conclusion is that, "while the court record does not explicitly state the outcome, it implies that Ahmed is considered guilty and must acknowledge responsibility for the pregnancy."[29] This conclusion is daring because if Ahmed was found guilty he was eligible for the death penalty. What the court decided at the end, we do not know, but it could not have been convicting Ahmed without proof. There is an additional interesting aspect of Peirce's analysis of this story; Peirce grapples with the question of why did Fatma claim so coldmindedly that she had illicit sex with someone? She adds that, in fact, this was a widespread phenomenon in Ayntab in 1540–1 (indeed, I never observed it in Bursa between 1600 and 1700). She again asks, why? She suggests a brilliant explanation, which at the same time for her sheds light on "the culture of the court". In her words: "These confessions need to be accounted for, as they contrast so starkly with the expectations of jurisprudence. Indeed, legal manuals insist that the judge do all in his power to discourage confession to *zina*..."[30] The explanation for why these confessions nevertheless occurred is a widespread custom in the Ayntab area of honor killing young women suspected of illicit sex. These women believed that the shame (and maybe punishment) incurred by a court confession would save them from the harsher popular retaliation. Peirce's explanation is insightful, but no law was compromised or negotiated in the process.

Like in Ine's story, here too, Peirce's brilliant point is social, rather than legal; we see how a girl in danger after sexual misconduct (not hers) uses the court to secure for herself a life insurance against an honor killing, and maybe even the willingness of a guy to marry her and give her future child legitimate social standing. This is all very interesting and very important, and shows how the law is implemented in one specific case according to its specific characteristics, rather than mechanistically—without really affecting the book law, which remains legally the guide, but slightly variable according to circumstances. Such variations existed in every court case studied: someone who killed a person was treated differently depending on the killing tool he used, on whether the killing was part of a highway robbery, on the killing record he might have had, and a

29 Peirce, *Morality Tales*, p. 355.
30 Peirce, *Morality Tales*, p. 364.

host of other circumstances. A certain amount of flexibility of perception existed, but all within the bounds of a certain law. Also, Peirce's point about honor killing is a bit sensational—not only is the logic of it open to different interpretation, there is no evidence presented of actual cases. Was it "borrowed" from modern anthropology?

Although Peirce's book is about gender and law, it also deals with other topics, among them criminal law, of special interest to me, since I believe it was the heart of the Ottoman legal system. Among the most relevant topics dealt with in this regard are five cases of murder that took place in 1540-1. Typically, Peirce seeks to see her general thesis in these cases as well. In her words: "These adjudications of murder are ... the record's most vivid demonstration that the study of legal culture needs to be grounded in the dialectic between action and prescription".[31] The reference here is no doubt to the dialectic between law and practice. The main finding is that in several of the cases no court punishment was applied, but arbitration between the parties took place, at the end of which an agreement was reached on compensation. There is some justification to talk here about interplay between the law and real-life processes, but again, it was a flexibility that was normal in murder cases that was part of the wrangling and difficulty of providing proof. In any case, punishment in murder cases was open to negotiation between the parties—as a part of the law: litigants in "private" murder cases could either demand retaliation (*kisas*) or bargain between themselves for a compensation (*diyet* or blood-money). This is well pronounced in every Islamic law manual and is the stuff of every *sicill* study written in the past. Again, however, there is some undeniable truth in saying that every specific case is decided, among other things, on the strength of the litigant's ability to marshal legal sources to substantiate their case, and in that sense, every case is a sort of law on the book and, at the same time, the law in practice, or interpretation of that law. But crucially, the deviation from the formal law is microscopic, if extant at all (since the law defines itself as negotiable).

The upshot of all this is that a careful reading of Peirce indicates that her documents contain some real negotiation of the law. It is still notable, however, that the main difference between Peirce's three stories and some other Kadi *sicills* that have been studied is that these records are characterized by a certain amount of free speech, with some hesitation, retraction of arguments, or rephrasing of them. I have not found any such cases in seventeenth century Bursa, and it is my understanding that no such recording was done either in seventeenth century Kayseri, Çankiri, or Aleppo. On the whole, the wording of the protocols is formulaic, without any personal detail of any sort, besides facts rel-

31 Peirce, *Morality Tales*, p. 336.

evant to the case. This was true as well for cases relating to divorce. In fact, in Bursa the largest group of documents related to *khulʿ* divorce (divorce on the initiative of the woman), yet all the cases were formulaic—the Kadi never tried to dissuade any of the parties from going on with the divorce, and none of the parties ever tried to argue; change version; or express emotions such as anger, hesitation, remorse, or what have you. Whether any wrangling took place in reality and was obliterated by the style of recording is anybody's guess. In all cases, however, the normative law was finally enforced, with but little deviation from the law book.

The bottom line is that in Ayntab we face a situation where more real-life details were for some reason supplied in the final protocol. All this shows that something in Ayntab was exceptional. I would guess that that something was the recent annexation of the area to the Ottoman state (which, as Peirce suggests, made the Ottomans eager to attract the legitimacy and support of the Ayntabans), and the still irregular nature of the court's affairs. The majority tribal population in the area may also have had something to do with this exceptionalism. In other words, Ayntab was different not only in its style of recording but also socially.

Be that as it may, it must be emphasized that on the whole, Ottoman Kadis tended less to negotiate about the law than Kadis in other systems of law. In the first place, unlike the wholly secular Chinese law,[32] Ottoman law was also Islamic in its main contours, and as such, sacred. A natural outcome was to be less willing to compromise on its content through negotiation. In the second place, there is a strong tendency among scholars to forget that the most basic administrative rule (obsession is a better word) that was noted before, the habit of transferring officeholders (including Kadis) from one place to another after one or two years of service existed. It is well known, and has never been disputed, that the reason for this was an eagerness to prevent the development of personal acquaintances between officials and local people, let alone people in possession of power. This was also helped by the fact that Turkish-speaking Kadis often served in Arabic speaking areas. The obvious communication problems thus created were sometimes overcome by Kadis hiring local deputy judges (*naibs*) to help them out, but, as we shall see clearly in the complaints, the Ottomans forbade this practice, enjoining Kadis to bring *naibs* from the outside that nobody knew locally, specifically because such relations created a tendency for corruption due to developing common interests between officials and local citizens. All this shows that at least the Ottoman administrative mentality was dead set against

32 The comparison is made by Ergene, "Why Did Ümmü Gülsüm Go to Court? Ottoman Legal Practice between History and Anthropology", *Islamic Law and Society*, 17 (2010), pp. 215-44.

the connections between Kadis and personal relations. All this must have surely exerted some influence on the functioning of the court in Ottoman society.

All this is not intended to negate Peirce's contribution, but to map its exact place according to my understanding. Peirce has shown that because every case was specific, every verdict was a new interpretation of the law. I still insist, however, that Kadis did not act in the Weberian mode of freely relying on ethical perceptions without any reference to any law. The law always remained the guide, and the Kadi apparently never left the code to the side.

In the final analysis, it is possible that the difference between this writer and Peirce is smaller than what might be thought. Something like this is suggested by various theoretical expressions made by Peirce in her book, in which she accepts the reality of Ottoman law. In one place, where she talks about familiarity in the Ayntab Region with Ottoman law, she says, "yet, the major principles of normative law appeared to be commonly understood, even if the language of the local community did not tally precisely with that of jurisprudence."[33] In another place, Peirce says, "the role of provincial court, at least in Ayntab in the mid-sixteenth century, was thus a complex one, for while it functioned as an instrument for the enforcement of normative law, it acted at the same time as an arena for negotiating the very law it was mandated to enforce."[34]

An important point proving the similarity of thought is concerned with mediation: the Kadi of Ayntab refused to serve as arbitrator between litigants point blank, although the law seems to have allowed him to do so. In other words, the Kadi refused to arbitrate even when this was fully acceptable morally and formally, but supposedly went on negotiating when he was supposed to be fully observant of the letter of the law. That sounds quite odd to me.

There is a further related issue that must be emphasized here: by enthusiastically underscoring that the only important aspect of Ottoman law was the study of the behavior of the Kadi on the ground, the legal realists may induce us to forget that there are additional important macro-questions that we want to learn from our study of Ottoman law. In order to learn about the quality of justice provided by the Ottoman system, we need to know who else, besides the Kadis, could meddle in the law? Were they provincial governors? And if yes, what role did they play? We also need to connect our studies to the study of Islamic law more generally, by finding out the nature of the law that was applied in Ottoman courts. There is also still interest in the questions posed by Weber—were the authorities in the habit of meddling in the affairs of the Ottoman courts? Was the Ottoman court riddled with corruption, as was its reputation throughout Europe in early modernity?

33 Peirce, *Morality Tales*, p. 372.
34 Peirce, *Morality Tales*, p. 374.

I argue that the fact that the Kadis had a tendency to be lenient to low-class, underprivileged women does not mean that Kadis brushed aside the whole concept of how a lawsuit should be conducted. Islamic law had an exacting logical model for this process, and it is time to add it as a layer to our analysis of how the court worked to find out whether this model was functioning.

This discussion can be further elucidated and sharpened by studying a verbatim ledger of a Bursa court record from the seventeenth century, published recently. The existence of this printed edition allows some in-depth investigation that is somewhat difficult due to the limited accessibility of the original court records (some technical problems, among them time shortage, precluded such detailed investigations in the early 1970s). Such research relates to the law of procedure of Ottoman-Islamic law. Such a study calls for the minute analysis of a large number of documents to find out whether this law was based on formless intuition or whether there was a systematic pattern followed. This minute investigation showed that in seventeenth century Bursa, the law of procedure was not haphazard, casual, or incidental as Weber and others might expect. Rather, it was well structured, constant, and entirely predictable (much as in seventeenth century Kayseri). A civil case would start with a claim (concerning a debt for instance). Sometimes the defendant admitted to the crime outright, and that was the end of the trial. If the defendant denied the claim outright, the court would require the plaintiff to produce two witnesses to prove it. If this was done, the case was concluded according to their testimony. If no such proof was forthcoming, the case of the plaintiff would be dismissed, but not before the defendant would be demanded to take an oath to the effect that his version of events was truthful.

Most civil cases, however, were somewhat different from this standard process. In most cases the defendant denied the exact claim of the plaintiff by producing an alternative claim, such as: "I did borrow the money, but I have returned it". In such cases, there was no longer any point in the plaintiff proving his point, as the defendant had already admitted it. The responsibility then shifted to the defendant, who had to prove his additional claim, with the onus of proof transferred to him. If he had the necessary witnesses, he won; if he had no proof, he lost, but not before the plaintiff was required to take an oath that his version of events was the correct one. The allocation of an oath was on the whole simple and logical—the defendant took the oath (and won) if he denied the charge totally and the plaintiff could not prove it; the plaintiff took the oath (and won) if the defendant claimed an alternative claim but could not prove it. This was found to be the procedure in scores of cases without exception. Thus, the structure of the court cases was more orderly and predictable than I had realized when I wrote my book on Ottoman law. Weber, whose modern supporters claim that the Kadi was basically improvising, could not be further than the truth. It was a highly professional and meticulous weighing of the claims, where easy-going personal considerations do not seem to have been a part of the process. Maybe my conclusion is a little naïve, but this is what is made clear by investigating the original documents.

At this stage, I wish to claim that there was actually a good reason why Ottoman Kadis and Ottoman law in general had every reason to be more legalistic in their approach to the Shari'a than their fellow scholars in former Islamic states. While the ideas of Weber, Rosen, and Peirce are based on the premise that the Kadi knew the litigants and was interested in their personal lives and wellbeing, there is reason to assume that this was not the Ottoman case. Their habit of swiftly changing the assignments of governors and Kadis seems to have been designed exactly for this purpose, viz., to prevent closeness between the Kadi and his clients, to avoid the possibility of influencing them. Also relevant, is the fact that the Ottoman state was more fully bureaucratized, including having a much higher level of bureaucratization of the *ulema*, which found expression in the well-known minute grading of all levels of the *ilmiye*, *muderrises*, and Kadis. If they were so thorough in grading all levels of the *ilmiye*, why should they not also be thorough in trying to be punctual in their enforcement of the law? There is in fact also empirical supporting evidence that they were more punctual in this than other Islamic states before them. It is well known that early in the formation of the Islamic judiciary, judges were often and easily dismissed when they were unable to attain the good will of the assigned community. A clear case in point is the story of Isfahan in the first half of the tenth century.[35] The Caliph wished to impose a Kadi from the outside on the city against the wishes of the community elite. The outcome was a six-months strike of the professional witnesses, which brought the work of the court to a standstill. To this we should compare the situation in the Ottoman Empire, where a Kadi sent from the outside, usually from the Bursa-Edirne area, was the common practice from start to finish. No one ever was heard complaining about this custom. Thus, the Ottomans were more bureaucratized than the others, and therefore, expecting more formalism on their part in applying the law is all but natural.

Up until now, I have been speaking about the law of procedure in order to show that there existed in the seventeenth century and onwards–at least in the central areas of the empire–a well-built legal system, where the Kadi worked more or less systematically to enforce the law. I want now to ask, who was responsible for the enforcement of that law? As we will see, this question is intertwined with the question of what the law was, in terms of Shari'a, *Kanun*, or

35 Nurit Tsafrir, "The Beginnings of the Hanafi School in Isfahan", *Islamic Law and Society*, vol. 5 (1998), pp. 9 ff.

customary law. The question of who enforced the law is crucial to sorting out the question of whether Ottoman Law was equivalent to the rule of law or not. This is because the alternative to the Kadi was usually provincial governors, and as we shall see in a next chapter, even top Ottoman bureaucrats thought that this possibility was a very pernicious idea indeed. I plan to concretize this discussion by talking about two areas of the law: criminal law, arguably the real core of the Ottoman legal system, and civil law, that is, the law managing economic and other similar relations between individuals.

It is well known that in the classical period, the Shari'a court was not in charge of enforcing the criminal law. Scholars such as Jansen, who studied the legal system of the Mamluk state, was entirely clear that it was not the Kadi's court that dealt with criminal justice, but instead, various government officials.

There is also the widespread opinion that the Islamic criminal law under classical Islam (up to about 1250) was not enforced at all. In any case, if anybody was enforcing them, it was governmental officials, not the Kadi. This was not the case in the Ottoman Empire. As part and parcel of the unwritten pact between the *ulema* and the state in that empire, it is easy to see from the start that the *ulema* enjoyed an adjudicative monopoly: there is no *mazalim* court in any real sense of the term, and we have seen that the Imperial *Divan* was dealing with legal matters only in exceptional cases. Even the medieval *udul* (professional witnesses, not of course the *şuhud udul* of the present study) disappear: in the story already cited from tenth century Isfahan, the *udul* were the cornerstone of the court. The strike brought the system to a halt. These *udul* (sometimes called notaries) shared many legal functions with the Kadi and were much more than just witnesses. Their disappearance necessarily means that the role of the Kadi was enhanced under the Ottomans.

From the little that was written on this, it seems that in the early Ottoman centuries, the Kadi may have dealt with all cases and may also have reached decisions, or verdicts. They did not, however fix punishments, possibly it was not considered their function to do so. This may have been within the jurisdiction of provincial governors and police officers (*subaşıs*). It is interesting to observe, however, that in the seventeenth century, in a large portion of the cases (maybe more than fifty percent), punishment was handed down in addition to the verdicts. It seems clear that the Shari'a court was becoming more and more important. (But there are views that Bursa may have been an extreme case, and that the role of the central government in other places may have been greater). In the Book of Complaints, there are a number of cases in which a statement is made by people that they had been judged in forums other than the Shari'a court and that, therefore, the whole process was illegal. Possibly they had in mind also sentences and verdicts, by governors and others. In all these cases, the complaint was found to be justified by the *Divan*. In recent years, there has been some discussion about this question. Michael Ursinus has published documents that are investigations of complaints conducted by the governor of the province of Rumeli in the late eighteenth century.[36] The complaints that came to trial were dealt with by the Kadi in the procedure to which they were accustomed, but the trials may have taken place in the office of the governor. Ursinus claims that this was no shar'i trial, a process that could only take place in a formal Shari'a court building. In my view, this is mistaken. Traditionally, Shari'a court could reside in buildings such as mosques, madrasas, or the Kadi's residence. In seventeenth century Bursa, numerous cases were conducted in fields or meadows, where a *naib* would be sent to deal with a localized issue that needed legal treatment and observation of landscape features. As long as the judge was a Kadi and the procedure shar'i, it was a shar'i trial.

It is interesting now to also pose the question of, what of the *hudud* was enforced in the central areas of the empire in the seventeenth and eighteenth centuries. Let us remind ourselves that the *hudud*, laws of God, the heart of the criminal code of the Shari'a, were five: drinking wine, theft, illegal sex (adultery or fornication), false accusation of illegal sex (including also the public swearing of such an act, where illicit sex was implied), and murder in the course of highway robbery (*kat' el-tarik*). I have found very few cases of wine drinking that landed people in court, and very few cases of proven theft. In any event, I have seen no case of the harsh bodily punishment that entailed the cutting off of a hand or stoning for adultery. This violation was of course particularly difficult to prove, since it required four witnesses. A punishment that we meet very often in seventeenth century Bursa is service on the Ottoman galleys as an oarsman for a number of years, as commutation of some of these offences. This punishment is neither Shari'a nor *Kanun*, but the act of the government at some unknown point of time in the seventeenth century (or even before). The issue that appears most commonly in our sources concerning criminal law, however, is killing as a part of a highway robbery. This violation was punishable by death by law, and this is what took place in real life as well. No alleviating circumstances were ever considered. Though we lack good realistic sources from the period of the formation of Islamic law, Ottoman sources from the seventeenth and eighteenth centuries make it quite obvious why this was the harshest law in the law book. Highway robbery was a huge problem with bands of unruly criminals roaming the countryside and making the life of passengers very difficult indeed. This offense was so common that it could be considered a strategic problem. The court procedure we find in all adjudicative cases against such criminals was the same

36 Michael Ursinus, *Grievance Administration (Şikayet) in an Ottoman Province*, London: Royal Asiatic Society Books, 2005.

—usually no proof was available against one specific perpetrator, but rather, a large group of citizens brought charges against the accused, invariably claiming that he was a, "seeker of corruption in the world" (*sa'i bi-fasad el-arz*), and that this was his continued habit. The last accusation was critical in establishing the criminal record of the defendants, and the death penalty was then imposed, as a matter of course. This procedure is not mentioned in the law manuals from the classical period or in *Kanuns*, and it seems to have been a customary law that somehow evolved in the Ottoman period. Yet, we can observe that *muftis* and Kadis lived peacefully with this fact. It must be emphasized that Kadis acted the same way in every case of highway robbery that came before them. They were not negotiating or making ad hoc decisions.

Something quite similar is apparent in the civil law. In the first place, various Islamic legal institutions that were supposed to be ossified on the book codes were discovered to be quite alive. Such is the case of the law of partnership, such as *commenda*, *mufawaza*, and the like, which scholars once believed was no more than staff for practicing casuistry. These were discovered in the court records of seventeenth century Bursa as practiced in real life. Did these institutions continue to exist from classical Islam to the seventeenth century or were they reintroduced during the Ottoman period? It would be hazardous to say, as there are almost no surviving Kadi protocols from classical Islam. What I want to emphasize here, in particular, is that while many civil law Islamic institutions were faithful to the Shari'a law code, many were not. An example is the double rent of endowment properties, which allowed for the long range rent of such pieces of real estate, despite the fact that it was squarely prohibited by the Shari'a.

This raises the question of the general commitment of the Ottoman state towards the Shari'a in those centuries. This may be the place to mention the legist Ibn Taymiyya (d. 1328) and his famous *fetva* against the Mongols, where he called upon his fellow Muslims to fight against the Ilkhanid Mongols and treat them as infidels or even heretics, despite the fact that they had become Muslims in 1295.[37] Seemingly, Ibn Taymiyya's argument is based on the fact that the Mongols deserve such treatment because they did not fulfill many parts of the Shari'a like proper Muslims, and this is the way many modern Muslims understand him.[38] This is, however, probably an incorrect understanding; for at the same time that he castigated the Mongols, Ibn Taymiyya was supportive of the Mamluks, who in all likelihood did not do better concerning the Shari'a. In fact, Ibn Taymiyya's intention was different;[39] it was mainly centered on the fact that

37 See Thomas Raff, *Remarks on an Anti-Mongol Fatwa by Ibn Taimiya*, Leiden: Brill, 1973.
38 Jansen, Johannes, J.B., *The Neglected Duty*, New York: Macmillan Press, 1986.
39 Ibn Taimiya, *Majmu'at Fatawa Ibn Taimiya*, vol. 4, Cairo: Dar al-Rahma li'l- Nashr wa al-

the Mongols claimed that they were not bound by the Shari'a of the Prophet Muhammad, but by what he calls Shari'a *kufriyya* (non-believers' law), specifically that of their historic leader Genghiz Khan. What he means, is that the Mamluks were well known to be bound by the Islamic Shari'a, and it means little if in practice they were unable to fulfill all of it. It seems that Ibn Taymiyya's ideas were paradigmatic in Islamic history (that is, shared by many if not all thinkers), and certainly this was true of the Ottoman Empire—what one needed was general, authentic, and well-publicized devotion and commitment to the Shari'a, not necessarily perfect performance of every law on the code book.

Up until this point, we have gotten a picture whereby the Kadi enforced the *hudud* more or less according to the format of the Islamic Shari'a, though not totally, or meticulously. It can be said that the Ottomans were keen on enforcing the Shari'a, but they were not persistent on its exact form, as inscribed in the major manuals. Somehow, the original laws were partially relaxed or negotiated, but it was not on an ad hoc basis. For individual litigants, the law seems quite stable and unchanging. On the macro-level, for whatever reason, some laws simply changed or were understood differently than in the classical period. We also observe that in contradistinction to classical and Mamluk Islam, the role of the Shari'a in Ottoman society was much more elevated, and with it, the role and position of the *ulema.* The question is, why? I have already dealt with this question and provided several explanations, but would suggest an additional one, that the Ottomans were obsessed with legitimation because of their low original status, and a major way to achieve a higher status was to draw near the *ulema* and attract their good will. All this was naturally enhanced after 1517, as the Ottomans came to shoulder responsibility for the wellbeing of the two sacred shrines of Islam, a task they assumed with the utmost seriousness.

Up until this point, we have spoken about the straight path of the Shari'a as the main body of law in the Ottoman Empire, and the kadi court as the main court in the public arena. It is time to introduce into the picture some elements that will show that Ottoman law was not foreign to legal pluralism, defined as a situation whereby the law contains more than one body of law, sometimes widened to the institutional arena, by including more than one legitimate set of forums to process disputes. I will only deal here with institutions and laws connected with the Shari'a system. Institutionally, one major element that has to be mentioned is connected to the concept of mediation, or *sulh*; in a large number of kadi court encounters in the Ottoman Empire, we find that mediators (*muslihun*) intervened in the process at a certain point, with the full consent of the parties, and suggested a compromise that was acceptable to the court and the

---

Tawzi', 1980, pp. 280 ff.

parties. It is a common error to claim that the Kadi himself mediated between the parties, but this has not so far been shown in the documents. That the situation was extremely widespread, however, is obvious, and it therefore introduces a clear element of pluralism into the system of Ottoman law.

A second element of legal pluralism evident in Ottoman law is the existence of a secular or state law (*Kanun*) within Ottoman law, law that could be thought of as introducing to the system state officials as legitimate actors. The Ottoman state started to enact non-Shari'a laws starting in the late fifteenth century, laws that covered mainly the penal area and land ownership, but also, obviously, taxation and state institutions and ceremonials, almost entirely neglected by traditional Islamic law. *Kanuns* were supposed to be enacted in areas not well covered by the Shari'a, but this is problematic, because the penal *Kanun* was handed to the Kadi for implementation, and many of the articles said specifically that the Kadi was authorized to implement the Shari'a if he preferred. Specifically, the *Kanun* added some fines to the usual penalties. The inspiration for this initiative may have originated, as is usually claimed, in Turkic culture in Central Asia, but the more important point I want to emphasize is that the *Kanun*, at least the all-important penal *Kanun*, was surprisingly short-lived. Heyd says that the first Ottoman *Kanun* was possibly enacted at the beginning of the sixteenth century, and it was in full decline in the 1560s. I have seen no signs of the penal *Kanun* in the Bursa court records of the seventeenth century. It is true that the land *Kanun* was much more resilient, and lasted until the nineteenth century. The reason for this was probably that Ottoman jurists, as much as their Mamluk predecessors, cared little for minor issues like the land regime.

Incidentally, although I have expressed a very reserved opinion of the Ottoman *Kanuns* as practical law above, ironically, it is the Sultanic orders in the *Şikayet Defteri* that show that the Sultans and their aides in the seventeenth century regarded the *Kanun*, generically speaking, as a highly important component of Ottoman law, next to the Shari'a. In the final analysis, if state officials were involved in the *Kanun*, their role remains a mystery until now.

An additional institutional body that worked to the side of the kadi court and also gave meaning to the term legal pluralism was the Imperial council or *Divan-i Hümayun*. The *Divan* was a sort of government, founded by the Ottoman center early in the state's history. This body was composed of the top Ottoman officials, including the Grand Vizier, the two military judges, the chief treasurer, and a number of top bureaucrats (*viziers*) with no formal function. The chief function of the body was to advise the Sultan on matters of policy, though the Sultan was of course under no obligation to heed their opinion. The body was crucial to the day to day running of the empire in several areas too low for the attention of the Sultan. One of these areas dealt with the thousands of complaints sent to the central government and were, of course, summarized in the Book of Complaints. An additional function was to serve as a court of law of sorts, a function still obscure due to the lack of studies on the subject.

The few documents on the *Divan* contained in the *Şikayet Defteri* can perhaps constitute a certain substitute for these missing studies. These documents make it clear that contrary to what is often maintained, the *Divan* was not considered a regular court of appeal, among other things because the very concept of appeal was not considered acceptable by the Ottomans. In any event, there is no case of appeal against a Kadi to the *Divan* in the *Şikayet Defteri*. The usual context in which the *Divan* is mentioned in this collection is in cases of an unusual crime and criminal, who had committed a heinous crime, or one the Kadi was unable to cope with. In many such cases, the *Divan* sent an order to send the suspect to Istanbul for further treatment. How exactly this was done, remains a mystery. It stands to reason that in the final analysis there was a trial, possibly conducted by the Kadi of Istanbul. Whatever the exact details, it is clear that the *Divan* constituted another court to that of the Kadi, and that it was a part of a legal pluralist web of courts.

Social Class in the Ottoman Court

In recent years, some studies have appeared that have sought to investigate anew the claim (also argued, as forcefully as I could in my own book, as well, and quite as forcefully, by Jennings), that the Shari'a court was a place where simple commoners could attain justice.[40] Two studies (Ergene[41] and Canbakal[42]) have challenged the conclusion of some former studies and claimed that it is unfounded that the Ottoman Kadi was, at least for the most part, unbiased in terms of social class. Canbakal, in particular, made the class bias of the kadi a focal point of her study, based on Ayntab in the seventeenth century. She collected information on lawsuits initiated by people with social titles like *haj*, *bey*, *çavuş*, *ağa*, and other titles preceding the names of *askers*, or members of the Ottoman administrative and political elite. Her conclusion from this exercise was that *askers* won their cases over commoners in substantially more than fifty percent of all cases. Ergene conducted a similar study for the towns that he studied, Kastamonu and Çankiri and reached the same conclusions as Canbakal. It is worthwhile noting again, that though class superiority was well known to the Ottomans and entirely accepted as legitimate, there was still the ideology that

40 See Ronald Jennings, "Limitations on the Judicial Powers of the Kadi in 17th Century Ottoman Kayseri", *Studia Islamica*, 50 (1979), pp. 151-184.

41 Boğaç Ergene, *Local Court, Provincial Society and Justice in the Ottoman Empire*, Leiden: Brill, 2003.

42 Hulya Canbakal, *Society and Politics in an Ottoman Town: Ayntab in the Seventeenth Century*, Leiden: Brill, 2007.

the state was supposed to provide a just legal system without class discrimination or biases. That does not in itself show, of course, that such biases did not happen in reality.

No comparable studies were done by scholars before Ergene and Canbakal, and certainly their conclusions go against the grain of my own study: in the 2,800 or so documents of the Book of Complaint, barely a handful of complainants noted that the Kadi acted unjustly within the courtroom. I went on and conducted a similar exercise (on the relations between class and the outcomes of court trials) in a verbatim register of the seventeenth century, recently published, in order to discover the role of class in the courtroom.[43] I found 43 cases of litigation of *askers* and *reaya* (commoners) in that register, the commoners winning some 51 percent of the total cases. In other words, in Bursa, the court was not another stage for the play of class supremacy. Beyond the dry statistics, maybe there is room to enter into some actual examples in more detail. On the whole, we find in these detailed cases a surprising assertiveness on the part of lower class people facing people from the elite. In this context, it is worthwhile mentioning some of Ergene's suggestions, whereby the Ottoman court was not only based on class bias in favor of the elite, but also on widespread corruption, since in his view plaintiffs in the Ottoman legal system won their cases as a rule because in this society there was no problem in finding people to bribe to give false witness in their favor.[44] Needless to say, cases like this sometimes happened and there was nothing special about the Ottoman legal system in this regard. It has to be kept in mind, however, that false testimony was considered a serious offence, moral as well as legal, punishable by ignominious public exposition. Additionally, it was also the Kadi's job to screen witnesses and block those suspect of possible false witnessing. I doubt if false witnessing was a big issue in seventeenth century Bursa (and similar cities in the central areas). Below I try to substantiate this claim.

Let us descend for a while from the level of the dry statistics to the concrete cases of encounters between commoners and members of the elite. Freed slaves are a case in point; quite a few of them came to court and made claims against their social superiors without fear or hesitation. An example is a freed slave who sued his former owner, a *sayyid* (descendant of the Prophet), and claimed that he was owed a sum of money for some time by the *sayyid*. The *sayyid* claimed that the sum was his, since the slave was his. The slave presented a valid manumis-

43 This study was based on the defter published by Abaci (using the translations is not recommended)—Nurcan Abaci, *The Ottoman Judges and their Registers: The Bursa Court Register B90/295 (dated* A.H. *1081*/A.D. *1670)*, 2 vols., Harvard, Mass.: Harvard University Department of Near Eastern Languages and Civilizations, 2007.

44 Ergene, *Local Court*, Chapter 6.

sion document, however, and the *sayyid* lost the case. It is not entirely clear what happened here; was the *sayyid* repentant for the manumission? The *sicill* does not give any hint. It is, in any case, a good example showing that lower class people did not think it was hopeless to present their cases to the court, and often even won.[45]

In the area of non-Muslims versus Muslims, we also encounter some surprises. Needless to say, non-Muslims in the society of the Ottoman Empire were part of the commoners, even the subalterns. It is sometimes, however, difficult to tell that this is indeed the case by judging the outcome of encounters in the Islamic court. In seventeenth century Bursa, most such encounters ended with the non-Muslims winning. It is true that Ergene claims that a *zimmi* (non-Muslim) in Ottoman society could not win a case against a Muslim without paying a bribe, because no Muslim would give witness for him of their own free will, but I disagree with this most emphatically.[46] Neither view can be proven definitively of course, but some documents seem to bear me out by supplying valuable hints. Thus, Bagos b. Bali, a *zimmi* carpenter, made a claim against a Kadi who was a resident of Bursa, that he had made some renovations in his house, but had not yet received his pay. The defendant's representative claimed that the debt was paid in full, but when called upon to provide proof, he failed to do so. Whereupon, the plaintiff was charged to make an oath, which he did, and he won the case. The situation here can be said to be surprising indeed—an Ottoman judge loses a court case to a *zimmi* in front of a Muslim judge, and nobody seems to be shaken.[47] It is evident that the defendant here could have more easily bribed someone or resorted to illegal tricks. Such tricks obviously did not happen here.

Jews also did not seem to be seriously biased against according to this register. An example is the case launched by the Muslim silk merchant, Ibrahim Çelebi b. Piyale, against the Jew, Kara Musi, in which he demanded 500 *kuruş* from him,[48] the price of the Persian silk he had sold to him. The Jewish merchant answered that until two years prior he had been submerged in debts that he could not pay, among them a debt to Ibrahim Çelebi. Then he reached an agreement with his debtors, whereby he sold his house and paid part of the debts, and the debtors waived the rest. When asked to prove his case, he summoned a group of Muslim witnesses who reiterated his words. It might be thought that in such a case the Muslim merchant would think that under pressure the Jew would come up with some more resources to pay him. When he saw that this approach was not working, he obviously did not seek false witnesses to advance

45 Abaci, *Ottoman Judges and their Registers*, No. 650.
46 Boğaç Ergene, *Local Court, Provincial Society*, pp. 114-15.
47 Abaci, *Ottoman Judges and their Registers*, No. 377.
48 Abaci, *Ottoman Judges and their Registers*, No. 512.

his case, but submitted quietly to the Kadi's decision. It is obvious that a bankrupt Jew would be unable to bribe anyone; the rich Muslim could, but did not—a clear indication, yet again, that the Kadi's court supplied credible justice.

Another category of people in Bursa that were, in effect, subalterns were women. Here too, we can see without difficulty that women were not passive or lacking in self-assertion when seeking to defend their rights in court. Their activity in all this was much more impressive than the modern image of these women would suggest. Women of course inherited property and were able to freely dispose of it by law because Islamic law prohibited husbands from obstructing women from freely disposing of their property as they saw fit. A fine document exemplifying this issue is the suit brought by one Salha Hatun against the husband of her recently deceased daughter, Sayyid Abidin Çelebi. He had two titles and, hence, was probably a distinguished member in the city. She was not impressed, and demanded the delayed bride money due to her daughter and some additional items. The defendant claimed that the sum was much smaller, but the woman called the imam of the quarter and the *muezzin* of the quarter mosque as witnesses. They confirmed her version of the story, and she won the case. If the defendant in this case had wanted to use illegal methods of argumentation, he might have simply claimed that he had paid the whole debt, which would have forced the Kadi to charge him with the need to supply proof, which he might have done by bribing false witnesses. That he lost the case in quiet should really stand to augment our confidence in this legal process.[49] Similarly, a woman who was the guardian of her under-age children after the death of her husband sued his father and claimed that he occupied a house the deceased gave his daughter before his last trip (which was to the Hajj). The defendant denied the charge completely, but two witnesses she summoned affirmed her case. This is interesting because the woman sued a male who must have been a leading member of her family.[50] As explanatory background, I want to note that I have shown in another study that the family in Bursa was a great deal less patriarchal than in many other places in the Middle East, and the two sets of facts may be related.[51]

Canbakal and Ergene have interpreted their findings to be that what we see in the court is a simple expression of class relations in Ottoman society—the system of law confirmed, and even strengthened, the existing class hierarchy in a more specific context. To my mind, this is a simplistic view, and I would suggest using a social model that better depicts Ottoman society at that time. In my es-

49 Abaci, *Ottoman Judges and their Registers*, No. 17.
50 Abaci, *Ottoman Judges and their Records*, No. 42.
51 Haim Gerber, "Anthropology and Family History: The Ottoman and Turkish Families", in idem, *State and Society in the Ottoman Empire*, Farnham: Variorum Reprints, 2010, Chapter V.

timation, it is a mistake to look at the Ottoman elite at this time as a homogeneous body of people or groups. It seems that the Ottoman elite of the time was, above all, fissured between several groups (top bureaucrats, *ulema*, and provincial notables), in such a way that they by no means saw themselves as sharing the same set of interests. It is a mistake, therefore, to assume that some *ağa* or *çavuş* appearing before a Kadi should receive special treatment. In all likelihood, the two groups felt competition with one another, rather than solidarity. My conclusion from this discussion is that there was, therefore, no objective reason why Kadis should give *askers* special treatment in court in the seventeenth and eighteenth centuries.

The last question to be addressed is how should we treat the differences in all these matters between Bursa and Ayntab? It seems to me that the situation in Bursa and Aleppo may well represent the situation in the core areas of the empire—the major cities, also those situated alongside the major highways. Judging from the case of Bursa, the social structure in those cities was less patriarchal, and based more on nuclear families and guilds (Canbakal's book makes clear that Ayntab at this time lacked guilds altogether, whereas in Bursa they were ubiquitous and all-important, both economically and socially). This is probably the explanation for the much more restricted importance of aristocratic families in Bursa in comparison to Ayntab (as is made evident by the lower prevalence of *zade*-ending names). It seems that Bursa's autonomy, which certainly existed and was real, was urban, not kinship-based, like in Ayntab.

Canbakal has also revealed a major new finding about the role of witnesses in the legal system that also necessitates a somewhat detailed treatment. Whereas studies of the former generation did not assign any importance to case witnesses, Canbakal found that witnesses had a focal role in Ayntab, most of them being scions of a small number of dominant families in the social fabric of Ayntab, returning to the role of case witness hundreds of times. These same people, and certainly their families, also dominated the life of Ayntab economically and certainly socially and politically. When it was required that somebody speak for the town of Ayntab in general, it was a member of one of these families who did so. Characteristically, people at this time in the Ottoman Empire had no family names, but old and "aristocratic" families had such names, usually ending with *zade*, "son of so and so". Needless to say, those semi-professional case witnesses always bore such names. I reviewed the newly published register of Bursa that provides an exact list of names of case witnesses, but no names in this register bear any family name. In other words, the Ayntab phenomenon of aristocratic families controlling the affairs of the court in some way or other simply did not exist in Bursa. Again, the conclusion from this comparison is obvious; Bursa was much less kin-based than Ayntab, and its law court was much more bureaucratic. Here, too, I believe it is more representative of the central areas of the empire, those adjacent to major trade arteries and imperial roads.

To conclude this chapter, I have dealt in this study with the law, since I think that the topic is relevant to the relative success and longevity of the Ottoman Empire, and to understanding the world of the complaints. I have said in many places that a crucial factor in this success was the key position awarded to the *ulema* in the state administration. In this chapter, we have seen that the *ulema* enjoyed an increasing hegemony over matters of law, at least until the beginning of the nineteenth-century Tanzimat. They also enjoyed a wide measure of administrative authority. In my estimation, this was on the whole beneficial to the state and the quality of administration. It constituted a serious limitation on the power of the civil authorities and created a multiplicity of forces that balanced each other and constrained the power of all involved. We have also checked the quality of justice supplied by the Ottoman legal system in this chapter. It was my finding that this quality was much higher than what was depicted as Ottoman justice in Orientalist literature of old. On the whole, the Ottoman court was not a tool of class oppression and it supplied justice to the subalterns, such as women. In my estimation, much of the population knew these facts and would agree with my findings. It is enough to recall that many complaints to the central government revolved around the fact that people did not receive the right of being tried in a kadi court. It is quite likely—and I for one firmly believe it—that the Ottoman legal system provided the Ottoman state with many points that augmented the positive side of the balance sheet in regards to its legitimacy and, thus enhanced its longevity. Furthermore, much of what was going on in the court in the seventeenth and eighteenth centuries was not only run by Kadis, but was run according to the Shari'a, roughly speaking. This was apparently unprecedented in Islamic history, and I believe that the Ottomans therefore had double the gains: the *ulema* had a positive image of them, unquestionably a better image than any state in Islamic history ever received from its body of *ulema,* and additionally, the stand of the *ulema* must have exerted some influence in augmenting the positive image of the common people towards the Sultanate.

Understandably, real proof of this is hard to come by, but a study of the Damascus (Arab) *ulema* towards the Ottoman judges that served in Damascus is a substantial contribution here.[52] The study, based on biographies and other materials written by Damascene *ulema,* notes that initially following the Ottoman conquest of 1517, the local attitude towards the Ottoman state was extremely negative, born of suspicion and apprehension at what the Ottoman policy could

52 Michael Winter, "Ottoman Qadis in Damascus in the 16th-18th Centuries", in Ron Shaham, ed., *Law, Custom and Statute in the Muslim World,* Leiden: Brill, 2006, pp. 87-109.

be, and what the attitude of the foreign (Turkish speaking) Kadis would be. More specifically, they resented a marriage tax that the Ottomans introduced and the interest bearing cash-*waqf* that the Ottomans allowed. After a short while, however, this attitude changed, and as time went by, it changed completely, becoming almost one of boundless enthusiasm and reverence. It was simply the case that most Kadis passed the test of performance with bright colors, and several aroused real admiration. The best remembered was the famous *Çivizade* (also of course *Şeyhülislam* before serving in Damascus). His Damascene biographer claims that Damascus mosque worshippers wept over his departure at his last Friday prayer in the city. More generally, a historian who studied this topic says, "The Ottoman chief qadis [Kadis in this book] of Damascus were judged by the historians on their own merit, and in the majority of cases they were described as pious, knowledgeable and just".[53] They were less appreciated in Cairo, but for purely "technical" reasons such as Cairo's distance and lack of care for Istanbul.

53 Michael Winter, "Ottoman Qadis in Damascus," p. 107.

Chapter 2: The Rise of Ottoman Scholars (*ulema*)

The Ruler

Introduction

One of the more distinct facts of the Book of Complaints, which is the main topic of this study and collection of documents, is the central role of the kadi, and oftentimes other *ulema*. To anchor this major fact in its proper historical setting, a short resumé on the development of the scholars in classical Islam and the early Ottoman Empire seemed necessary.

Like so many states in the pre-modern world, the Ottoman Empire was also what may best be termed a patrimonial, bureaucratic state. This is a Weberian model, which was fruitfully employed by Stephen Blake to analyze the Mughal Empire, and that can also be used for the Ottoman Empire. A patrimonial state is a state where the ruler controls a state as he controls his own family. In fact, many states like this began as a family venture. When the state grows, however, the family model begins to be insufficient–bureaucratic functions necessarily appear, requiring soldiers, tax collectors, judges, and the like, who cannot all emanate from the ruler's household in the strictest sense. In some such states, the ruler nevertheless strives to keep alive the fact or myth that the state continues to be his virtual household, and this may be true to various degrees in different cases. Most of these states end up being a kind of mixed bag of bureaucracy and patrimony, hence the title of this model. Many historic Islamic states were, in fact, much less patrimonial and much more bureaucratic than states in other pre-modern empires for the simple reason that the scholars in Islam were always free of any trace of bondage. This was a fact, the importance of which can hardly be exaggerated. This was even more so in the Ottoman Empire because hardly any state in Islam had such close relations with the *ulema*. Again, to see how these relations came about, it is important to go back to the formative stages in classical Islam.

The Ruler as an Islamic Ruler

This topic seems not to have been discussed much since the maligned Gibb and Bowen discussed it, and although I do not share most of Gibb and Bowen's views on the Ottoman Empire, it seems a serious mistake to leave this topic out of this book. It is important and is an interesting topic in itself, but even more so, when trying to understand the role of the *ulema* (scholars) in this state, which in my view, constitutes a key (possibly the key) to understanding Ottoman bureaucracy and Ottoman history in general.

The Ottoman ruler was called *Bey* during the time of the first two rulers, and

Sultan thereafter, although the term *Padishah* (Persian, literally king of kings) meaning roughly the same, was the most common for most of the Ottoman Empire's history. At least chronologically, there is a continuity between the Ottoman rulers and the Caliphs and Sultans of classical Islam, and it seems imperative to evaluate the measure of substantive continuity and change involved here. More important, inspection of the ruler's role as an Islamic ruler will reveal that it was more important a role than meets the eye. Although all this may be connected on a certain level with "religiosity", strictly speaking, this is not my own level of analysis or area of interest. I am interested in Islamic institutions as legitimizing institutions, or as more or less effective institutions to run a state in a viable manner. As I will show, the Ottomans used Islamic institutions and Islamic scholars for administering their empire more than any other Islamic state, which was a crucial factor in their history. For this reason, an introduction to the evolution of government in Islam would seem to be in order.

Unlike Christianity, which appeared on the margins of an existing empire, Islam appeared in an area and time devoid of state and government.[54] Every tribe in the area was ruled independently by its chief as a political entity. Mecca itself was devoid of any government and every clan looked after its own affairs. It would have been difficult in such circumstances for a religious group not based on kinship to rise and thrive, even exist, unless they could enlist the support of one of the tribes. A tribe in al-Medina agreed to extend such support to the early Muslim community in return for mediation services, and in such a way, Muhammad became a political leader and even a leader in war. In time, the tribes also accepted his religious message. We, thus, get a model of a state, which is at the same time a religion; the political leader was also the religious leader of the group. It is only natural that the leader of the community, the successor of the Prophet, became crucially important ideologically, even as a theological figure. It was also natural that the identity of the ruler and his right to rule became the focal point of political thought in Islamic history. Crone poses the interesting question of what sort of things a Muslim in the middle ages expected of his government? She suggests that it certainly would have been the provision of law and order in the first place, as a medieval European would likely answer. For Muslims of the medieval period, however, this would not be a sufficient answer. For them, the government was also, and mainly, the tool used to maintain a moral order, and it was the role of the ruler to provide that service. Without that service, the community would lack the rescue vehicle that was necessary to cross the main road that was made evident by the Prophet (Meaning crossing the road to attain the hereafter). Only the rightful ruler (an imam in medieval

54 Patricia Crone, *Medieval Islamic Political Thought*, Edinburgh: Edinburgh University Press, 2005.

Muslim parlance) could serve as the proper vehicle. Any other type of ruler could check internal anarchy, but not supply the moral basis needed. Without an imam, the Muslim community would not be based on true law (Shari'a), and would resemble a non-Muslim community. At the beginning, all went well because the rulers were effective and legitimate, and able to meet the expectations of them. In time, this ceased to be the case and some debates ensued. All of this shows how crucial the head of the community was to the early Muslim community's self-perception.

Since Muhammad left no son, his successor had to be elected by the leaders of the community who naturally chose an elder statesman and a close companion, Abu Bakr, to be the successor. A group of Ali's supporters (Ali was the Prophet's nephew and son-in-law) objected and supported Ali for the leadership position, which in fact was the initiation of the Shia as separate from the Sunni. From that time on, for reasons that are not entirely clear, there is no primogeniture in Islam, but designation—it is the decision of the exiting ruler to decide who from among the legitimate candidates will be the next ruler. This situation continued smoothly until 945 C.E., when the Shiite dynasty of the Buyids took the center of the Abbasid Empire. At first, the constitutional situation was not so problematic since, as the Buyids were Shiites, their rule was fundamentally lacking in legality anyway. The situation, however, became more dubious in 1055 C.E., when the Sunni Seljuks took over the Abbasid Empire, receiving the title of Sultan from the Caliph, thereby creating a new constitutional situation. In this situation, the legal imam, that is, the Caliph, was no longer the real ruler. The situation was rendered even more complex when the Seljuks accepted the formal sovereignty of the Caliph and also accepted the fiction that they were ruling by his permission. Clearly, the jurists had to try their best to clarify the situation legally. Al-Mawardi suggested that there would not be a problem with the legality of the Sultan if he accepted the supremacy of the holy law. For the eleventh century, however, this was still a premature solution, since much of Muslim political theory still depended on the place of the Caliph. Al-Ghazali's solution was, therefore, more in tune with the times, when he claimed that a compromise was appropriate, whereby the Sultan would be the legitimate ruler if he indeed accepted the sovereignty of the Caliph and admitted to the religious-spiritual superiority of the Caliph, which was the chief consideration of the Muslim community.[55]

This was more or less the situation until 1258 C.E.—the Caliphs remained the imams, the legal heads, but lacked real power, which devolved on the Sultans, who were the actual rulers, but not the imams. In 1258 C.E., however, the Mon-

55 H.A.R. Gibb, "Constitutional Organization", in Majid Khadduri and Herbert J. Liebesny, eds., *Law in the Middle East*, Washington: The Middle East Institute, 1955, pp. 3-27.

gols sacked Baghdad and the last Caliph was executed by the Mongol Hulegu. The Abbasid Empire and the Caliphate were no more, and Islamic theorists had to face some grim realities. The Egyptian Ibn Jamaʿa now suggested one solution to the predicament, claiming that as there was no longer a Caliph, Muslims had to accept any ruler who happened to take over the government and establish himself in power as imam (defined as the true Muslim ruler), whatever the nature of that power. This was an extreme and even mindless solution, however, since it suggested the dismantlement of the entire moral foundation of the Muslim faith, as a community dedicated to the execution of the moral message of the Prophet Muhammad. Soon, a more sensible solution appeared. The famous one was by Jalal al-Din Dawwani, who suggested that any effective Muslim ruler could now claim the imamate, provided he saw as his purpose the enforcement of the Shari'a. Such a ruler could even consider himself to rightfully be a Caliph, but it was well understood that the original meaning was transformed, and the reference now was to Caliph in his own territory, rather than a universal Caliph as in the Abbasid period.[56]

Indeed, new types of Caliphs then started to appear that did not purport to be equivalent in value to the Abbasid Caliphs, but merely imams—even Caliphs—in their own territories. These rulers had a new legitimizing basis of power, which stemmed no longer from their descent from the tribe of Quraysh but from their enforcement of the Shari'a and the pride of place they were willing to accord to the bearers of the Shari'a, the *ulema*, in running the state, the judiciary first, but then also other areas.

An example of a writer who composed a treatise in this spirit is Abu al-Khayr Fadl Allah b. Ruzbihan from Isfahan.[57] The writer was a Hanafi thinker from the Iranian region that lived and worked in central Asia at the end of the fifteenth and the beginning of the sixteenth century. He saw himself as a close follower of the great Islamic philosophers of the Abbasid period, who simply had to adapt his theories to the changing times, that is, to the lack of a Caliph. Ruzbihan closely followed Dawwani, though; more than that he seemed to reflect the current opinions in the later fifteenth century of those who worked on redefining the political ideal. The effective ruler was then seen as the imam, but only provided such a ruler undertook to implement the Shari'a, which maybe for a state in this twilight zone was not considered a natural thing to do. In addition, such implementation should be carried out in close cooperation with the *ulema*, the natural bearers of the Shari'a. As Lambton says, "Justice ...is laid

56 Gibb, "Constitutional Organization".

57 Ann, K.S. Lambton, "Changing Concepts of Authority in the Late Ninth/Fifteenth and Early Tenth/Sixteenth Centuries," in Alexander S. Cudsi and Ali E. Hillal Dessouki, eds., *Islam and Power*, London: Croom Helm, 1981, 49-69.

down by the Shari'a; and for the execution of its ordinances and the protection of all its laws, to which are due the continued existence of the human race, there is need of a person singled out by divine support, who is endowed with ability to manage affairs...and who will protect the laws of the Shari'a. Such a person is the king".[58] Further, she said, "[T]he *ulama* play an important part in Fadl Allah's theory: it was the ruler's duty to defend the shar'i sciences but it was through the ulama that knowledge of these sciences was preserved."[59]

The upshot of these developments was that with the disappearance of the Caliphate, Muslims were in need of something new to hold on to as the central component of their worldview, and this was the need of the ruler to embrace the *ulema* as a central element in his state. Whether the Ottomans were fully aware of all this, is hard to say at present, but they certainly behaved as if they were.

If we pass now to the Ottomans, the first thing to note is that some of the early Ottoman rulers called themselves Caliphs in their correspondence with other Islamic rulers, particularly in the fifteenth century when the Ottoman Empire was a small principality in the northwestern corner of Anatolia. As Arnold shows, it is obvious that the reference was to the second meaning of the term, the one that came into being after the disappearance of the original Caliphate (that is, a Caliph in his own little kingdom). At that time, a large number of obscure Muslim rulers adopted the same appellation in all corners of the Islamic world. The "problem" for the Ottomans appeared in the early sixteenth century, when the Ottoman Empire had good objective reasons to see itself as one of the biggest countries in the world, if not the biggest. Such a feeling was unquestionably enhanced in 1517, when the Ottomans came to control not just the prestigious Muslim centers of Damascus and Cairo, but also Mecca and Medina, the religious and cultural centers of Islam.

An important Ottoman text, relevant to our story at this stage, is a treatise by Lutfi Paşa, a historian and former Grand Vizier.[60] Lutfi says he composed his treatise as a response to commonly encountered questions on the part of various people as to whether the Ottoman Sultans were legitimate imams, that is, proper Muslim leaders. One can surmise that such a question could pose a serious dilemma for the Ottomans in the sixteenth century, since the Ottoman Empire lacked authentic Islamic-legal origins but was too important a state to be treated as the principality of old, a mere statelet on a par with other Muslim principalities. The author had to find some sort of justification to account for Ottoman greatness in Muslim terms. In particular, he had to contend with the famous legal argument, based on a well-known hadith (a saying by the Prophet) that

58 Lambton, "Changing Concepts", p. 57
59 Lambton, "Changing Concepts", p. 59
60 H.A.R. Gibb, "Lutfi Paşa and the Ottoman Caliphate", *Oriens*, 15 (1962), pp. 287-295.

says that Caliphs should only come from Quraysh. He found a proper argument, saying "the imams from Quraysh" refers only to the first thirty years of Islam, not more. As for the latter rulers, Lutfi freely admitted that while Süleyman himself inherited his kingdom from his forefathers, who were already legitimate rulers, the original Ottoman ruler simply seized his position by force. His legality was based on the twin points that he not only kept public order, but that he did this by employing and enforcing the Shari'a of Islam. Thus, Lutfi joined those thinkers who held that after 1258 it was not the original Caliph who ensured legitimacy, but enforcement of the Shari'a and keeping effective law and order. On the other hand, Lutfi did not insist that the Ottoman Caliph was equivalent in stature to the original Caliph; hence the conclusion should probably be that he should be considered a Caliph in his own territories, rather than a universal Caliph.

The Ottoman claim for the Caliphate received a considerable boost from the treatment of Ebu Suʿud Efendi, *şeyhülislam* of Sultan Süleyman (in office 1545–74).[61] Rather than delve into complicated and dubious legal arguments, Ebu Suʿud simply presented Süleyman's claim to the title in all sorts of documents where the Sultan presented his titles, such as, importantly, the entrance Porte to the Süleymaniye complex in Istanbul (housing a number of Islamic institutions and the all-important Süleymaniye Mosque), as well as in some written documents like preambles to state laws (*Kanuns*). In these documents, Ebu Suʿud used the term Great Caliphate in referring to Süleyman, so it is clear that he had in mind the historic Caliphate rather than the local-territorial one. Ebu Suʿud does not explain the logic of this new usage, but simply employs it. It seems that by the time of Süleyman, the Ottomans had already thought of themselves as the real leaders of Islam. Apparently, Sultans after Süleyman did not claim the title of Caliph any longer, at least not until the early eighteenth century.

It is necessary at this point, however, to remind ourselves again that we are not dealing here with the question of the Caliphate per se, but with the way the Ottomans came to develop (and for centuries maintain) special relations with the *ulema*. We might begin dealing with this issue by saying that the Ottomans forgot about claims to the Caliphate for a number of centuries after Süleyman (d. 1566), understanding that their association with the Caliphate was really no more than tenuous. It is probably true to say that for them, finding an alternative prop to the Caliphate remained an issue, and that they may well have found it in their connection with the *ulema* in other ways than through the Caliphate.

It must be emphasized at this stage, that so far I have not discussed the *ulema* in Islam per se, but only the position of the Caliph. In order to understand

61 Colin Imber, *Ebu's-Su'ud: The Islamic Legal Tradition*, Stanford: Stanford University Press, 1997, Chapter 4.

the story from all its sides, we need to enter briefly into the sociology of the scholars themselves, starting again with classical Islam.

The *Ulema*, Scholars of Islam

It is one of the main arguments of this study that the *ulema* were the crucial institution that explains the relative success of the Ottoman Empire in the world, at least in terms of legitimacy, maybe even longevity. To substantiate this point, we shall make a small comparison between the social situation in the Ottoman period and in other Muslim countries, mainly classical Islam. The story begins where it began in the last section. On the whole, it can be said that until the Ottoman period the *ulema* developed independently of the Islamic state. They must have developed early on in the Muslim state as collectors and interpreters of *hadiths*, the sayings of the Prophet, designed to help develop the Shari'a, Muslim law, embedded in the Quran and *hadith.* These early scholars were not employees of the Muslim state, and they abhorred the laws enacted by the state to facilitate its own work. As they went further into the business of tracing sayings of the Prophet, they developed (or discovered) further Muslim law, and they furthered the notion that the law had nothing to do with the Caliph, who was therefore forbidden from touching it or going near it. The outcome was a centuries-long animosity towards the Caliph and the government, despite the ironic fact, noted above, that for the scholars, an Islamic state needed a Caliph, an imam, as a religiously legitimized ruler.[62]

As we go along, in time things were patched up between the state and the *ulema.* Thus, Frank Vogel tells us that under the Abbasids, the *ulema* learned to live amicably with the state, began to serve it as advisers, and soon monopolized most state positions that had any connection with the law—a monopoly given as a price for legitimacy. Things took a considerable turn for the worse, however, in the eleventh century, when both the Caliphate and Sultanate entered a period of chaos that soon looked long lasting and irreversible. The *ulema* started to notice that the Caliphate was not even mentioned in the Quran, hence it was no more than a tool to fulfill God's commands. Then, however, says Vogel, "When it no longer served that purpose, in a time of political chaos, the *ulama* set about to minimize the role of the ruler by depriving him of true legitimacy, marginalizing his functions, obstructing his institutions, and in the end reducing his mandate to the lowest level of justification, that of sheer military force."[63]

The Ottoman period was by no means a continuation of this situation. The main change characterizing the Ottoman period, as far as the organization of the *ulema*—to start with that technical area—was concerned was the annexation by

62 Crone, *Political Thought*, Chapter 11

63 Frank Vogel, *Islamic Law and Legal System: Studies of Saudi Arabia*, Leiden: Brill, 2000, p. 200

the state of an important part of the *medrese* and kadiship system (*ilmiye* for short) and rebuilding it on a new bureaucratic basis.[64] While in classical Islam *madrasas* were entirely independent of the government, from the time that Mehmed II rebuilt Istanbul, a change in organization was evident; around his Fatih Mosque built in the city, eight new *medrese* were built, and they became the top layer of the entire Ottoman *medrese* system, which were all graded hierarchically, according to the daily salary of the chief *muderris* (teacher). This went a little further in Süleyman I's time, when the Sultan added an additional layer of top *medreses* around his own Mosque in the city. The institutions not only became part of the state bureaucracy and were given a relative amount of importance in the hierarchy, they were somehow (it is difficult to pinpoint what that was) made more important institutionally in that formerly a student would come to study with a certain famous scholar, wherever he taught; now a student came to a certain *medrese*, and the diploma he eventually got was from the institution itself, not the individual scholar. Possibly, one reason for this was the fact that due to the new custom of the swift transferring of bureaucrats, including *muderrises*, from one *medrese* to another, no student could expect to get his diploma from the original scholar with whom he had started his learning some years earlier. A bureaucratization also took place in the organization of the Kadis. They too were placed in a strict hierarchy that gave meaning to the notion of a promotion, a concept that no bureaucracy can live without. What we find is that some twenty kadiships were elevated from the rest and announced as particularly important. They were the kadiships of the most sacred cities such as Mecca, Medina, and Jerusalem, along with the kadiships of the central cities in urban and political terms—Istanbul, Edirne, Aleppo, Cairo, Damascus, Bursa, and some other of lesser importance. This development reached its peak in the early eighteenth century, when the *ilmiye*, or scholarly institutions, became organized in such a way that there were two career paths open to an aspiring scholar. The first path was that one could accept a job of a low Kadi in the outlying provinces upon graduation from the *medrese*, with the requirement that they stay there for the rest of their career. In other words, there was no possible promotion from a low kadiship to a senior position of kadiship. The second line of career progress open to the aspirant was to accept a post as a *muderris* in a centrally considered *medrese*, from which they could be promoted to higher *medreses*, eventually to cross the line and be promoted to the position of Kadi in a

64 Richard Repp, *The Mufti of Istanbul*, Oxford: Ithaca Press, 1986; Gilles Veinstein, "Les Ottomans," in Dominique Longa-Prat and Gilles Veintstein, eds., *Histoire des Hommes de Dieu dans l'Islam et le Christianisme*, Paris: Flammarion, 2003, pp. 179-202; Michael Winter, "Ulama between the State and the Society in Pre-Modern Sunni Islam," in Meir Hatina, ed., *Guardians of Faith in Modern Times*, Boston: Brill, 2008, pp. 21-45.

centrally located city whose kadiship was considered of top importance. If everything went well for this imaginary scholar, eventually he could attain the office of *kezasker* of Anatolia and then Rumeli, and then the top position of *şeyhülislam.*

This was a chart on paper, and many things in Ottoman history and bureaucracy could be said to have remained on paper, but there are studies of nominations stretching across two centuries that show that in this case, the policy worked in real life, despite hitches and inevitable cases of corruption. There were few cases of serious distortion of this model along the way, including the case of Feyzullah Efendi, the *şeyhülislam* who incensed everyone and paid for it with his life in the rebellion of 1703.[65] This *şeyhülislam* nominated his children as *muderrises* while small children. This was a travesty, but it was not representative: the general level of jurisprudence made apparent in kadi court records (for example in seventeenth century Bursa) and in *fetva* collections of Ottoman *şeyhülislams* was respectable—to say the least. I did not find in any of these sources any legal absurdities or bizarre decisions, so the stigma usually put on the forehead of Ottoman scholars in the period after the sixteenth century seems to me no more than the outcome of the old superstitions relating to the Ottoman Empire in general.

This was a description of the bureaucratization of Ottoman *ulema*, which while important, is only one side of the development. We have seen above that in classical Islam, after a period of rapprochement between the scholars and the ruler, things turned sour, and something like animosity developed. From the very beginning, none of this was to be observed in Ottoman history, and on the contrary, what seems to be operative is the best possible symbiosis, even warm and friendly relations, in all likelihood unprecedented in Islamic history. The major question, however, is, why? One reasonable factor, is one that I have already suggested: after the disappearance of the Caliphate, Islamic states needed a new basis of Islamic legitimacy, particularly states that had no kinship relationships with the Prophet, which was certainly the situation of the Ottomans. I would suggest, however, that there was another important factor, one that is more down to earth. We have seen above that Vogel suggested that starting in the eleventh century, the Caliphate entered a stage of anarchy and chaos, which was in fact the period of the disastrous wars and decline of the Seljuk Empire and it was possibly this that sent the post-Abbasid *ulema* into despair about the situation in the first place. Indeed, the situation improved considerably under the Ottomans, who for about four centuries knew mainly victories, optimism,

65 Madeline Zilfi, *The Politics of Piety*, Minneapolis: Bibliotheca Islamica, 1988, pp. 215 ff.

and a bright-looking future ahead. It is small wonder then that the *ulema* were not hard to win over under these conditions.

What did the importance of the Ottoman *ulema* consist of? After all, one often sees studies of classical Islam where Ottoman *ulema* are depicted as inferior creatures for having lost their autonomy to the state. None of this is of course true. For while the Ottoman *ulema* were bureaucratized, they were given serious roles in state affairs. One major point concerns the role of the Kadi. Unlike the Kadi in classical Islam, who had to share the stage with the *mazalim* court and the *muhtasib*, who together dealt with most matters of the law, the Kadi in the Ottoman Empire bore sole responsibility for all socio-legal affairs. The *mazalim* court never existed here, and the *muhtasib*, though sometimes encountered, was of minor importance, mainly in charge of collecting a certain tax. It is even more interesting, however, that the Kadi was charged with much of the business of the Ottoman administration. The Kadi was expected to achieve something which was no less than herculean—to be the trouble shooter of the provinces and to face provincial governors and their staff single handedly, with no means of enforcing their authority. In documents in the Book of Complaints, we observe the Kadi dealing with every kind of state official to stop abuses narrated in the complaints. With all that, Ottoman Kadis managed to preserve their legitimacy and prestige.

A lucid case study showing the internal logic of society-*ulema* relations is the case of Syria after the Ottoman conquest of 1517 as conducted by Michael Winter.[66] I cannot refrain from more or less repeating Michael Winter's finding on the view of public opinion in Syria in the decades following the Ottoman conquest. I discussed this view once in the chapter on law, as there the focus was on opinions about Ottoman-Turkish Kadis; here, I wish to emphasize opinions about the Ottoman Turks and the Ottoman Empire more generally. Though the Ottomans were Sunnis like the Syrians, the first impression created by the Ottoman conquest of the area was quite negative and the whole experience of the change in 1517 was traumatic. Egypt went from being the central land of an Empire to a far-away province. A large majority of the bureaucrats who ran it in Mamluk times were local, rather than Turk. At this point, much of this changed: the kadis, the governors and the officers of the army were Turks, sent from Istanbul. The language constituted a major barrier to understanding. The first Ottomans were described as ignoramuses, bad Muslims, and cruel conquerors. There was much resentment against the *Kanun*. That the *Kanun* actually sought reconciliation between itself and the Shari'a was not heeded. The Ottomans an-

66 Michael Winter, "Ottoman Qadis in Damascus in the 16th–18th Centuries", in Ron Shaham, ed., *Law, Custom and Statute in the Muslim* World, Leiden: Brill, 2006, 36 ff.

nounced the introduction of a new tax on marriages, which particularly incensed local opinion and that of the *ulema* even more.

In a matter of few years, however, opinion shifted drastically. The approach and opinions of Arab public and of the *ulema* changed towards favoring the Ottomans. The Ottomans were more and more perceived as the sole power protecting the world of Islam from the West and from the newly created Safavid Iran. Ottoman respect for traditional Arab culture was now appreciated much more, as expressed for example in the respect awarded for the complete independence and autonomy of the Al-Azhar educational complex in Cairo. As time went by, all writers in Syria became sworn admirers of Ottoman policy in general. Appreciated in particular, was the execution of a serious and sincere Islamic policy, unprecedented—in their opinion—in Islamic history. All enthusiastically commended the Ottoman positive approach to the *ulema* and the religious institutions in which they taught. The great value of these sources is that in them, top Syrian *ulema* speak their mind freely and in a frank and sincere way; there was no coercion for them to express any particular opinion, and not all of their views were positive.

The *Şeyhülislam*

The best example attesting to the special position of the *ulema* in Ottoman society is the role of the *şeyhülislam*, an office that started from the very bottom in the 1420s, to eventually reach the top of special legal advisers to the government, who was able to depose Sultans, particularly when working together with other top state officials.[67] This office is a serious blow to the popular thesis of Ottoman absolutism, since it was in effect a major weakening factor of the unlimited power of the Sultan.

Already, the fact that such an official function existed, is a notable fact by itself. If the original role of the *mufti* in Islam and Islamic law was to supply applicants with *fetvas* (answers to legal questions), then it is to be kept in mind that there was no such official post in classical Islam; *muftis* were entirely independent and unrelated to the state in any shape or form. Like the bureaucratization of the *medrese* system, the appearance of an official *mufti* expressed a development in the relations between religion and state in Islam after 1258.

The *şeyhülislam* held the key position in the Ottoman bureaucratic structure because they functioned as a legal adviser to the government that was, to a certain extent, independent of the Sultan from a certain period in its development, and certainly independent of the Grand Vizier and military factors in the Otto-

67 The best description of the rise of the *şeyhülislam* from obscure origins to greatness is that of Richard Repp. See Repp, *The Mufti of Istanbul.*

man elite. The *şeyhülislam* became a sort of neutral factor between all these forces, which proved critically important in times of crisis.

To repeat and emphasize even more, the *şeyhülislam* was decidedly an officeholder that limited the power and authority of the Sultan, and made him less than an absolute despot, which is the usual appellation of the Ottoman monarch. It is, therefore, justified to claim that the *şeyhülislam* was an Ottoman wonder, as was rightly said of the Ottoman palace school for professional bureaucrats (*enderun mektebi*), erected not at the time of Westernizing reforms but at the time of the earliest Sultans. Only here, the fact is immeasurably more important because the Sultans were willingly building a power that would restrict their own power with their own hands, and they did this willfully and even cheerfully.

Finally, another point that must be raised here shortly is the question of, why? What on earth could push such a powerful despot like the Ottoman Sultan to undertake such an astonishing venture? One possible explanation was brought up earlier, when I spoke about the Sultan as an Islamic ruler; I showed there that one major point in the intellectual world of the Ottoman Sultans and the Ottoman elite in general is the feeling of gloom in the wake of the disappearance of the Caliphate after 1258, a mere generation before the rise of the Ottomans. Before 1258 it was the Caliph who represented and symbolized Islam. After 1258, something extremely important in the intellectual structure was missing, and as we have seen, Muslim theorists suggested that the void should be filled by rulers, elevating the role of scholars and the Shari'a, that is, a more earnest enforcement of the Shari'a. Under these conditions, nominating a head for the *ulema* who would also be the top Shari'a expert, seems like a reasonable thing to do.

The *şeyhülislam* was the head of the *ulema* in the Ottoman state. From a meager start in around 1420, the officeholder rose in the fifteenth century to reach a kind of apogee in the sixteenth, retaining his supreme importance in the next two centuries, crucial for the continued existence of the empire for another century. The only detailed study of the office of the *şeyhülislam* is the exemplary analysis of Richard Repp, still very much valid today, though I have some disagreements over his personal interpretations. There are only some minimal details on the career of the earliest *şeyhülislams*, so the secrets behind the early history of the office remain obscure. Repp claims that most *şeyhülislams,* until about 1545 (the rise of Ebu Su'ud), did not behave at all like we would expect, that is, like top—and only—legal advisers to the Sultan. He suggests, alternatively, that the *şeyhülislam* was nominated to represent the spiritual leadership of Islam, as his rise came close to the disappearance of the Caliph. It is well known that Islam, like Judaism, as *halakhic* religions, and is not particularly keen on abstract spiritualism, and see morality as incarnated in the God-given holy law, the Shari'a in the case of Islam. It seems more probable that the *mufti* was simply nominated to serve as *mufti*, the state being small at the time, with one *mufti* being enough for its purposes.

It is also the case that reading afresh some materials on the early *muftis* does reveal some involvement of them in stately affairs of the highest importance. At the time of Fahr-i Din-i Acemi, there was the story of Fazl-i Tabrizi, a *Kızılbaş* propagandist who managed to get into the Sultan's palace and exert influence on the Sultan himself (Mehmed II). The Grand Vizier and the *mufti* discussed the matter and decided to leave it to the *mufti*, who was invited to a public discussion in the great mosque of Edirne, where he (Tabrizi) incensed the congregation present, whereupon the *mufti* gave a *fetva* for his execution as heretic. Of Molla Husrev (one of the earliest *şeyhülislams*), it was said that he was personally friends with Mehmed II, who used to refer to him as, "the Abu Hanifa of our time". Molla Husrev, of course, also had an impressive list of publications, and his being the foremost scholar of his time was never in doubt.[68] There are clear signs then, that the role of the *mufti* underwent an historical development that made some sense, rather than appearing ready made out of the blue at the time of Ebu Suʿud.

In any event, it is clear that with Ebu Suʿud (mufti 1545–1574) the *şeyhülislam* reached its unquestioned apogee. Again, there was personal friendship between the *mufti* and the Sultan (Süleyman the Magnificent). In addition, the *mufti* was a most valuable adviser; when he asked permission one day to go on the *hajj*, the Sultan refused, saying he could not manage without him. More important, of course, the *mufti* reached the height of his authority—he became the undisputed legal adviser to the Sultan, who consulted him on every important matter. Toward the end of his term and life, the *mufti* also received the right to suggest to the Sultan names of candidates for the major legal scholarly posts. In the seventeenth century, the *şeyhülislam* was to reach the apogee of its power and prestige, in the Ottoman Empire and in Islam as well when this officeholder deposed six different Sultans, as part of a prolonged crisis situation that gripped the Ottoman Empire in its entirety.[69] No one ever suggested that *şeyhülislams* were trespassing the bounds of their authority, though no one actively awarded them with that authority. It was an incremental process, that developed naturally out of the earlier special treatment awarded to the *ulema* in the wake of the decline of the Caliphate, and, I would say, the effort to counterbalance the growing strength of the high men of state.

68 Abdülkadir Altunsu, *Osmanlı Şeyhülislamları*, Ankara: Ayyıldız Matbaası, 1972, pp. 6-7.

69 See Baki Tezcan, *The Second Ottoman Empire*, Cambridge: Cambridge University Press, 2010.

Chapter 3: State, Bureaucrats, and Scholars: the Evidence of the Book of Complaints

This chapter deals with various insights that can be extracted from a book of complaints of citizens presented to the Sultan in 1675 (the so-called Vienna Book of Complaints), containing complaints launched by citizens against the wrong done to them by state officials.[70] Roughly, the documents used in writing this chapter are the same as those used in translating the real documents in part 2 of this study, but the equivalence is only partial, as I had to discard documents that I was unable to decipher in full. Containing some 2,800 complaints, the book as a whole, is a sample of hundreds of similar legers in the central Ottoman archive awaiting the attention of researchers.[71] The very existence of such a literary and administrative genre within the Ottoman bureaucratic world is, to my mind, another case of an Ottoman wonder. There are three such wonders in my estimation: the *enderun mektebi*, or school for administrators, and the office of *şeyhülislam*, a real check on the Sultanate and other forces, voluntarily introduced into the system by the Sultans themselves. The Ottomans may have been more dependent on popular legitimacy than other Turco-Iranian or Muslim states (because of their grass-root social origins) and hence, were probably more committed to the institution of complaints than the others.[72] For example, in the biographies of eighteenth century Grand Viziers, sometimes such high-placed persons sustained a severe blow to their career as a result of people in a province complaining against them.[73] In any event, currently there is no sign that any other Muslim state took the business of complaining as seriously as the Ottomans. It certainly attests to the centrality of justice (to the poor, in particular) in their belief system, a purely ideological issue, but also part of the circle of justice, where the issue was also one of material importance—justice was no less than tantamount to the survival of the state.

The kadi record (*sicill*) is, without any doubt, the most important source for understanding the working of the Ottoman legal system, but it is a source that suffers from the fact that it looks at this system from the inside. By itself, it cannot tell us anything about the place of the kadi court in Ottoman society of the time, or what other players in the political field thought of it and its proper role

70 Majer, ed., *Das osmanische „Registerbuch der Beschwerden" (Şikayet Defteri) vom Jahre 1675*, Vienna: Verlag der Österreichischen Akademie der Wissenschaften, 1984.

71 Zarinebaf-Shar ("Ottoman Women and the Tradition of Seeking Justice") wrote what seems to me the only study based on actual archival *şikayet* documents. See: "Ottoman Women and the Tradition of Seeking Justice in the Eighteenth Century", in Madeline Zilfi, ed., *Women in the Ottoman Empire*, Leiden: Brill, 1997, 253-64.

72 Linda Darling, *A History of Social Justice and Political Power in the Middle East*, New York: Routledge, 2013, p.

73 Taib A. Osmanzade, *Hadikat el-Vuzera* [reprint], Freiburg: D. Robischon, 1969.

in that society. A source that can supply a ray of light on the kadi court is this complaint literature that thrived in Ottoman society, to an astonishing extent. I have used this literature in the past to shed light on the kinds of abuses people complained about and to single out the major culprits of these abuses, basing my findings on the same Vienna Book of Complaints from 1675, which, as I said, contains some 2,800 orders, each narrating a complaint and orders what to do about that complaint.[74] In this study I revisit this source, as I want to look more closely at some of the legal aspects of the complaints, aspects that reveal something of the relations between and among groups in the Ottoman elite—the Sultanate, the scholars (*ulema*), and the high officials. I believe the source also sheds some light on the position of the kadi court (and the *ulema* more generally), the Sultanate and the provincial governors in the eyes of the Ottoman public and within these groups.

Halil Inalcık made the point that in its ideological self-perception, the main function and raison d'être of the state was justice, which in turn consisted in firstly defending the subjects from abuses coming from state officials.[75] This was not, of course, a topic invented in the Ottoman environment; scholars have shown that it is a topic that harks back to pre-Islamic Iranian states, where it found expression in what was called the mirror of princes literature (a symbolic mirror was placed in front of the ruler, allowing him to see what he looked like).[76] While the absolute authority of the kings was a corner stone in the political thought of the Sassanid state, political philosophers who advised the kings were emphatic in pointing out that too much emphasis on the implications of absolutism were counterproductive, and could result in the king losing his reign, or a weakening in his position. This perception was not based on an ethical principle of commitment to justice per se, but was a matter of expediency. The preoccupation of the intellectuals of the time was, how could the ruler preserve his state and dynasty from ruin. These philosophers made the observation that though the citizens were necessarily the "golden goose" to be fleeced by the king, overdoing it could kill the goose and, with it, the kingdom. Stable polities required satisfied citizens, and one essential need that had to be satisfied was justice. Legal justice meant many things: it meant that the king did not arbitrarily seize citizens' property; that he judged justly among them, not discriminating in favor of the stronger and richer; and most importantly, that he kept a close eye on his officials and curbed their excessive appetite for resources and

74 Haim Gerber, *State, Society and Law in Islam*, Albany: State University of New York Press, 1994, pp. 154-173.

75 Halil Inalcık, *The Ottoman Empire: The Classical Age, 1300–1600*, London: Weidenfeld and Nicolson, 1973, pp. 65-66.

76 Patricia Crone, *Medieval Islamic Political Thought*, Edinburgh: Edinburgh University Press, 2005, Chapter 13.

power, which were invariably at the expense of the common people. There are clear signs that rulers from Sassanid Iran to the world of Islam took this exhortation to heart, and devised policies to implement it. It was only natural that these perceptions and axioms made their way to the Turkish and Ottoman world: we have seen above that the Sassanid world exerted a great deal of influence on Islam via the resurgence of Iranian born bureaucrats under the Abbasids and the later Turco-Iranian states, and this influence no doubt was transmitted further into Anatolia. Mirror books were not only written in Turkish; some Iranian books were translated into Turkish, including into Ottoman Turkish.[77]

Some writings on this topic appears under the banner of "the Circle of Justice" (also called advice books, among other names). This famous approach, a variant of the topic of mirror of princes, referred to the specific need of the ruler to protect the simple folks from the depredations of officials, usually aided by an army.[78] Some treatments of the circle of justice in the Muslim context speak of justice in a generalized way, but in Ottoman society the above rendering of the "circle" has a specific and exact meaning that may at first sight elude us. The true gist of the Ottoman "circle" is the obligation incumbent upon the ruler to restrain his officials and prevent their depredations against the common people.[79] Again, at a base, this idea probably came from pre-Islamic Iran. It is especially associated with the famous Sassanian King, Khosraw Anushirvan. As such, it was part of the general recipe for dynasty longevity, since justice would strengthen people's love for the ruler, and his rule would persist.[80] This idea would also no doubt appeal to the Ottomans and may have propelled them to encourage the existence of a respectable legal system. Some treatments of the question of justice in pre-Islamic Iran, however, devote special attention to the problem of powerful officials and what to do about them. The best example may be the Seljuk Vizier Nizam al-Mulk's treatment of the question of justice in his *siyasat namah*, Book of Government. This book, of course, draws heavily on the perceptions of the Iranian world. While Nizam al-Mulk speaks also about justice in general, oftentimes he is quite specific in speaking about the term in the sense of the need to supervise the officials and check their excesses.[81] All of this probably indicates that Ottoman Sultans were fully acquainted with the problems

77 See Eleazar Birnbaum, ed., *Kai Kaus Ibn Iskandar, The Book of Advice: The Earliest Old Ottoman Turkish Version of his Kabusname*, Duxbury, Mass.: Harvard University Printing Office, 1981.

78 Darling, *A History of Social Justice.*

79 Cornell Fleischer, "Royal Authority, Dynastic Cyclism and Ibn 'Khaldunism' in Sixteenth Century Ottoman Letters", in Bruce B. Lawrence, ed., *Ibn Khaldun and Islamic Ideology*, Leiden: Brill, 1984, 48-50.

80 Ann K.S. Lambton, "Islamic Mirrors of Princes", in Lambton, *Theory and Practice in Medieval Persian Government*, London: Ashgate, Variorum, 1980, Chapter 6.

81 Ann Lambton, "The Dilemma of Government in Islamic Persia: The Siyasatnama of Nizam al-Mulk", *Iran* 22 (1984), pp. 55-66.

that could emanate from the power of officials from early on, and earlier studies of complaints, in fact, show that they were aware of these problems.[82]

Awareness of the contents of the mirror or advice books certainly existed in the minds of Ottoman rulers and high men of state, who portrayed the political system as a field in which the Sultan was a shepherd, and the citizens were sheep needing the shepherd to lead them to safety and happiness. The fact is, without wishing to sound too naïve, it is difficult to locate many oppressive policies by the Ottoman Sultans, besides the basic fact of having to pay taxes, which nominally were not terribly onerous. The point was that the sultan merely devised a policy, and it was the officials who implemented it, and here lies the rub.

One of the major administrative tools used by the Ottomans (possibly also by others before them) to empower the common people in curbing officials was the complaint sent to the ruler.

Though the variety of complaints in the Book of Complaints, in terms of content and structure, is wide-ranging and includes many private complaints of individuals against other individuals, a large part of the 2,800 complaints studied revolves around collective complaints of citizens against officials of all sorts. Complaints were, of course, mainly against provincial governors and their aids, which extended their tax levying authority to collect illegal taxes. Starting from the bottom up, we are talking about tax collectors of various taxes; police chiefs, or *subaşıs*; deputy district governors, or *mütesellims;* district governors, or *sancakbeys*; and provincial governors, or *beylerbey* (or *mir-i miran*). Complaints against provincial governors were quite rare, in fact, and it would seem that these people were particularly keen not to jeopardize their chances of advancement to the very top, so they played it by the rules. Most of the complaints were against *sancakbeys*, and particularly *mütesellims*, people hired by *sancakbeys* to do the job for a specified period of time, and may not have been part of the official hierarchy of the provincial service.

As said above, although the variety of documents in the book of complaints is large, and contains many complaints about supposed grievances committed by individuals against other individuals, most of the complaints, and certainly the more interesting among them, revolve around collective complaints of groups of citizens against state officials that have caused them various wrongs. More often than not, such groups consisted of either villages or the citizens of a *kaza*, an area that may have included several, possibly scores, of villages. Probably in the latter case, what was meant is that a group of citizens came to court and claimed to represent the entire *kaza*. In any event, most such complaints re-

82 Suraiya Faroqhi, "Political Activity among Ottoman Taxpayers and the Problem of Sultanic Legitimation (1570–1650)", *Journal of the Economic and Social History of the Orient*, 35 (1992), pp.

volved around allegations of tax extortion, often involving many additional abuses. In general, maybe half of the complaints were sent solely to the kadis. The other half of the complaints was sent to both the kadi and governor of an area. The outcome was that no more than a handful of the orders (emanating from the complaint) were not sent to a kadi. Already, from these statistics it becomes clear that kadis were really supposed to carry almost the entire burden of dealing with administrative abuses and legal rights of the citizens on their shoulders.

On the most general plane, the book makes it clear that at least in the eyes of the central government, the kadi was the key figure in running all areas of life that were even slightly connected with legal or quasi legal questions, including many areas that were purely administrative. There is no single document where the sultan calls on a governor to put his authority into action and adjudicate among the people, or even try hardened criminals. Even in cases of gangs of robbers threatening neighborhoods and even killing people, governors are called on to bring alleged criminals to the Shar', rather than using their own authority.[83] The only exception here, are cases that are directed to go to the Imperial *Divan* (a group of cases treated below). I will claim in this study that the extreme approach of the central government towards preserving an adjudicatory monopoly at the hands of the Kadi was not merely a theoretical interest and empathy shown to the common people, but also an outcome of an effort to separate the powers, or more correctly, to keep the *umera* (high officials) in their place.

Most of the complaints revolved around a claim of a group of citizens that the *mütesellim* of the district went on a tour (*devir*) of his area—a strictly forbidden activity on his part—and in doing so extracted illegal "dues" from the citizens. This was, for example, a topic of complaint by the citizens of Aydın.[84] The order was directed to the Kadi alone, who was ordered to see to it that nobody was to transgress the Shari'a and *Kanun,* and that sums extracted illegally were to be repaid. In another case, a group of Yörüks from the *kaza* of Kangari came to the Shari'a court and complained against the *mütesellim* that while they were perfectly content to pay their legal dues on their animals, he had charged them substantially higher rates. Formerly, they had already secured an order against him, and had also summoned him three times to a trial before the Kadi, all to no avail; he failed to show up. The order was, therefore, to summon him to court again, by whatever means available, and force him to repay the people. Again, the order was sent to the Kadi alone.[85] It is impossible at present to know just how the Kadi managed to handle a governor, supplied as he was with military forces, and one might conclude that such orders were only theoretical, but such

83 *Şikayet Defteri,* 56a-6.
84 *Şikayet Defteri,* 94a-5.
85 *Şikayet Defteri,* 120a-1.

a conclusion would be harsh and exaggerated; if ordinary citizens came to the kadi court and activated this long process, it must have been effective to a certain extent. Common people would not buy into possible Ottoman state propaganda about justice, rights, and the like, if those were merely empty slogans. It would seem that a Kadi armed with a Sultanic decree conveyed something to state officials. There were probably hundreds of such examples in the Book of Complaints.

There were also other examples, some of a different kind. One was a complaint sent from Diyarbekir, where a person told the story of some people in the area, formerly known as heretics (*rafizler*), who had been witnessed against by a large body of impeccable Muslims during an inquiry by the Kadi. They were then jailed by the provincial governor, but later escaped and were at large for three years. They were then apprehended after engaging in highway robbery, among other things, like assaulting the house of the complainant and killing his servant. He asked that this group of people be summoned to the Shari'a court and that they be punished according to the law, and this is indeed the order given.[86]

A number of orders delineate the exact relation between the Kadi and the provincial governor in the legal process. In one case, a villager in the area of Hurpishta[87] in Rumeli Province complained against his *sipahi*, who one day decided to arrest him for no apparent reason. The case was brought to the Shar' and the villager won his case, but the *sipahi* disregarded the verdict, whereupon the villager complained to the central government. The order called on the governor (*mir-i miran*) to bring the case to the court, do justice as transpired in the kadi court, then implement the verdict and not let such an occurrence happen again.[88] Here the order was directed to both the governor and the Kadi, but the governor was explicitly directed to see to it that the case was brought before the Kadi, then the judgment implemented. There is a careful delineation of the governor's authority, and it does not include adjudication. In another case, an order was sent to the provincial governor of Diyarbekir and to a certain Kadi, telling the story of Ahmed, who formerly gave a large sum of money to Mansur Bey to serve as his *mütesellim*, but this man later excused himself and claimed he was unable to fulfill the job. He also refrained from returning the money. The governor was called upon to look into the issue with the help of the Shar' (*marifet-i sha'rla görüp*), and later implement what was decided and proven in the Shari'a court.[89] Again, the governor was clearly ordered to stay out of legal matters, but

86 *Şikayet Defteri*, 115b-2.
87 In modern Greece.
88 *Şikayet Defteri*, 3a-4.
89 *Şikayet Defteri*, 10a-5.

enjoined to look over the process from the side, then step in to implement the Kadi's decision. In a third such example, a scholar (*alim*) from the region of Saruhan, Western Anatolia, complained that in the Hamze Baba covenant (*zaviye*) in this region, the residents (*abdallar*) drink wine, as reported by trustworthy people (*thikkat*). The *Sancakbey* of Saruhan was called upon to bring the case to the Shar' and then implement the law accordingly.[90] Again, the order was clear and insistent that the governor should not solve the issue using his own authority. In a rare case, the Governor of Aziz in Eastern Anatolia complained about a gang of highway robbers in the area, composed mainly of Turkmen and Kurdish tribesmen. He asked that they be brought to the Shar' and punished in accordance with their crimes. This is the only case that I noted where a governor launched a complaint of this sort, and the only one where a governor asked for the involvement of the Shar' in such a blatant case of public insecurity.[91]

I will end these introductory remarks by analyzing some cases that might look too important to be dealt with by the Shari'a court, yet this is nevertheless where they were directed. In a complaint that came from the *kaza* of Kara Ferye near Selanika, someone died and left some property to his orphans, then a relative took hold of the property. When summoned to the Shari'a court, he expressly refused the claims, and also shunned the legal opinion (*fetva*) issued against him in the matter. When he was arrested, some highway robbers attacked the prison, released him, and he disappeared. This was plainly a serious violation of the public order and of Ottoman authority, but what was the order to the local authorities? Find him and bring him to the Shar' for trial, then report to the *Divan*. Apparently, it took something really exceptional to jump over the authority of the Kadi.[92] In another example, we find a quarrel between two *janissaris*, at the end of which one of them was stabbed to death. Though we are told that members of the military and administrative elite were exempt from the Shari'a court, this is exactly the place where the case was dealt with, and where a *kisas* verdict (execution by retaliation) was given.[93] In a third, surprising case, we find a complaint launched by the manager of a *hass* fief inhabited by Danişmendlu Turkmens, probably in Eastern Anatolia. The manager claims that Mufettiş Ahmed Paşa, in passing through or staying in the area, extorted illegal exactions from the inhabitants. The order, addressed to the Kadi of Istanbul and to the deputy Grand Vizier, called on them to bring the case to the Shari'a court. It also said that should the *paşa* be found to be in the wrong, he should return the sum collected illegally. The point here is, of course, that even an Ottoman *paşa*

90 *Şikayet Defteri*, 163a-1.
91 *Şikayet Defteri*, 114b-7.
92 *Şikayet Defteri*, 47a-4.
93 *Şikayet Defteri*, 114a-3.

was not immune from having his case being examined by the Shari'a court.[94] Finally, on this topic, in an interesting complaint that came from Ayntab, we hear of a *sayyid* who claimed that his brother was unjustifiably murdered by another *sayyid,* also a resident of Ayntab. His request, however, was quite bizarre. He claimed that the said killer was from among the powerful and the overbearing (*muteghalibadan ve zikudret olmağla*), and that there is a realistic fear that he is in cahoots (*yekdil ve yekjihet*) with the *naib* of Ayntab and, therefore, he asked for the case to be transferred to Maraş, the provincial center—which is why the order was directed to the Kadi (*molla*) of Maraş in the first place.[95] Again, here, one might expect some sort of administrative intervention, but despite the complication, the monopoly of the Shar' is preserved.

A Note on the Agent (*mübaşir*)

In Michael Ursinus' study of the complaints presented to the province of Rumelia in the latter part of the eighteenth century, there is a serious, though enigmatic, part assigned to an officeholder called the agent (*mübaşir*).[96] After narrating the complaints, more often than not it is stated that the matter was entrusted to *mübaşir* so and so, though what exactly he was supposed to do remained elusive, with the possibility that he had certain legal authority to adjudicate people. It is important, therefore, to say that the *mübaşir* in fact appear also in the *Şikayet Defteri,* not very often, but definitely about twenty times. In no instance was his role even remotely near to adjudication, though he played an extremely important role in enabling the Kadi to function properly. A *mübaşir* was usually appointed for ad hoc purposes to bringing people to the court in situations requiring intelligence or travel in several areas, possibly using force and the like. Usually the reference was to situations where a band of highway robbers or their leader needed to be apprehended, or brought back after they had made their escape. In such conditions, a special-task expert was needed, and this was the *mübaşir.* The order was always that he was supposed to bring people to the court, nothing more. Obviously, therefore, the *mübaşir* in no way diminished from the adjudicatory monopoly of the Kadi.

The Kadi Court and Big Crime

It might be surmised that the Kadi would be absolved of dealing with substantial crimes (for the most part highway robbery by gangs of criminals), and that those would be the appropriate province of the various provincial governors to

94 *Şikayet Defteri,* 34a-2.
95 *Şikayet Defteri,* 32b-3.
96 Michael Ursinus, *Grievance Administration (Şikayet) in an Ottoman Province,* London: Royal Asiatic Society Books, 2005.

be dealt with according to the *Kanun* or by administrative methods (torture and the like). This is far from being the case, however, and the Shar' is never left out. There is never a call to employ the *Kanun* alone. For example, in an order to the Kadi and *Sancakbey* of Dukagin, there was a complaint sent by the soldiers (*nefrat*) of a castle, who sent a man to "our gate" and reported a gang in the area that was assaulting and looting, and so far 45 people had been killed. The order addressed the governor and called on him to stop this lawlessness and bring all the culprits to the Shari'a court to get what they deserve.[97] Telling, is also the story of large scale brigandage in the region of Aydin, that also prompted the order to the local authorities to make every effort to stop it, and then get all of those involved to the Shari'a court.[98] A group of 40 robbers, made up of villagers from various villages in the Aleppo region, was terrorizing the countryside, and had killed at least one person. Some officials, possibly the *mütesellim*, gave them refuge. The order called on the authorities to put a stop to the situation and bring the criminals to justice, that is to the Shar'.[99] These examples can be multiplied.[100] Exceptional here, was the case from the Rumeli Vilayet, where a villager was said to have gathered 50 or 60 *sekban* (soldiers, "dog keepers") around him who terrorized the countryside together. It was the request of the governor of Rumeli himself to bring the case to the Shar' and stop this reign of terror.[101]

The Kadi in Administrative Areas of Life

One of the fascinating aspects revealed by the *Şikayet Defteri* is the degree to which the role of the Kadi was administrative rather than just adjudicative. He seems, in fact, to have been the major trouble-shooter of the vast Ottoman administrative apparatus of the time. An example is a quarrel between two Ottoman *paşas*, one member of the *Divan* and the other *Beylerbey* of Anadolu, seated in Kütahya. The *beylerbey* received a loan of 10,000 *kuruş* from the complainant, but failed to repay it. The Kadi of Kütahya was ordered to see to it that the sum was retrieved from the assets of the governor in the identified city.[102] In this case, an explanation might have been sought because of the fact that the governor himself was involved in the affair, so maybe an objective official should solve it. This explanation does not hold in many other cases. An example is the complaint of a village head (*zabit*) in the *kaza* of Irmiye[103] against a person who refused to pay taxes claiming he was a *yeniçeri*, hence exempt. The *zabit* claimed

97 *Şikayet Defteri*, 28a-1.
98 *Şikayet Defteri*, 70b-1.
99 *Şikayet Defteri*, 45a-5.
100 Examples: *Şikayet Defteri*, 19b-6; 4a-1.
101 *Şikayet Defteri*, 10a-2.
102 *Şikayet Defteri*, 76b-3.
103 In modern Greece.

he had no documentation attesting to the fact that he was a *yeniçeri*. All this is purely administrative, yet addressed to the Kadi alone.[104] In many cases, there is a quarrel between two *sipahis* over the rights of ownership of a village, or the rights of ownership of the taxes of a certain village. All such cases go to the Kadi, and to the Kadi alone.[105] Also important is the complaint of the people of Kara Ferye near Selanika against owners of fiefs in the area, for meddling in the affairs of weighing the load of taxes on specific individuals in the region, a job traditionally in the hands of the Kadi. Their complaint was found to be justified.[106]

All this is more than just surprising; it is, in my view, astonishing. One might expect that minor conflicts between two villages about their borders, or between two fief holders about "ownership" of a fief would be classic cases for the governor to solve. Yet, apparently they were not. Not once is a conflict of this nature addressed to a governor, or to any official in the provincial administration other than the Kadi. The Kadi was really the herculean multi-purpose functionary who was supposed to be able to solve any problem.

Shar'ia Court Decisions—Final?

Many complaints (and orders) in the Book of Complaints deal with suffering and damages caused to people by the fact that a kadi court decision provided in their favor in the past was not carried out and the legal adversaries continued to harass them in all sorts of ways, among other things, by denying them their rights. It is appropriate to recall at this point that there is some discussion of this issue in the literature on Islamic law in general, with one scholar claiming that Islamic law in fact had no concept of finality of the legal process; meaning claimants could pursue their cases indefinitely.[107] More recently, David Powers studied this issue (particularly in the context of North Africa) and came to the conclusion that though there was an assumption of prohibition of review, a closer look at the original texts revealed that in many cases it was nevertheless possible.[108] This raises the issue of the Ottoman approach to this subject. Luckily, there are some references to this question in the *Şikayet Defteri*. I have found a number of documents that relate to this subject, and not surprisingly, they show a strict policy on the finality of the Kadi's decisions. In one case a *vakıf's* manager had a quarrel with two Istanbul residents over a piece of property inherited by them, a

104 *Şikayet Defteri* 10a-6; for a similar case, 99b-6.
105 *Şikayet Defteri*, 8b-1; 78a-1.
106 *Şikayet Defteri*, 104a-4.
107 Baber Johansen, "Legal Literature and the Problem of Change: the Case of the Land Rent", in Chibli Mallat, ed., *Islam and Public Law*, London: Graham and Trotman, 1993, pp. 34-35.
108 David S. Powers, "On Judicial Review in Islamic Law", *Islamic Law and Society*, 2 (1992), 315-41.

fact that he emphatically denied. When they obtained a court decision in their favor, he demanded another hearing by the court, saying, in the language of the order: "he went on bothering the two, in contradiction to the Shari'a court document (*huccet*), against the *Kanun*, and without Imperial Order, saying: 'let me sue you again'". The two also presented a *fetva* of the *şeyhülislam* saying that, "it is not permissible to hear a claim which had been once dealt with by a Shari'a court, decided upon, (and) a *huccet* given concerning it".[109] The structure of the other cases is exactly the same: one party to a kadi law suit refuses to accept the verdict, would proceed to sue the other in another court, to which the central government retorted by emphatically reiterating that, "according to the *Kanun*" only an order of the Sultan can open the gate to a reiterated hearing of a case in a court of law.[110]

On the other hand, however, there are also a number of documents that testify to the fact that this prohibition was far from being strictly enforced in practice. This took place on two levels: in the first place, there are quite a few documents that show that people managed to get a second hearing by using all sorts of tricks and excuses, often implicit and not detailed;[111] and second, the government itself often issued a warrant for a second hearing without any compelling explanation. An example is the complaint of Mehmed from Istanbul, who lent 800 *altun* (gold coins) to a relative, who died while on the *hajj*. The deceased man's wife and daughter seized the estate, and refused to pay the debt, even after they have lost a kadi court hearing. Mehmed was, therefore, asking for another chance to pursue the issue in court, though he had won the first time. The request was granted, although the logic was not clear at all.[112] In another case, freed slaves claimed that their former patron, now deceased, left them a third of his estate. Though they lost in a court hearing, they persisted in their claim. The heirs asked for an order against them, but what they got was an order to take it to court again. Again, the reason, which is not self-evident, was not given.[113] The most disturbing case is the conflict between two villages in an unidentified place in Anatolia, where the villagers of one village claimed they had found free water on the mountain (*mubah dağ suyu*) and had started to use it, but then a neighboring village claimed that the water was their summer pasture (*yayla*) water, according to the defter. This claim was found by the court to be false and the Kadi decided in their (the claimants) favor. The other village went on persisting with the case, so that by now the first village had received two *fetvas* and two

109 *Şikayet Defteri*, 95b-3.
110 *Şikayet Defteri*, 207b-1; 167b-6; 170b-5.
111 One example is *Şikayet Defteri*, 80a-2.
112 *Şikayet Defteri*, 99a-4.
113 *Şikayet Defteri*, 76a-2. Similar cases: 101b-2; 80a-2; 114b-6.

Sultanic orders, and they were asking for another order that will put an end to the saga. The order merely sent them to the Shari'a court again. Maybe the kadi court was looked at as a panacea to every problem and all conflicts. Or, possibly, the officials thought that the Kadi would show the strong hand that seemed needed here.[114] All this may smack somewhat of inefficiency, but I also find it noteworthy that the mighty Ottoman state chose here an unmistakable path of leniency rather than a tough approach to its citizens.

In only one case did I find a rough approach taken. In this example, villages in Etranos, not far from Bursa, complained that a tax collector had overtaxed them, then run away, and did not pay them even after they chased him to Edirne and sued him again. The order was to the effect that if he did not obey this order to pay his house would be sealed off.[115]

The Kadi and the Common People

Most of the complaints in the *Şikayet Defteri* were by citizens against abuses done to them by government officials, mainly provincial bureaucrats. Many of the complaints were also sent directly to the central government, no doubt by a special person sent there. However, a very substantial number of complaints present a group of people who complained in the court of the Kadi. They complain of the abuse, probably asking for it to be forwarded to the central government, hence, its final appearance in the Book of Complaints.[116] Incidentally, this is the only alternative to direct presentation to the central government. Also noteworthy, is the fact that many groups of complainants ask in their complaint that their case be assigned to the kadi court.[117] An exceptionally lucid and emphatic example is the case of the common soldiers (*nefrat*) of the castle in the *kaza* of Bolvan,[118] who claimed that in the past, when some of them committed a violation that necessitated a legal procedure, their officers would bring them to court and then carry out their penalties. They said that now, all sorts of state officials (*ehl-i örf*) interfere and extort additional sums from them and cause a lot of suffering. They asked to return things to what they used to be.[119] Here again, no case was found where a complainant (one or several) asked for the involvement of the civil authority. These facts seem to constitute a weighty vote of confidence in the office of the Kadi, although some rare cases were directed against Kadis themselves. For the most part, these complaints revolved around allegations of excess impositions of taxes, but sometimes we come across even worse

114 *Şikayet Defteri*, 78a-4.
115 *Şikayet Defteri*, 71b-6.
116 Examples: *Şikayet Defteri*, 33a-6; 38a-6; 117b-4; 117b-7; 45a-4.
117 *Şikayet Defteri*, 29a-6; 83b-5; 66b-7.
118 In modern Serbia.
119 *Şikayet Defteri*, 73a-3.

cases, such as the case of the people of a *kaza* in the province of Bosnia, who demanded that the treatment of a dangerous gang of robbers in the area be assigned to the Shari'a court.[120]

Adjudication by Provincial Governors and the Question of its Legality

One of the discussions taking place in the literature on Ottoman Islamic law is the role of state officials (usually—governors or their deputies) in adjudication. In his study of eighteenth-century Aleppo, Marcus found that while the Kadi was the normal judge, people sometimes were summoned to the governor, who judged according to much harsher and arbitrary terms and laws.[121] Marcus found these references in the Kadi's deliberations; another important source in this regard is the *fatwa* literature, where the same problem of adjudication by governors is found and is strongly denounced.[122] Such trials were referred to as trials before "an administrative judge" (*hakim al-siyasa*), and were considered by *muftis* to be strictly forceful, arbitrary, and illegal procedures; so much so that people were liable to be indemnified for harm done them by defendants in such trials.[123] These "judges" turned out, on closer inspection, to be none other than provincial governors. All this certainly shows that such a procedure was considered by the *ulema* as a most serious perversion of justice, not as a legitimate process. In light of this, it is strange that Ursinus takes the case of Aleppo to mean that it was part and parcel of the governor's job to adjudicate by whatever means he saw fit.[124]

In light of this, it might be thought that people would turn this problem of adjudication by governors into a topic of complaint, and in fact, about ten such cases were discovered in the book of complaints. These cases are important, in that they reveal most clearly what the *Divan* and the Sultan thought about this issue in general, not just with relevance to one particular complaint. It might be useful to look more closely at some of these cases. Before delving into the examples, it may be necessary to emphasize that I have made a careful distinction here between abusive behavior of governor (such as cases related to tax extortions) and cases that look like adjudicative behavior. The best measure of discerning this is simply the wording of the complaints: tax extortions were said to be violations of the *Kanun* and the Shar'; when mention was made of meddling in adjudication, reference was made to an imposition of penalties without any specific allegation, without proof being supplied by righteous and legitimate

120 *Şikayet Defteri*, 22b-3.
121 Abraham Marcus, *The Middle East on the Eve of Modernity*, New York: Columbia University Press, 1989, pp. 107f; 114f; 116f.
122 Haim Gerber, *Islamic Law and Culture, 1600–1848*, Leiden: Brill, 1999, pp. 57-58.
123 Gerber, *Islamic Law and Culture*, pp. 56f.
124 Ursinus, Grievance Administration, p. 6.

witnesses, and without recourse to the Shari'a court. This precious collection of just a few documents is the clearest indication that we currently have of how the central Ottoman government in the late seventeenth century viewed the kadi court vis-à-vis the rest of the state administration.

A clear case of a governor who saw himself as qualified and empowered to adjudicate is found in a petition sent from the Kadi of Istrumca. The citizens came to court and complained that a dead body had been found in the city's mosque; the killer was not known. While no one was prosecuted in the Shar' and no valid proof was put forward against any of them, backed by upright witnesses, the governor nevertheless apprehended some of them and charged them with murder. The order takes the governor to task for imposing a penalty on people without a prior, proper shar'i trial. All this was also backed by a *fetva* of the *şeyhülislam*.[125] The conclusion is obvious—the central government did not at all see it as part of the authority of a governor to play the role of a judge. Another case came to light in a petition sent from the Kadi of Kurşunlu (in the area of Kangari, East Anatolia). In this case, the common people of the *kaza* came to court and complained about oppression committed against them by the governor of Kangari. The governor's deputy was accused of going out on "tours" (*devir*), against the law, extorting sums of money from the people, then arresting people from among them, whom his employees had arrested without shar'i trials and without witnesses, beat them up and took fifty or sixty *kuruş* from them, under the name of *carima* (a fine for some sort of crime). The Sultan ordered the case be brought to the Shar' and that they do justice according to what had transpired.[126] An even more appalling case came to light in a petition sent from Aleppo, filed by a private person. A certain Haci Ahmed complained that some time ago his son Isa had arrived in the *sancak* to trade in grapefruit juice syrup (*pekmez*). The *subaşı* of the said place, without proper shar'i trial, arrested him and executed him (*salb*). The order called on the Kadi and the governor of Aleppo to bring the case to the Shar'.[127] An illegal meddling in adjudication was also made known in a petition sent from Raqqa, Eastern Anatolia. The governor of this province, the *beylerbey* in person, was alleged to have gone about in the *kaza* of Birecik, extorting various provisions, but additionally subjecting some people to severe beatings and jailing some, from which they were released only upon the payment of 600 *kuruş*. All of these atrocities were committed, it was emphasized, without any shar'i process or any proof of wrongdoing. This conduct was strongly condemned and the Kadi was called upon to rectify the situ-

125 *Şikayet Defteri*, 86a-2.
126 *Şikayet Defteri*, 38b-3.
127 *Şikayet Defteri*, 89a-2.

ation perforce. Ha was also warned not to allow such a situation to be repeated in the future.[128]

In another case, the former *mütesellim* of Beğ Şehri was a subject of a complaint—the complainant claimed that without the testimonial of righteous witnesses, he had extorted from him the sum of 1359 *kuruş*. The order was, again, to bring the case to the Shari'a court.[129]

In a somewhat exceptional case, a person named Ibrahim filed a complaint against the governor of Karasi: his brother was trading in the region of Izmir, when an unknown person killed him. The complainant, being the sole heir, captured his brother's estate, but the governor extorted a large sum of money as *uşr-i diyet*, claiming a person had been killed in the affair (*diyet* being the fine paid by a neighborhood where a murder had been committed, the culprit not being apprehended. If anything, of course, the complainant should be the beneficiary of such a "fine"). Again, the Kadi was ordered to bring the case to the Shar' and order a repayment, should the complainant be found to be in the right.[130]

Bearing in mind the relative importance of Aleppo in the meddling in judicial affairs, some cases do indeed come from that city (the number is by no means large enough to prove that Aleppo was truly a special case). In one such complaint, one Ebu Bekir, a resident of Aleppo, complained against the former *mütesellim* of the town, claiming that the said official had arrested him and extorted 700 *kuruş* from him without any due process involving righteous witnesses. The Kadi and the then *mütesellim* were called upon to bring the affair to its due process in the Shari'a court. It does not even cross the mind of any of those involved that the governor may have been within the bounds of his authority when behaving in such a manner.[131]

If we possibly thought that the central government related more harshly in this respect to lower-level officials (such as deputy governors, *mütesellims*), some complaints show that this was not the case. Even a *beylerbey* was not immune from such censure. In one relevant complaint, a group of *janissaris* from Lefkoşe (Cyprus) complained against the *beylerbey* of the province for extracting sums of money from them, again, without any shar'i process and without anything being proven against them. Again, the Kadi was ordered to bring the case to a hearing before him.[132]

In another complaint that comes from the same place, we observe a different kind of problem, also probably an area of abuse of the law by governors and

128 *Şikayet Defteri*, 36b-7.
129 *Şikayet Defteri*, 30a-5.
130 *Şikayet Defteri*, 86a-6.
131 *Şikayet Defteri*, 30a-3.
132 *Şikayet Defteri*, 3b-2.

their aids. In this case, *yeniçeris* from Lefkoşe sent a man to Istanbul to complain against the current governors of the island, claiming that in the past the custom was that when one of their number committed a suspected violation of the law, their own officers (*zabitler*) would jail the suspect and bring the matter to the Shari'a court. While this was the "old *Kanun*", the current governors disregarded it, without recourse to the court, and without the testimony of acceptable witnesses, and imposed on them their own penalties. The Kadi was ordered to prevent that kind of violation.

In an order to the Kadi of Lipova,[133] it became clear that the people of the area presented a petition where they complained against the officials in general, saying that when a *curm* was proven against one of them, as attested by a Shari'a court verdict (*huccet*), and this was collected by the governor or the *mütesellim* in accordance with the *Kanun*, no more *curm* was to be imposed by government officials, as had happened in the past.[134]

In none of these cases were the central government officials interested in the details of the case, and they did not delve into the issue of whether the governor had the authority to meddle in judicial matters. In all of the cases, the behavior was ruled as illegal as it is, for itself and on itself, simply on the strength of the statement that no Shari'a court procedure had been involved. It, therefore, becomes clear that the central government saw it as a serious violation of duty for provincial governors to impose penalties on people by preempting the legal process before the Kadi.

In all the cases I have presented in this section, the procedure (if it is to be called that at all) was clearly outrageous, though remotely and superficially resembling a shar'i procedure (for example by using the terms *carima*, crime-money, or *diyet*, blood money). It could possibly be surmised at this point that perhaps there were honest governors out there who adjudicated fairly, thus not giving a pretext for a complaint, and obliterating the topic from the eye of the historian. I rather doubt this, and suggest that losing parties in trials before a governor would in any case feel wronged and tend to file a complaint—at least sometimes. There is not a single case like this, however. The more likely conclusion is that honest governors would send legal business to the Kadi, or have a Kadi conduct a shar'i trial in the government's office, which to my mind is more or less the same thing.

Complaints Against Kadis

It would be naïve and unrealistic to expect that the Kadis in this period of economic hardship and rife in administrative abuses would be entirely blameless as

133 In modern Romania.
134 *Şikayet Defteri*, 103a-6.

a group. The focus of my argument in this chapter is that they functioned much better than usually depicted, but that does not mean that the situation was flawless: To round out the picture, these flaws must be shown as well. I cannot emphasize strongly enough that the number of complaints against Kadis was vastly smaller than those directed against the other levels of the administration, particularly provincial governors. Most of the complaints against Kadis were that they had exacted expenses for issuing court documents that were higher than the legal rate. Some Kadis also participated in exactions of taxes from the populace of a *kaza*. It must be emphasized that, as I have found in a former study of this source, there were almost no complaints that a Kadi took bribes or was suspected of handing out intentionally one-sided decision for some other hidden reason.[135]

As in the case of provincial governors, the lower the grade of the Kadi, the more prone he was to suspect or downright illegal and corrupt behavior. This means that *naibs* were much more involved in exactions and extortions than real Kadis. Apparently, a particularly problematic category was *naibs* locally drafted by Kadis to work with them from among the local population. The abuses involving this group were famous enough for the central Ottoman government to ban the employment of such local *naibs* altogether, a ban that apparently was never effective. Thus, in a complaint sent from an unidentified place, it was claimed that, "while it is forbidden for naibs to be locals" a local *naib* was nominated despite complainants, and the outcome was that he made a deal with some officials to rob the common people of substantial sums of money. The order confirmed that, indeed, such employment of *naibs* was forbidden.[136]

The Role of the Imperial *Divan* (*Divan-i Hümayun*)

It is well known that the Ottoman Imperial *Divan* doubled as a kind of cabinet and Supreme Court. We are only interested here in the second function. That the *Divan* did some adjudicatory role is not in doubt or up for debate. What this role was exactly is much less clear. It certainly was not a court of appeal, the Kadi's verdict being in theory final, open to revision only under special circumstances and with Sultanic sanction (as we have seen above). In these unclear situations, and with a total lack of studies, it is important to note that the *Divan* is sometimes mentioned in the *Şikayet Defteri* as an alternative tribunal to the Shari'a court or, more correctly, as a forum for hosting a shar'i session, conducted by a Kadi according to "his" procedure. In fact, it was the role of the high state offi-

135 Examples of abuse cases by Kadis include: *Şikayet Defteri*, 98b-3; 36b-1; 71b-3; 100b-6; 95b-7; 153a-3.

136 *Şikayet Defteri*, 103a-5.

cials, probably those sitting on the *Divan*, to decide on cases to be sent to that body. Careful perusal of these documents reveals the logic behind these cases.

It seems clear that the most important consideration for directing cases to the *Divan* rather than the Shari'a court (where the vast majority of cases went, or should go in the perception of the government) was the centrality of the crime or violation raised in the relevant complaint. Chief among those issues was crimes involving the interests of the state itself. Several gangs of criminals, with or without the appellation *haydud eşkıyası* (the famous robber bands in the Ottoman Balkans, some say specifically anti-Ottoman robbers), specifically targeted tax collectors laden with sums of money, whom they wished to rob—often with success.[137] Another type of case found where various social leaders incited villagers against paying all or part of the taxes demanded by the government. One such case even happened in the area of Bursa, which was considered relatively easily controlled and orderly. An interesting, though obscure aspect of this case[138] was that the incitement was done after the suspected culprit, a man named Abdi, assembled a *cemiyet*, which is a forbidden act. Another case happened in the Janik area, where a man appeared, incited the people, made a *dernek* and *cemiyet*, and aroused a social disorder (*fitna*).[139] My understanding is that *cemiyet*, in this context, must be a rally, maybe even a sort of demonstration. Sometimes peasants made such demonstrations without a clear leader. The wrath of the central government was nevertheless unmistakable, as shown by the summoning to the *Divan*.[140] The situation appears in the *Şikayet Defteri* at least ten times, so it must have been a rare, but extant phenomenon that certainly calls for further research.[141]

Maybe the most bizarre "political" crime in this Book of Complaints was the outcome of the complaint of a private individual, who notified the authorities about a document forger who "gave" legal and governmental jobs to people for payment, possibly on order, and made a lot of money through this "entrepreneurship". We might imagine that the authorities in Edirne (where the sultan was staying at the time) did not like this initiative at all, and called for the immediate summoning of the case to the *Divan*.[142]

In the second place, the *Divan* seems to have assumed cases involving particularly pernicious bands of criminals to himself. Such bands were reported on from all areas of the state, probably most often from Rumeli and the Turkmen

137 Examples: *Şikayet Defteri*, 100b-5; 214a-1; 212b-1, where *haydud eşkıyası* are specifically mentioned.

138 *Şikayet Defteri*, 60b-6.

139 *Şikayet Defteri*, 99a-5.

140 *Şikayet Defteri*, 89a-3.

141 For another case involving high state sensitivity see *Şikayet Defteri*, 100a-2.

142 *Şikayet Defteri*, 154a-3.

areas of Southeastern Anatolia, and many of these cases were directed to the *Divan.*[143]

In the third place, cases that local Shar'ia court seemed unable to solve, for a variety of reasons, went to the *Divan* as well. For example, in a village in the *kaza* of Gümülcina,[144] a Christian woman converted to Islam and married a Muslim man, but as the man went to war, she returned to Christianity. When her husband showed up in the village to summon her to the Shar', the village people prevented this by force. Now an order was issued to summon her to the *Divan.*[145] In several cases people simply refused to attend a case against them in the Shar', and the *Divan* arrogated the case to itself.[146]

Other cases that went to the *Divan* were private conflicts involving high men of state. A son of a *beylerbey* owing a large sum (and not paying it back) was summoned to the *Divan.*[147] Intra-familial conflict over the proceeds collected from a *ziamet*-fief was also directed to the Divan.[148]

In more minor cases, the order went out merely to present the details of a case to the *Divan* after it had been dealt with by the Shar'. In some of these cases, the Kadi or *naib* were only called upon to investigate (*tefahhus*), and then to forward the case to the *Divan.*[149]

The *Divan*—Shar'i Trials

While materials are beginning to accumulate about the role of the Imperial *Divan* as a court of law, some complaints in the *Şikayet Defteri* point at the surprising possibility that many, if not all, the actual cases of adjudication that took place there were shar'i type adjudication, no more and no less. A case in point is an order sent to a Kadi of an undisclosed location, which revolves around the complaint of a guardian of a six year-old girl. It sets forth the story of a person, Ivaz, who by some deceit and the help of a certain Kadi married the girl to his son, without the consent of the guardian or the child's mother. Upon the complaint, they said Ivaz disappeared from the area. The order directed the Kadi to find and summon the parties to the *Divan*, "and there let them engage in a shar'i confrontation".[150] A second relevant example is a quarrel between a moneylender and a *yeniçeri* who had borrowed the substantial sum of 2280 *kuruş*, and made all sorts of excuses for not returning the money. The order nominated a

143 *Şikayet Defteri*, 44b-4; another example, 154a-5.
144 In modern Greece.
145 *Şikayet Defteri*, 120b-4. For a similar case see *Şikayet Defteri*, 73a-4.
146 *Şikayet Defteri*, 156b-2.
147 *Şikayet Defteri*, 6a-2.
148 *Şikayet Defteri*, 205b-6; for a similar example in *Şikayet Defteri*, 110a-3.
149 *Şikayet Defteri*, 2b-2; 3b-3; 12b-4.
150 *Şikayet Defteri*, 210a-5.

mübaşir to summon the two parties to the *Divan* in order to conduct a shar'i trial there.[151] In a third case, a village in the *kaza* of Vize complained against a moneylender for trying to exact a sum in excess of a thousand *kuruş* from them, entirely unjustly. The order says: "An order has been issued that now, if he has a shar'i answer, let him come to the Imperial divan and let them have a shar'i encounter", "*ecelden, şarʿi cevabi var ise gelüp divan-i hümayunumda murafaa-i şarʿ olunmak içün yazılmıştır*".[152] In some additional instances, cases involving refusals to attend a shar'i trial or involvement of unusually large sums of money also led to an invitation to shar'i trials within the *Divan.*[153] It is not at all clear what this means for all the cases of summoning to the *Divan* where no mention is made of a Shari'a court hearing. My guess is that many, or most, of these cases also went through this phase, but only future research will be able to resolve the issue once and for all.

151 *Şikayet Defteri*, 49b-6.
152 *Şikayet Defteri*, 102a-4.
153 *Şikayet Defteri*, 8a-7; 210a-6.

Part II:
The Şikayet Defteri: The Documents

Chapter 4: Oppression and Brigandage

Preliminary Remarks

The most distinct topic in the Book of Complaints, both substantively and statistically, is the aggressive, large scale abuse by state officials, of rights of the peasantry when it came to taxations laws and limitations. The late great Turkish Ottomanist, Halil Inalcık, has said that in several places that, in the self-view of the Ottomans, the obligation incumbent on the government to protect the poor subjects from the rapacity of state officials was the most important pillar both of Ottoman law, and of the justification for the existence of the state. The contents of the Book of Complaints indeed shows that there was much truth in this statement. Hence, a collection of document such as the present one has to devote great deal of space to the phenomenon. Distinct in this set of documents is both the amazing extent to which officials were ready to go to achieve their goals, but no less amazing was the resolve of high state officials to curb the tide.

"A distant relative" of the official abuse of taxation was the equally widespread topic of organized highway robbery, carried out not by individuals alone, but by organized groups of scores of members, probably led by charismatic leaders, that made the life of wayfarers hell on earth. This was also a major problem of law enforcement in the empire in the seventeenth century.

Documents

No. 1

36a-6

Order to the Kadi of Nezib[154]

The Kadi of Nezib, Abdulbaki, has sent a letter, saying: the people of the town of Nezib and the people of the villages around it came to the Shari'a court and said: the current general governor (*beylerbey*) of Rakka, Ali Paşa, came together with about 500 mounted, armed men and "settled" [in village areas], demanding a thousand *piasters.* Formerly I gave an order to them to prevent any intervention demanding "taxes" such as *konak* (way station), ... *zahira* (provision), and other pretexts. But he did not obey my noble order, and against the Shar' took from them a horse [worth] 300 *piastres,* later captured and arrested some of them. They were so afraid, they ran away, [so this group] set on the families [of those escapees], for five days, plundering their money and provisions.

The order was written to say that if he took from the poor citizens that much

154 In South Central Anatolia.

money, contrary to the Shar',[155] the *Kanun,* and the old custom, he must be made to return all of it.[156]
16-25 February 1675

No. 2

222b-5
Order to the Kadi of ? [empty] and to the [governor] of Niğbolu[157]
Ibrahim Paşa, may God prolong his glory, sent a letter saying: Mustafa, Mehmed, known as Hatib Ali-zade, Veli, a *sipahi,*[158] another Mustafa, and the rest of the people of the village of Boranli (?), situated in [x] *kaza,* of the *kazas* of the said *sancak,* of which he is the holder, as well as Omer, the *voyvoda*[159] of the said village, all made a revelation of oppression (*izhar-i tezalum*). Suleyman, being a citizen of said village as well, is not behaving properly: [thus], he takes from the hands of some [of the citizens] the land deeds given them by the *voyvoda,* slit them in half, and gave[160] [the lands] over to whoever he wished. He also took by force sheep and cattle from the poor, and attacked the road taken by those wishing to go and complain against him, beat them and incarcerated them for many days, and said to some of them—"You belong to those wishing to cause me harm" ... and he cursed the *imams* and *hatibs* of the said village with ugly

155 The documents of the Book of Complaint usually refer to the Shari'a system of law and courthouse by the name of Shar' and I have chosen to do the same.

156 In this document, we find one of the amazing aspects of the Book of Complaints, that is, the autonomous organization of a large group of people coming from the same area for the purpose of coming to the court of law to present their claim against a high-placed official. They often did this via the Kadi, thus showing the Kadi's exceptional prestige. I have not, however, found a single case of complaint via a provincial governor in the Book of Complaint. We have no information on how popular organization was done in practice. That it was not entirely spontaneous is quite possible; at present we simply do not know. The phenomenon, however, is nevertheless striking. This complaint was also exceptional in that it was launched against a general governor of a province (*beylerbey*), a rare occurrence among the abusers, maybe because these people were high enough to see the greater picture of the entire state, rather than their own tiny interests.

157 Modern Nicopolis in Bulgaria.

158 A *sipahi* was the holder of a quasi-feudal estate, either of the type of *timar* (tax income up to 20,000 akçe) or *ziamet*, providing an income of up to 100,000 *akçe.* The exact term *sipahi* refers more exactly to the military side of the holder, since in exchange for the income awarded, the *sipahi* was expected to supply the sultan's armies with a well-equipped number of soldiers in times of war. The estate was state land rather than private in any sense of the word. On the land system of the Ottoman Empire see Halil Inalcık, "The Ottoman State: Economy and Society, 1300–1600", in Halil Inalcık and Donald Quataert, eds., *An Economic and Social History of the Ottoman Empire, 1300–1914,* pp. 103-179.

159 A *Voyvoda* is an administrator of an estate of special kind, either of endowment or sometimes of a *ziamet,* a quasi-feudal estate yielding up to 100,000 akçe.

160 It is a common practice of the secretary of the *Divan* to write extremely short summaries of the complaints and to change tenses midway through documents, which was probably done to save space and time. Gratefully, they often kept vivid personal expressions, thus giving an appealing flavor to many *Şikayet* documents.

curses, and threatened them with death, and usurped by force the properties and money of some. Things like these have no end. It is quite clear that they will eventually scatter and die. They asked for an order that will stop and repudiate such acts.

The order was written to summon the above [to the *Divan*].[161]

21-30 September 1675

No. 3

47a-4 (transcribed in Majer, *Şikayet Defteri*, pp. 24-5)

Order to the Kadi of Kara Ferye and to the *mütesellim*[162] of Selanika, and the *voyvoda* of Kara Ferye

The *naib* of Kara Ferye, Mustafa, sent a letter, saying: Ibrahim, the representative (*vekil*) of Dimo and Kosta, the children of Manul Faguma, of the *zimmis* living in the suburb (*varoş*) of Selanika, who had died formerly, came to the Shari'a court and said: Formerly, the *zimmi* Yano veled-i Dimo, who was the guardian and general economic agent of Dimo and Kosta concerning the money they have inherited from their father, "ate" and consumed all the said money, and his debt to them [as a consequence] is 5 *kise akçe* (about 375,000 *akçe*). When he [the complainant] asked to see the [written] calculations of expanses, in accordance with a *fetva* that he has, the said one did not agree to show his calculations in a Shari'a court, and said: "I am not ready to work according to a *fetva*", thereby violating the Shari'a. In order to see the calculations, and with approval of the Shar'ia court, the said *zimmi* was put in jail, for "safekeeping" (*emaneten*). But in the month of Zilkade of the year '85, at night after sunset, the son of the said *zimmi*, together with a group of brigands belonging to his own state of mind, broke into the prison, injured the guards, freed the said Yano and he escaped. His affairs were then looked into by a number of people, and the answer came that Yano, the said *zimmi*, is a robber deserving to be eliminated.

A decree was written to order that the matter must be dealt with by the Shari'a court in place. The said *zimmi* must be captured by any means, and have a legal

161 This document ends with a directive to summon the culprit to the *Divan*. Not many abusers earned this honor, and it is clearly a case of a special nature, being described as "exposure of oppression". It was a combination of brigandage and oppression, featuring exceptionally harsh expressions, like tearing of land ownership papers, blocking the way of villagers seeking ways to complain, verbal abuse of religious officials, and so on. Blocking the way of would be complainants is a particularly interesting element, as it reveals that complaining was effective, at least to a certain extent.

162 The *mütesellim* was the deputy of the governor of the sub-province, fulfilling the jobs of the *mirliva* while the previous one was away from the province. It was a temporary assignment, with no permanence of employment and probably no prospects of advancement or career opportunities, hence, *mütesellims* seem very unconnected to the well-being of the Ottoman state or the citizens entrusted to their care. It is therefore, not a real wonder that they were the worst abusers in the Book of Complaints.

encounter with his opponents, and if the situation is as described, and it is legally proven that his corruption is as described, the Shari'a has to be applied to his case, and whatever becomes apparent must be made known to the *Divan* as it is, and you must be careful that such a complaint is not [launched] against you in the future.[163]
3-12 August 1675

No. 4

28a-3
Order to the Governor of the Morea and to the kadis of... [two places in the area]
The people of the village of Kandilli, situated in the said *kaza*, have sent a petition, saying: a person known as Kablan Mehmed, citizen of the said *kaza*, paid the taxes imposed by my order in a partial way. Besides, he has attacked the village of the said people, and has extracted [from them] the sum of 80 *piastres* under the heading of penal violation (*curma*). And another citizen of the said area, someone called Abdallah, has assaulted their village, plundered all their possessions, and has, in addition, beaten up and killed one of them, with no justice. [Thus,] he has committed major oppression, violation of rights, and corruption.
The order has been written so that the case be dealt with by the Shari'a court in situ, including all other relevant circumstances [*şurutile*].[164]
16-25 June 1674

No. 5

120a-1
Order to the Kadi of Kangari[165]
You have sent a letter, saying: the *yürük* living in that *kaza* came to the Shari'a court and said: the sheep tax and bechelor (*benak*) tax imposed on them is going to the income of the *sancakbey*, and the aforementioned are satisfied [to pay in this way], but now the *mütesellim* of Kangari is not satisfied with this,

163 This is an interesting story about a non-Muslim (*zimmi*) guardian of children, who "ate" the inheritance left for them by their deceased father. When asked to give an account of his spending, he refused to do so. Then an investigation yielded that he was a well-known brigand, who was liable for execution because of his criminal record. Finally, he broke out of prison by force with outside help and disappeared, something exceptional in the Book of Complaints.

164 This is also a story about brigandage, *eşkıyalık*, told very succinctly. It is exceptional case of two brigands acting independently. Most likely, here, we are dealing with two brigand leaders who assaulted a village and robbed the people of much property, using pseudo-legal terms like *curma*, [illegal] fine.

165 Modern Çankiri, in Eastern Anatolia.

and charges them, contrary to the land register, six *akçe* per sheep and five *akçe* to a *benak*. Formerly there already was an order issued forbidding taxation in excess of the register and the Sultanic order. In addition, [those doing the over-taxing] have [already] been summoned to the Shari'a court for an encounter on three occasions, but they did not obey the Shar', but rather, beat up the subjects in a strong way, and committed major oppression and molestation. They asked for an order of mine.

An order was written to summon [those involved] [to the Shari'a court] by any means. After establishing by proof the excess sums he [the *mütesellim*] has collected, whatever they are, he must be made to return them through the means of the Shari'a court, and he is not to be allowed tricks of avoidance and obstinacy.[166]

5-14 June 1675

No. 6

30a-6

Order to the Kadi of...[empty]

The *naib* of Kaçanik *nahiye* sent a letter, saying: the citizens of villages of Kaçanik mountain pass came to the Shari'a court and said: they are registered in the land register as keepers of mountain pass (*derbend*).[167] They fulfill their services to the full as pass guards, and while there is no place to disturb them with illegal complaints, the citizens of the city of Skopje, contrary to the Shar' and *Kanun*, and merely to meddle [in the affair], have started to harass them and molest them with demands of [a certain tax]... and tax of irregular Tuna brigands (*martelos*),[168] and of a tax on houses, and other illegal versions of [various] taxes, which is harassment on their part.

The decree was written so that no money should be extracted contrary to the Shar' and the *Kanun*, and against the formerly extant custom.

16-25 June 1674[169]

166 This document complains against the *mütesellim* of Kangari. One major point of interest in it is the popular initiative shown by the citizens, who come to the Kadi's court and presented their complaint. The complaint itself shows that the *mütesellim* beat up the villagers seriously, the term used being *darb şadid*, strong beating. This term was taken from the parlance of shar'ia manuals or *fetva* books, to describe a serious punishment that falls short of the serious *hadd* punishments (the so-called Quranic punishments on harsh crimes, involving execution or amputation). The terms appear in our documents a large number of times, probably used by state officials in their self-styled role as quasi-judges.

167 Certain communities in the Ottoman Empire that lived near dangerous mountain passes paid their taxes by providing armed men to guard the pass against brigands.

168 Pre-Ottoman Balkan forces incorporated into Ottoman armies, which in time deteriorated into private armies of bandits. See Halil Inalcık and Donald Quataert, eds., *An Economic and Social History of the Ottoman Empire*, p. 17.

169 This case of possible abuse may be just a demand for a more justified distribution of the tax-

No. 7

3a-5

Order to the *Beylerbey* of Rumelia and the Kadi of Hurpishta[170]

A man named Hasan presented a petition, saying: While I am tilling a piece of land in the estate of *sipahi* named Huseyin, of the citizens of the said *kaza*, he said to me [one day]: "You are a peasant tiller, [come], together with your oxen", and arrested me. And despite the fact that he [the peasant] sued in the Shari'a court, the *sipahi* did not obey the court's decision. [The peasant also] notified that he has a court decision in his hand. He asked for an order of mine that would seek to achieve justice, which [would also mean] work according to the court verdict.

Now, my order has been written so that you, who are the aforementioned provincial governor, make sure that this affair is dealt with in the Shari'a court; and if the corruption of that nature, which stands against the Shari'a, is duly proven, justice has to be done in this matter. And you should beware of being again subject of such a complaint.[171]

8-17 January 1675

No. 8

92a-3

Order to the Kadi of Samakov

You sent a letter reporting: the entire citizen body (*umumen reaya*) of the *kaza* of Samakov came to the Shari'a court, together with those among them who are miners and said: in order to defend themselves, and since every year there come the freebooters of the Danube (*sekban-i tuna*)[172] [to attack them], and this year too, in order to fight the *haydud*[173] brigands, with the agreement of their social

load. Money was certainly extracted by city people from villagers without due process, and the interesting point is that this was fought by none other than the *naib* of the area, a figure that will come under much fire in the following pages. Obviously, many *naibs* were honest.

170 A town in modern Greece.

171 In this document we observe another type of abuse—here the abuser was a *sipahi* and the victim was a peasant of his. The order directed the Kadi to take charge of the affair, despite the fact that it was an affair internal to the Ottoman administration. Though the order was also directed to the general governor of an *eyalet*, this governor has no role to play.

172 *Sekban* means a keeper of dogs, literally. As so often can be seen in Ottoman history, the original term changed over time, and in the seventeenth century *sekban* came to denote a "new style of army", made up of recruits from the common people, rather than the Sultan's slaves. Their salaries were much lower, and most of them were fired when the campaign came to an end. As a consequence, the term changed its meaning again, to refer to irregular and disorganized troops, and even to mean no more than brigands. In this document, *sekban* are referred to as both irregulars working for the forces of law and order and brigands. On the *sekban* see Suraiya Faroqhi, "Crisis and Change", in Inalcık and Quataert, eds., *Economic and Social History*, pp. 119, 419, 436.

173 This is one of the few references in the Book of Complaints to the famous *haydud* or *hayduk*

leaders [*ayan*] and with the help of the Shari'a court, from each village *sekban* were drafted (each village according to its abilities), and each village being legally responsible for the behavior of the other villages, and they hold every seven-eight villages as one unit, and with no regard to the borders of villages, they conduct war against the *haydud* brigands wherever these can be seen. On both sides, people were killed, and a *mübaşir* came from the governor of Rumeli with his caretaker, who said to them: "blood was spilt". [Saying that], he exacted a fine (*tacrim*) from them under the name of blood money (*uşr-i diyet*). [Doing this] he transgressed their legal rights, and they strongly (*ilhah*) asked for an Imperial order that would prevent and repudiate [such behavior].
Now, an order was written so as to prevent the poor people from among the citizens from being hurt and wronged in their legal rights.[174]
26 April-5 May 1675

No. 9

129b-1
Order to the *Sancakbey* of Izvornik and to its Kadi
You who are the Kadi sent a letter to My Porte, saying: the citizens of the villages in the said *kaza* came to the Shari'a court and said: agents accompanied by 5-10 mounted, armed men, sent by the *mütesellim*s of Bosna and Bana Luka came to their villages, saying: "In your villages something happened in the past", and [under this pretext] settled in the houses of the poor citizens and their families, and sat there for five to ten days, ate food and drank drink for free, and in addition beat them and cursed them and their families, and without bringing them to court, tied them and took them to the pasture areas or to areas outside of the villages, and took from them so much money that most of them had to leave their traditional area of living (*terk-i vatan*). They asked for an Imperial order that would direct the governors of Bosna and Bana Luka not to send again mounted soldiers and agents that would come with drafts [of tax orders] and they also demanded that the governor of Bana Luka would not

bandits, often presented by historians as early national revolutionaries. Obviously, for the poor and hardworking miners of Samakov, who were Christians, they were just plan bandits. See Eric Hobsbawm, *Bandits*, London: Weidenfeld and Nicolson, 1969, especially Chapter 5 (entitled "Haiduks").

174 This is no doubt one of the most amazing documents in this collection. There is a story here about the town of Samakov, the main, if not only, source of iron in Ottoman society. The complainants, described as the entire citizenry of the town, claimed that every year this city used to be attacked by *hayduks*, the famous Balkan brigands (sometimes styled social bandits). The *hayduks* would assault the iron miners who countered by raising their own voluntary militias to defend themselves, with the knowledge and apparent support of the Ottoman Shari'a court and the Ottoman state. This is the only case known to me, where such a case existed in Ottoman history.

come again with an agent, contrary to the *Kanun*, to demand justice (*dava-i haq*), and likewise, that the governor of Bosna would not again send an agent to call someone to court, but would take someone like this to the local Kadi (*toprak kadısı*), according to the Shar', thus implementing justice, and would not take a legal matter to another area contrary to the *Kanun*. They demanded that such acts be banned and pushed aside.
My order has been written according to its usual elements (*şurutile*), so that no such transgression of the Shari'a and the *Kanun* is committed [again].[175]
15-24 June 1675

No. 10

17a-6
Order to the Kadi of Ivraça[176]
The citizens of Ivraça presented a petition and said: these [people] behave properly, and nothing criminal (*curm*) has been proven against them by honest witnesses (*şuhud udul*), and they did not, therefore, deserve any fine (*carima*). [But while this was true], the current *mütesellim* of Niğbolu, just for the sake of capturing and summoning them, and under the heading of the draft, imposed on them monetary fines, contrary to the Shar', and in addition, extracted from them [taxes] under names like *avret* tax (Women tax?)... a pasture tax, turban tax, and provisions tax. He also took money for nothing, without Sultanic order, thus causing a major violation of their rights. He also caused them dispersal and death. They asked for an Imperial order of mine to prevent and repudiate [such behavior].
Now, the order was written so that no one will violate the rights of the citizens, contrary to the Shar' and the *Kanun*.
27 January-5 February 1675[177]

175 This is a document of exceptional importance. It is, first of all, a major case of abuse and deprivation of justice. The *mütesellim* sent his mounted soldiers to settle in villages for days on end, extracting free resources at will. The pretext is, as usual, some kind of a crime that they all had to pay for. He did some other extreme things also, like capturing and tying up some villagers, and transporting them to other places, which had placed the entire local society in a state of psychological horror. This forced many of the villagers to leave their places of original and emigrate, which the villagers described as the worst possible measure that could be taken against them, in terms of justice. This is why they also demanded to be judged by their local Kadi (*toprak kadısı*), a point echoed in almost every document in this collection and emphasized particularly by the officials of the *Divan*.

176 In modern Bulgaria.

177 This is another oppression document, perpetuated again by a *mütesellim*, the quintessential abuser, using the same "legal" pretext of a criminal violation committed by the citizens of the area in the past. The citizens in question employed an argument used here for the first time, but extremely often in the Book of Complaints: to be liable for the criminal fine demanded by the *mütesellim*, they needed to be convicted by a Shari'a court, using a regular Islamic law methodology. This means, in the main, with the testimony of impartial and righteous wit-

No. 11

15b-7

Order to the Kadi of Bayramiç[178]

The inhabitants of the *kaza* presented a petition, saying: Hasan Çavuş, in charge of collecting the cart tax (*araba bedeliyesi)*, part of the taxes of the said *kaza*, has collected it illegally: he has not taken into account the 336 *piastres* that they have paid as cart tax, and now has taken from them, against the Shar' and *Kanun*, 260 additional *piastres*. This is an injustice and a violation of their rights. They asked for an Imperial order that would direct [all involved] to deal with this [issue] in the Shari'a court, so that justice is done.

Now, an order was issued so that the affair be brought before the Shari'a court in situ. If it is true that he has taken more than is allowed by the Shar' and the *Kanun*, he has to be made to return it, and there is no permit to extract a profit (*faiz*), contrary to the decree and the land register.

27 January-5 February 1675

No. 12

72b-2

Order to the Kadi of Izmir and the *mütesellim* of Suğla *sancak*

The citizens of the *kaza* of Sifrihisar Çeşme sent a man and a petition and said: [ordinarily] they pay their *avariz*[179] tax, which they are obliged to pay, and the rest of the taxes due from them according to [Sultanic] decree to those in charge of collecting them on the basis of the decree and the land register, and there is no fault in their payment. But now, their kadi, a kadi named Mustafa, took 400 *piastres* more than is allowed by the decree and the register for himself. Besides, he took more than is allowed by the *Kanun*, 15 and 20 *piastres,* for the issuance of Shari'a documents. And while the tax on the division of estates is 15 to every 1000 [of estate value], he charged 150 and 160, thereby creating a major case of oppression and violation of rights. They asked for an order in this matter.

[My] order has been written so that if the claim of him extracting contrary to the Shar' and *Kanun* is right, he has to be forced to repay, and let me not hear of such a claim again.

7-16 April 1675

---

nesses, who have been thoroughly checked by the Kadi for these qualities. Without this, no conviction could be legal.

178 Situated in the Biga *sancak*, south of the sea of Marmara.

179 The *avariz* tax was an irregular tax that became entirely regular. It was a real-estate tax, where the value of a citizen's house was assessed and paid accordingly.

No. 13

37a-3

Order to the Kadi of Kangari[180]

The Kadi of Milan, Mevlana Ramadan, sent a letter and reported that: the citizens of a *kaza* of Milan came to the Shari'a court and said that: the current *mütesellim* of Kangari sent 50 mounted, armed men and he himself went out on a tour (*devir*), visited village after village, settled in the houses in which they and their families were living, and took from them, without pay, food, as well as 50 and 60 *piastres*, and black barley, and what was not registered in the register as earmarked for the *mirliva*, that is, *yaylakiyye* tax on every piece of summer pasture. Facing their legal opponents, they said: while nothing about them was proven as wrong in the Shar' and according to just witnesses, the said persons, using draft [alone] captured and incarcerated them, and beat them severely, and every three months they sent to them *subaşıs* who took from them sums of money under the name *aylık*. Doing [all] this they committed oppression against them and violation of their rights. They asked for an order that would put an end to [such behavior], which is against the Shar' and the *Kanun*.

Now, [my order] was written so that the matter be investigated in situ by the Shari'a court. If it is true that he has extracted from the poor of the citizens sums of money contrary to the Shar', *Kanun*, and the land register, he is to be forced to return the sums to the owners of the rights. A court document [*huccet*] should be issued, describing faithfully the things that unfold [in the investigation].[181]

16-25 February 1675

No. 14

19b-6

Order to the *Beylerbey* of Rumelia and the Kadi of Konica[182]

You who are a Kadi, you sent a letter and said that: the *sipahi* Nazir living in the *nahiye* of Konica, that is in the said *kaza*, together with Dimo and Shabo and

180 The modern Çankiri, in Eastern Anatolia.

181 This is another case of oppression through tax extortion. The term introduced here is tour (*devir*), which is a tour by a unit of soldiers from village to village that is made in order to extract resources and illegal taxes. Considered highly illegal by the state, and subject to numerous orders trying to obliterate it, it was still very much alive at this time. Another important element in this document is the importance attached by the *Divan* to narrating exactly the facts discovered by the investigation conducted by the court. This is one of several cases in this collection of complaints where we see that *Divan* members would disagree completely with statements claiming that the authorities in classical Islam did not keep Kadi records because these things had no practical value. The insistence of the *Divan* on the necessity of writing a *huccet* is intended to allow retrieval of the facts of the case for reuse.

182 In modern Greece.

Hristo and Niko and Hiba [?] and a thousand Christians living in the same *nahiye*, came to the Shari'a court and complained against a case of major oppression. [Some people] from village [?] belonging to the *nahiye* of Kolonya, together with 5-10 brigands belonging to their state of mind, set fire to the village of Balgat, belonging to the *kaza* of Konica, in the year 1080 and something, and robbed the money and property of the said people. The people of the said village dispersed and died. [With this], they committed a major oppression and violation of their rights.
[My order] was written so that the matter will be dealt with by the Shari'a court in place, so that the criminals will be caught by any means, and so they will get their true shar'i punishment, whatever that may be.[183]
27 January-5 February 1675

No. 15

114b-8
Order to the Kadi and the *Sancakbey* of Aziz[184]
You who are the said *mirliva*, you have sent a petition in which you claimed: in that area between Alicak Belend, Murad Paşa bridge, the river, Arslan Belend and Kara Su, Kurdish and Turkmen tribesmen, together with local brigands, descend on the roads and act as highway robbers, there being no end to the anarchy and lawlessness which they create. He asked for an order that would direct [all concerned] that if there is shar'i proof of their lawlessness, as described above, they would get their proper [punishment], as prescribed by the Shar'.
[My] order was written so that [everyone] is directed to behave in accordance with what was described above.[185]
26 May-4 June 1675

No. 16

44a-4
Order to the Kadi of Valonya, to its *mütesellim*, and to the commanders of the fortresses of Sevandes and Kalas?, and to *voyvoda* x (empty)

183 This is again a document that can be unsettling to some people—here a group of brigands attacked a village and pillaged its properties, and then set the entire village on fire. The villagers claimed that the citizens scattered and some of them died. At least some of this sounds reliable. The document is important from an additional point of view, here one of the addressees is the provincial governor, as befits a situation of major crime. It might be expected that the governor would be called upon to exercise some judicial function, but this does not actually take place. The case is instead entrusted to the Shari'a court.

184 In Eastern Anatolia.

185 In this brigandage document, complaining is done to the central government about the difficult nature of the phenomenon in the area. The interesting thing, though, is that not the common people (its common victims) did this complaining, but the provincial governor himself, who obviously expressed his frustration at the impossibility for him to control the situation.

Hasan sent a petition and said: three *zimmi* brigands named Duka, Yako-oğlu and Lazri? Attack and plunder day and night the villages in the vicinity and steal their money and properties. Some of them also beat up these villagers with arms of war and even kill people, thus committing a great many acts of crime and oppression. They ask for an order that will direct that this matter be investigated by the Shari'a court, and that justice will be done.
Now, [my] order has been written so that the matter will be dealt with by the Shari'a court, and if the corruption and evil nature of the [suspects] are proven, what they deserve according to the Shar' should be carried out.[186]
8-17 March 1675

No. 17

11a-4
Order to the Kadis in the sub-province (*sancak*) of Ruha[187]
The citizens of the Imperial estates, endowments, and feudal estates in your areas of jurisdiction presented a petition to My Porte, saying: the *avariz* and other taxes which the said citizens of the villages are obliged to pay, are calculated on the basis of high, middle, and low [income], and each person pays according to their ability, and there is no fault with their payments, and there is not a thing in their behavior giving any reason to bother them. [While this was so], a demand came from the provincial governor (*mir-i miran*) and the other state officials, without an order [by the ruler] to pay irregular taxes such as *subaşılık*, summer pasture, fire-wood, and other taxes. They have thus committed a major transgression, have extracted from them a large sum of money, and committed oppression. [They asked for an order] to stop the said people from doing [all this]. But they [also notified] that the said people did not obey the order and molested the citizens in the said way.
Now, an order of mine was given in order to prevent the aforementioned from committing [further] violations.[188]
18-27 January 1675

186 This document is special in the sense that those who are accused of brigandage are three Christian leaders, brigands from the Avlona area in Albania. Some of their victims are said to have been killed by war-tools, knives, and rifles, crimes that are all potentially punishable by death according to Islamic law.

187 In South Eastern Anatolia.

188 This tax extortion is not as graphic and shocking as many others in the collection, but it is nevertheless special in the sense that it again shows the illegal activity that sometimes took place even at the hands of general governors of provinces (*beylerbey*).

No. 18

28a-5

Order to the Governor General (*beylerbey*) of Rumelia and the Kadi of Ivranye[189]

The *voynuks*[190] who live in the said *kaza* presented a petition to My Porte, saying: they claim that they used to pay their taxes and dues (imposed on them according to the Shar', the *Kanun*, and the land register) to their officers, and that they are happy [with that arrangement]. But in the year 1080 and something, their officers were no longer satisfied with this [arrangement], but extracted additional taxes from them, like *çift* tax of 12 *piastres* for a *çift*[191] and [an additional] tax of 130 *piastres* and added to their *ispence*[192] 8,000 *akçe* and a big sum under the name of *carima*, and in this way created an oppression with no end. They asked for an order of mine.

Now, [the order] was written so that whatever was taken against the *Kanun* and contrary to the Shar' should be given back, and in the [future] taxes are to be taken [only] according to the Imperial treasury.[193]

6-15 February 1675

No. 19

36b-7

Order to the Kadi of Ruha

The citizens of Birecik *kaza* came and argued: the Governor General (*beylerbey*) of Rakka, Ali Bey, came in the year 1080 and something, and settled "on the shoulders" of the citizens and ate bread and drank free of charge, and took sheep and lambs and other kinds of food and provisions of theirs, then beat up some of them severely, and contrary to the Shar' incarcerated some of them. He also took from them 600 *piastres* and caused a major injustice.

The order is that that case should be dealt with by the Shari'a court in situ and if it is true what is said he has done, against the Shar' and against what was customary, he has to be made to return [the money], and you should be careful not to be [the reason] for such a complaint in the future.

16-25 February 1675[194]

---

189 In modern Serbia.

190 *Voynuks* were soldiers of pre-Ottoman Balkan units, incorporated into the Ottoman armies, who then settled on the land. See Inalcık and Quataert, *Economic and Social History*, p. 16, and glossary.

191 The basic land tax of the *timar* system.

192 A poll tax in pre-Ottoman Serbia, continued under the Ottomans as a customary tax in some areas. See Inalcık and Quataert, *Economic and Social History*, glossary.

193 This tax extortion document deals with the situation of the *voynuks*, state soldiers settled on the ground and performing a service to the state. As part of the state administration, they might be expected to be above worries about taxation. As this document shows, however, this was hardly the case.

194 This case of tax oppression, too, comes from Eastern Anatolia, and involves the general gov-

No. 20

38a-3

Order to the Kadi of Kurşunlu[195]

You have sent a letter and said: the poor citizens in this *kaza* came to the court of the Shari'a and reported a major case of oppression: the present *mütesellim* of Kangari, Mehmed, contrary to the Shar' and the *Kanun*, sent to the area a commander of irregulars (*ağa*) with 150 mounted, armed men called *martelci* [*martolos*]. These settled in the houses of the local people and their families, ate food of various types without pay, and in addition took 15-20 *piastres* from every village. And though [armed] tours (*devir*) are forbidden, and though formerly an order was issued banning [tours], they cared little for this order and went out on tours with 300-400 mounted, armed men, went from one village to another and extracted from every village 50-60 *piastres*. And once every two months their *ağa* nominated someone to subaşı, who came to the villages with a force of 40-50 mounted men and extracted by force 20-30 *piastres* as subaşı money from each village. And although they pay summer pasture tax, earmarked for the *sancak* governor, according to their ability, the said person is not content with this and extracts from them as summer pasture tax much more than they can afford, that is, 700 or 800 *piastres* that he takes from them, using arguments that have no basis in reality, and using [merely] a draft [of tax-decree], he sent [against] many of the poor, groups of mounted, armed men, 15 and 20 big, headed by an agent, none being citizens of the area. And while nothing has been proven against them in Shari'a court by just witnesses, some of them were captured and arrested contrary to the Shar' and without a Sultanic order, were badly beaten, and besides, sums of 50 and 60 *piastres* were taken from them under the name of *carima*. Violation of rights and oppression of that nature know no bound and the citizens of many villages have dispersed and died. They insistently asked for a decree that would put an end and repudiate all these illegal innovations (*bidaatlar*).

Now, [my] order was written so that whatever they have taken that is proven and is against the Shar', the *Kanun* and the land register, should be returned.

26 February-7 March 1675[196]

---

ernor of a province. Here the oppression was stark and narrated in great detail. Interestingly, however, even in this case, where the accused is the Supreme Governor, the clear-cut order is to bring the case to the Shari'a court in situ, where the governor might possibly influence the outcome. I choose the optimistic interpretation that the *Divan* people did not intend to stifle the process of justice, but to withstand any illegal behind-the-scenes machinations.

195 In sancak Kangari, Eastern Anatolia.

196 This story of tax oppression is obviously one of the worst, including as it does, all the despicable repertoire of the tax abusers, from the illegal tour (*devir*), to extortion of money with the help of a draft, rather than a real Sultanic order. The abuses in this case went so far that the victims dubbed them as *bidaatlar*, illegal innovations that are more than strictly legal, being

No. 21

75b-4

Order to the *naib* of Gölbazar Bursa

You who are *naib*, you sent a letter and said: the poor citizens of Gölbazar Bursa came to the Shari'a court and reported a case of oppression (*izhar-i tezalum*) against them: Ismail, the *mütesellim* for the holder of the post of Governor General of Anatolia, came to the Shari'a court with a draft [of taxation order] (*musevvede*), and demanded money under the name of blood money (*uşr-i diyet*), and tax for the government house (*konak*). [In addition], his people took [some] of the citizens as simple workers to other provinces, and he [also] took from them 1436 *piastres* in six months. And on the part of the Governor [himself], it was said to the citizens: "You used to pay to the said province tithe (*uşr*) for spilled blood (*kan*)", and [saying this], took from them as much money, as well as the tax of 300 chickens and [an unspecified amount for another tax]. They claimed that they thus remained without the ability to defray their taxes, what would cause the poor citizens to disperse and [eventually] to die. All these were major [cases] of oppression and violation of their rights. They asked for an order that would direct to prevent and push aside [such abuses.]

The order was written so that no action would be possible against the Shar', the *Kanun* and the old custom.[197]

7-16 April 1675

No. 22

58a-1

Order to the Kadi of Antalya

The citizens of the said *kaza* sent a petition, claiming: Kusar-oğlu Haci Ahmed, Ilyas Kethuda, Vazan [?] Halil, and Turkmen Mahmud, also of the inhabitants of the said *kaza*, extracted from the poor citizens of the said *kaza* 100 *piastres* under the name of camel money, contrary to the Shar' and the *Kanun*. Under the regular taxes they [took] 100 and 110 *piastres*. They also told them, "We paid 100 *piastres* as blood money to the officials for you, and also took from them one time 120 *vukiyye* of coffee". Similar violations of the law are endless. They ask an order that would direct [transgressors] to give back what they have taken to their poor owners contrary to the Shar' and *Kanun*, thereby achieving justice.

---

in fact theological.

197 This document is just another ordinary tax extortion, carried out, almost as usual, by the *mütesellim*. This time, however, the popular movement against the oppression is led by the *naib*. As I have already alluded to, many *naibs* at this time were a lot less inclined to put their neck on the line to side with the poor in their fight against extortion from highly placed state officials (*ehl-i örf*).

Now, [my] order has been written so that they are to be made to return what they have taken contrary to the Shar' and *Kanun*, with the help of a *mübaşir* nominated for this purpose.
23 August-1 September 1674

No. 23

55b-3
Order to the Kadi of Akhisar[198]
You have sent a letter and said: the inhabitants of the said *kaza* came to the court and said: the present *voyvoda* of Akhisar, Furhad, and his affairs' manager (*kethüda*), Ahmed, undertook upon themselves the tax farming of a number of *timars* from their *sipahis*. They did not content themselves with the taxes approved by the Shar' and the *Kanun*, but under tithe they extracted from them much produce by force, and under the name *carima* they have squeezed large amounts of money from them. These types of oppression and legal violation have brought about the destruction of some villages, and many Muslims who worked as simple workers have perished. They have not obeyed the Shar' at all. They asked for an order that would stem and push aside such behavior.
Now, [my] order has been written so that the case be brought to the Shari'a court in situ. They are to return the sums they have taken from the poor citizens contrary to the Shar' and the *Kanun*. Afterwards, they are to refrain from usurping the rights of the citizens, contrary to the Shar' and the *Kanun*. They are to refrain from interfering in the business of the area. And if they do not refrain [from such behavior], their case ought to be registered in the *sicill*, a *huccet* ought to be issued, and their case should be presented to the *Divan*.
18-27 March 1675

No. 24

3b-2
Order to the Kadi of Lefkoşe[199]
The pensioners of the corps (*ocak*) of Janissaries guarding the island of Cyprus sent a petition to My Porte, saying: while these persons mind their own business, and create no problem justifying anyone to molest them in contradiction to the Shar', the General Governor of Cyprus for the year 1080 and something, Abdulkadir, without anything being proven against them in a Shari'a court, extracted from them a great deal of money, totally illegally.
[My] order has been issued so that whatever he has taken from them against

198 There were three Akhisars in the Ottoman Empire, two in Western Anatolia and one former Yugoslavia.
199 Today's capital of Greek Cyprus, Nicosia.

the Shar' and the *Kanun*, and against the old custom, should be returned to them, provided it is proven in the Shari'a court.[200]
8-17 January 1675

No. 25

10a-2
Order to the *Beylerbey* of Rumelia and the Kadi of Bihlishte[201]
The Kadi of town [?] [in that province] sent a letter, reporting that the people of the *kaza* came to the Shari'a court and complained that when they go to the bazaar of the town of Kurce, situated in their area, the brigand Mehmed, citizen of the village of Vazana [?], situated in their administrative region, together with 50-60 armed irregulars [*sekban*] belonging to his own state of mind, came and captured a number of people of the same administrative area, put them in chains, and beat up the Deputy of the *yeniçeri* commander [of the region] really hard and chained him [as well]. In this way, they have committed major oppression and deprivation of rights. They asked for an order of mine that would decree to bring the matter for consideration by the Shari'a court, so that justice can be made.
[My] order was written that the matter is to be brought to the Shari'a court in the place [of the events]. And if it is proven according to the Shar' that the [suspects] committed the crimes alleged, justice should be applied to them.
18-27 January 1675

No. 26

15b-4
Order to the General Governor (*beylerbey*) of Rumelia and the Kadi of Konica[202]
The scholars, the sufi poor (*suleha*), rich, and poor, sent a memorandum (*mahzar*) saying: in this year, 1085, the *mütesellim* of Yanya, went out on a tour (*devir*) of *nahiye* [x] of the said *kaza*, and took 70,000 *akçe*. Not being satisfied with this, he came to the said town with 120 soldiers and settled in it for three days, extracting from them food, drink, barley, straw, wood, sheep, oil, honey, and other provisions to the price tag of 28,000 *akçe*, which together comes to 98,000 *akçe*. He also arrested many people among them, whom he put in chains, and also took from them a tax for criminal misdeeds [*carima*] of 20,000 *akçe*.

200 In this little document there are several important points to study: retired fortress guards complained against a high-placed state official, who was supposed to be equal to them socially and in terms of class and status group; yet, surprisingly, these look like two separate groups. Moreover, the governor, who was supposed to be able to judge cases like this, was himself dragged to the Shari'a court, where his power was quite negligible.
201 Bihlisht in modern Albania.
202 In modern Greece.

[They thus] announced that he has committed a major oppression against them. They asked the issuance of a decree that would direct to bring the matter to the Shari'a court and that justice should be done.
[My] order has been issued so that what he has taken from the poor citizens, provided this can be proven in a court of law, in the place where it all took place, should be given back.
27 January-5 February 1675

No. 27

119a-7 (transcribed in Majer, *Şikayet Defteri* p. 26)
Order to the Kadi of Selanika
The inhabitants of the village of Kadi that belongs to the said *kaza* presented a petition in which they claimed: they are the citizens of the feudal estate (*ziamet*) of Halil, a *muteferika* of My Sublime Porte (receiver of a Sultanic medal of mine). They are independent (*serbest*), which means that no one can meddle in their [affairs], but while this was the situation, the said Halil, contrary to the Shar', extracted 800 *piastres* from them, and again imposed a tax of 40,000 *akçe* as foot tax on them. [In addition] he extracts from them every year 80 lambs with their sheep. And besides, he extracts from them the money-value of 100 *kile* barley (local village measure), as well as 30,000 *akçe* as a wood tax. He also imposes on them a *çift bozan*[203] tax of 3 *piastres* per person, and marries their under-age girls to whomever he likes, and he takes 5-6 citizens of theirs to be his personal servants, as well as [allowing himself] to impose on them punishments of up to two strokes of the whip. In addition, though he has an old house, he destroyed 5-6 houses of the citizens [to enlarge his own house?], and in this way extracted from them 40,000 *akçe*. Illegal acts and usurpation of rights of that nature have no end. This being the case, they formerly sued [the above mentioned] in the Shari'a court, which ruled in their favor, awarding them the sum of 120,000 *akçe* as compensation. They have [already] received 100,000 *akçe* [of this sum], the rest remains unpaid. They ask for my order.
An order was written so that the issue will be investigated by the Shari'a court and justice will be done.
5-14 June 1675[204]

203 A tax that should be paid by a peasant who deserted the land, not by others.

204 This document presents an unusual record of abuse, of an exceptional nature: the "hero" in this case is the *sipahi*, possessor of the quasi-feudal estate, a direct employee of the Sultan and recipient of a medal of honor. The *Divan* people might have "forgotten" that part of his biography, in light of the dismal tale of abuse they were about to tell. He extracted large sums of money from the peasants in the area, just like other state officials, but he did some "original" things as well. For example, he married off small girls at will to whomever he chose and inflicted whip lashes on (innocent?) peasants. Another aspect of this document that is more important theoretically is that we hear that the peasants have already sued this *sipahi* in a court

No. 28

170b-2

Order to the *paşa* and Kadi of Diyar Bekir

Someone named Ali has presented a petition to My Porte and claimed: he is dealing with his own affairs, not molesting anyone or hurting the rights of others against the Shar', refraining from creating any situation justifying restraining him. But while this was the case, a certain Ahmed...[illegible title], citizen of [x ?] *kaza* seized all of his money and property, in the year 1080 and something, against the Shar', unjustly. Besides, he said to him: "You complain against me." [With this pretext,] he arrested him for four months and sealed his house. And besides the fact that he caused a great fear in this way, another inhabitant of the same *kaza*, Isa Bey, the *bey* of Kork (?), took the daughter of the said [complainant] forcefully and against the Shar', thereby causing him a great deal of oppression. He asked for an [Imperial] order against this.

An order was issued to direct that: you, who are the said vizier, in accordance with my Imperial order which is coming to you, and in accordance with what was detailed in the petition, if the usurpation of rights committed by the [subject of complaint] is right, ask [more about this], and [then] see to it that [those concerned] are brought to the Shari'a court, and facilitate the attainment of justice.[205]

3-12 August 1675

No. 29

205b-2

Order to the Kadi of Bursa, and to the *naibs* of Yenişehir, Inegöl, and the *mütesellim* of the Hüdavendigar sub-province [*sancak*]

Mustafa and Ibrahim, citizens of Bursa, presented a petition, saying: the mother of the two, Aişa, was on her way to a Saturday market one day in 1080 and something, when some brigands from Bursa, Yenişehir, and Inegöl, Mustafa and... [three more unspecified names], together with some more brigands belonging to their own state of mind, hit their mother with a war tool (*alet-i harb*),

of law and the peasants not only won but had already received 100,000 *akçe* from the 120,000 awarded to them in the decision. This is highly significant, since there are extremely few cases of complaints judgments actually made good in real life. This is one of these rare cases.

205 This document is of particular importance to this study. The complainant here claimed he was a simple man interested only in his own affairs, but a socially strong man captured part of his property unjustly. Interestingly, the abuser is on record explaining himself—he felt that the complainant was about to complain against him. So again, we are provided proof that the complaining process was taken seriously by all those involved. More ominous is another aspect of this complaint; a friend of the abuser is said to have kidnapped the complainant's daughter, maybe as a threat and maybe for a short while; we do not know, but it certainly looks bad.

killed her, and plundered the things she had with her. They asked for a decree that would order to find the said ones in any of your districts and attain justice. Now my order has been written so that the matter be investigated through the Shari'a court. Whoever has done this immoral act must be apprehended by any means, and if there is proof of what they did, the Shar' has to be executed concerning them, in accordance with what they deserve.[206]
1-10 September 1675

No. 30

193b-1
Order to the *paşa* of Erzerum and its Kadi
A brigand (*şaki*) called Bardal (?), concerning whom there is a complaint in the form of a written testimony (*şehadet name*), and who is from the Tacirlu subtribe, belonging to the tribe of Boz Ulus, united with brigands belonging to his own state of mind. Formerly, an order of mine was given to *timar* holders from Erzincan and Kemah who complained of him, saying: he beats us up and robs our property, against the law. Taking Ahmed as agent (*mübaşir*), they sued in the Shari'a court, before kadis responsible for hearing their complaints, but [the object of the complaint] was not content with this, made one hand with the agent, and just in order to capture and give trouble, said: "We shall deal [with this matter] in another place." And while convening assemblies is forbidden, he made one. And he put one kadi in chains, and he drove away the Kadi of Kemah by force and removed [him to another place], contrary to the Shar'. In this way, he committed major acts of molestation, and brought about the dispersal and death of the citizens. There is no end to such acts of illegality. You, who are the aforementioned vizier, [know] that these things were reported by the poor people with insistence and feeling coming from the heart.
Now, [my] order was written so that brigands who did not obey the Shar' in the said manner, as described above, and did not obey the Sultanic order, are to be summoned to the Provincial Council of Erzerum, where a shar'i encounter is to be held; those holding rights that find proof and approval are to be given what is theirs. A court document (*huccet*) is to be issued on what becomes clear in this way. Those who organize assemblies and create social corruption (*fasad*), should receive their due according to the Shar'. But care should be taken to

206 This document is a small case of brigandage, but it is one with grave consequences. An old woman on her way to a Saturday market was assaulted by brigands, killed, and her property stolen. The ominous aspect was that the culprits vanished. One interesting aspect of this document is that the Shari'a court is given the directive to conduct an investigation in an effort to locate the suspects.

avoid a situation where citizens unrelated to the issue are damaged illegally in their rights.[207]
22-31 August 1675

No. 31

32b-2
Order to the *paşa* of Istanbul[208] and to its Kadi
You who are *naib* in the *kaza* of Ünye, you sent a letter to My Porte and reported that: Musa, of the inhabitants of the village of Çavuş, which belongs to the *kaza* of Ünye came to the Shari'a court and complained that Haci Ibrahim, *amin* [of beytulmal?][209] said to the aforementioned Musa, in the area of Biga, in the year 1084—just in order to capture and drag, "You have found money [which is not yours]", and incarcerated him for fifteen days, then brought him to another *kaza*, and took from him 1,092.5 *piastres*, a horse, and a rifle. Then he escaped to Istanbul. He asked for an order that would direct to bring the matter to the Shari'a court and for his money to be returned to him, sums that, as detailed, were taken from him contrary to the Shar' and in violation of his rights.
Now, my order is that [the suspect] must be made to return what he has taken unjustly.
16-25 February 1675

No. 32

29a-6
Order to the Kadi of Gradçanica[210]
You sent a letter to My Porte saying that: people of the said *kaza* came to the Shari'a court and said: since olden times, the governors of Izvornik never used to go out on tours (*devir*), and the [institution] of the tour has also been outlawed and declared to be among the forbidden things. [But now], the current *sancakbey* of Izvornik went in the year 1084 on a tour among the citizens of the said *kaza*, without an order of mine, took from them more than 100,000 *akçe*, under names like provisions and way station (*konak*). In addition, he also took

207 This document takes us back to the grave issue of abuses connected with the forced transfer of people to a place other than their own. Here, these things were done by a brigand who had the courage to deport Kadis to other places and to agree to judicial encounters in another place. Both of these things were anathema to rural people in Ottoman society, as we have seen in several documents. Not surprisingly, the approach of the citizens to such a brigand was put in exceptionally emotional terms.

208 This could only be a reference to the Deputy Grand Vizier, usually referred to as *kaimakam*, filling in for the Grand Vizier when he was absent from Istanbul. On this office, see Uriel Heyd, *Ottoman Documents on Palestine*, Oxford, Oxford University Press, 1962, p. 18.

209 The public treasury.

210 In modern Serbia.

the sum of 164,000 *akçe* from *ziamets* and *timars* in the said *kaza*, contrary to the Shar' and in violation of their rights. There is no end to the acts of transgression and oppression of this nature. [If such acts] continue, there is no doubt that the people of this *kaza* will scatter in all directions. They asked for an order that would stop and push aside such activities.
Now, my order is that they are not to be allowed to act contrary to the Shari'a and the *Kanun*.
6-15 February 1675

No. 33

153b-6
Order to the *monla* [Kadi] of Sakiz[211]
The people of the island of Değirmenlik[212] came [to the court] and said: the aforementioned pay the taxes imposed on them to the hands of their officers, when the Sultanic order arrives [directing them to pay], as well as to the hands of the tax collectors, and there is no reason to bother them, against the Shar' and the *Kanun*. [But while this was so], the deputy of the commander of the Mediterranean fleet (*kapudan*), *mir-i miran* Mehmed, against the Shar' and the *Kanun*, took from them 1,300 *piastres* and also took some of their children by force, thereby causing them a major injustice. And the current deputy head of that fleet is saying to them: formerly you gave 1,300 *piastres* and some of your kids (*evlad*) to the deputy *kapudan*; now give that to us as well. Doing this, they are not clean of causing a denial of their rights, against the Shar' and the *Kanun*. They asked for an order that will prevent and push aside such illegal molestation.
An order was written to clarify that it is not permissible to violate the rights of the poor *reaya*, against the Shar' and the *Kanun*, and against the custom, current from olden times.[213]
15-24 July 1675

---

211 The island of Chios, close to Izmir Bay.

212 In the Aegean Sea; the Greek name is Milos.

213 This is obviously a case of exceptional oppression. Since this is an area of natural closeness to the sea and the Ottoman navy, we can assume that the reference in the document is to a draftee into the Ottoman navy. The language of draft by force is entirely clear, and we probably have to take the document at face value and realize the harsh realities facing the poor subjects (*reaya*) of the region.

Appendix—Social Banditry or Hidden Regular Banditry?

No. 34

3b-3

Order to the Kadis of ... (empty), ...(empty) and...(empty) and to the *mütesellim* of Aydın *sancak*

Mehmed, the acting *majordomo* of my acting second vizier, my *musahib*,[214] Mustafa Paşa, may God prolong his glory, presented a petition, saying: people from the *kaza* of Nazili, which belongs to the *sancak* of Aydın, which the aforementioned vizier holds as *arpalik*,[215] Numanoğlu Ahmed ...[and five other] are men of bad character and are also malicious reporters (*ghamaz*). Together with brigands (*eşkıya*) belonging to their state of mind, they create assemblies; they prevent the collection of taxes imposed by Sultanic decree and are in accordance with the Shar', the *Kanun*, and the land-register, and are legally due as rights and impositions, and do not allow their collection. And they themselves diminish the *hane*[216] imposition of certain villages and augment the imposition on others, and take their money, thereby committing a major injustice. Formerly, my order went out that if they do not behave themselves; if they do not stop meddling in affairs foreign to them, or in the affairs of the area, then they are to be expelled. But now, [it has become clear] that they do not take notice. They asked for a decree that will investigate the situation of the aforementioned by the help of objective people from adjacent administrative areas and will present and make known the truth.

Now, an order was issued so that the affairs of the aforementioned be investigated by the Shari'a court, and the crimes that can be proven be registered in the kadi *sicill*, whatever these crimes are, and all this information should be passed on to the Imperial Council.

8-17 January 1675[217]

---

214 The reigning Sultan had a number of personal friends, each called *musahib* or companion, who were probably old acquaintances from the Ottoman officialdom whom he had met while a young boy. Usually, these people were remunerated by feudal estates, as was done in this document.

215 A feudal estate, held by a non-military official. From the word *arpa*, barley.

216 *Hane*—literally a house. The term was often used within the context of the *avariz* tax, which was a complex but highly logical structure of elements. On the one hand, the overall number of *hane* imposed on an administrative area was decided in Istanbul, roughly according to the size and wealth of the relevant population. The individual assessment and the communal (quarter, village) assessments were decided in the provinces by the Kadi and the leaders of the communities, always relative to individual prosperity. Any outside intervention in this process would mean chaos and major resentment. On various aspects of this term and institution, see Haim Gerber, *Economy and Society in an Ottoman City: Bursa, 1600–1700*, Jerusalem, The Hebrew University, 1988, Chapter 1.

217 This document deals with the activity of a group of brigands working in the area of a quasi-feudal estate. This group assembled peasants and called upon them to refrain from paying

No. 35

100b-3

Order to the Kadis of Yenişehir and ...[empty]

Yusuf Ağa, my acting head of the *Der-i Saadet*,[218] presented a petition in which he stated: when the citizens of the villages of Karaca Su, Şeyhler, and Kerban-saray, and other villages depended on them, situated in your areas of jurisdiction, [all] forming part of the endowment of the Mosque of Ebu Eyyub el-Ansari, which is under my supervision, were required by their officers to pay the tithes and the rest of the impositions and dues for the years 1084–5 (the payment being due in accordance with the *Kanun*, the land register, and the extant custom), most of the citizens willingly agreed to pay. But while this was so, Abu Bekir and Abd al-Nabi and Ivaz Efendi, citizens of Karaca Su, incited the citizens by creating a large gathering (*dernek*) and assembly (*cemiyyet*), which are forbidden in my Protected Domains (*Memalik-i Mahruse*). Besides, the citizens of the endowment are "independent" (*serbest*),[219] which means that no one from the outside has the right to interfere in their affairs, but [while this was so], the [said three] relying on some [flimsy] excuse, arrived to the side of the *mütesellim*, and the *mütesellim* even helped those said heads of the *cemiyyet*, so that the tithes and the rest of the taxes due from the citizens in favor of the said endowment were not paid, the sums remaining in the hands of the citizens. [All this] means major damage to the endowment. He asked for an order that will direct that the legal tithes and the rest of the taxes and dues that were imposed on the citizens of the villages of the said endowments for the said years, will be paid to the officers. And the villages of the said endowments are independent, hence the acting governors and the other officials are to refrain from interfering in the affairs of the citizens of the villages of the said endowment. [These things] are to be prevented and repudiated.

Now, [my] order was written to direct that, in accordance with what was said above, the Shar' and the *Kanun* are to be followed.

26 April-5 May 1675

---

taxes. Was this true social banditry, that is, robbing the rich to transfer resources to the poor? One has to doubt it, since we also hear that they were robbing money from the poor. The nature of this interesting question is still unclear.

218 This is the head of the Imperial harem, traditionally, also doubling as the supervisor of Sultanic and semi-Sultanic *vakıfs* in the empire.

219 Independent, that is, from taxation forming parts of other legal frameworks, such as the *timar* system.

No. 36

98b-3

Order to the *paşa* of Erzerum and the Kadi of Kara Hisar

You who are the kadi of Kara Hisar Şarki, you have sent a letter to the Porte and said: Halil Sayyid Mehmed, citizen of the said *kaza* and one of the *sipahis* [of the region], does not behave respectably—he always comes to the side of the kadi, the *naib*, the *voyvoda,* and the chief of police (*subaşı*), and every month he is a factor in taking the money [of the poor people], contrary to justice. In addition, he joins people of a like turn of mind, with whom he makes one hand, and while convening an assembly (*cemiyet*) is illegal, he creates [such] assemblies, and he meddles in affairs that do not concern him, as well in the affairs of the area. And he is active in representing his people in Shari'a court cases, [in which capacity] he is not free from usurpation of rights and harming the poor. In all this there is a former signed letter by the *ağa* of the *sipahis*, Mahmud. They ask for an order that would direct to bring the case to the Shari'a court for consideration, in order to stop and push back [such behavior].

Now, my order has been given so that if there is truth in the claims about his corruption, as described above, and in the claim about harm caused to the poor, these things are to be prevented and pushed aside.

26 April-5 June 1675

No. 37

208a-4

Order to the *paşa* [governor] and Kadi of Diyar Bekir

The kadi and *naib* of Malatya, Mevlana Yahya, sent a letter to My Porte, saying: Hasan, manager (*voyvoda*) of the *hass* estate of Malatya, one of the *hass* estates of Hasseki Sultan, came to court and said: a number of people... [from unidentified places in the Malatya area] came formerly to Istanbul and claimed: "The managers of the said *hass*, demand from us more things than is legally allowed by the Shar', the *Kanun,* and the land register, contrary to what was ordained from high places." They somehow got a Sultanic order supporting their case. When [the messengers] came [with the new order], and the order was read in the presence of the said *hass* manager, he said: "There is nothing in my behavior against the Sultanic order." And thus, while good relations existed between the *voyvoda* and the people, the *mufti* of the said town, and the commander of the janissaries, Ahmed Çavuş, and the *alay bey*, Ahmed, together with people belonging to their state of mind, got all of them together, and during three whole days (*ala el-tevali*), had a big gathering (*cemiyet*), in which they told [those present,] "What you paid is oppression; whatever was collected beyond the

fixed liability (*maktu*) whether by the *binbaşı*[220] or the other taxes collected from olden times, or in the past, after today their collection must cease, not one *akçe* being given for them, and what was collected must be returned." And in this way, forming a gathering, they came to the Shari'a court, and put pressure on the said *naib*, saying: "Write to engage in correspondence [with Istanbul]" (*murasele tahrir öyle*). The said *naib* answered that, "It is impossible (*olunmaz*) to engage in exchange against a Sultanic order." After this answer, they did not disband the gathering, and in this way were not free from organizing a gathering and corruption. He asked for an order of mine in this matter.
Now, my Sultanic order is that you, who are the aforementioned vizier, the taxes that used to be collected of old, whatever they were, continue to be valid. You are to take care not to be the cause of harm and reduction in the income of the said Hass, and those who create gatherings and corruption of that nature, you should apprehend and prevent their corruption and gathering activity, and you should take care not to allow a situation in which another complaint like this is sent against you.[221]
11-20 September 1675

220 A military officer.

221 This document is another strange example of what may look like social banditry. We see here three Ottoman officials who organized a sort of demonstration, where they tried to convince their listeners to refuse to pay taxes beyond a certain historic minimum. They also tried to convince the *naib* to take the issue forward and pursue the discussion with Istanbul. That these activities never brought any change in the extant Ottoman taxation institutions is evident enough, but it is more interesting to think about what the intentions of those organizing those quasi-demonstrations might have been. As I have said above, I am still unconvinced that their true purpose was social banditry in any real sense.

Chapter 5: The Kadi and the Common People

Preliminary Remarks

Though brigandage and oppression may be the main topics of the Book of Complaints, it is important to pay attention to some topics that are less distinctive. Here, there is first the topic of complaining itself. Citizens in large numbers gave up on their instinctive passivity and obvious fear for their own lives and those of their families, and approached the central government with demands to rectify wrongs done to them. No one complained anonymously, and complaints were more often than not sharp, avoiding any soft terms to mitigate what had happened. More than this, a large part of the abuses committed were done to collectivities of people, and it is interesting to observe how these collectivities reacted. Many of these collectives were villages, but many of them were supra-village entities, like the people of a *kaza.* Oftentimes, these collectivities came together and sent petitions to the central government. Quite often, they came to the Shari'a court in their area and complained to the kadi. A striking point here, is that in the Book of Complaints they never complained to a provincial governor of whatever rank. In any case, I am interested in the many complaints where the common people approached the kadis and complained via them. We also have to bear in mind that besides direct contact with the kadi court, in many other complaints, sent directly to Istanbul, the complainants asked the Sultan to solve the problem via the kadi court. It is thus clear that many citizens throughout the empire had full confidence in the kadi and his court, and saw them as the Dutch boy putting his finger in the crack in the dam to save the whole country from disaster.

It is important to bear in mind that many of the complaints were resolved through a legal process, and the only qualified judge in Ottoman society was the kadi. In fact, a major theme in this book is that as far as the Ottoman center was concerned, only the kadis had a legitimate authority to judge. Every implementation of such quasi-authority by somebody else, even the highest provincial governor, was considered to be illegal.

Documents

No. 38

102a-6

Order to the Kadi of Galata

You have sent a letter and said: the manager of the endowment (*vakıf)* of Sehzade Sultan Mosque of Istanbul, [x]... came to the Shari'a court and said: the people of the village of Biga, which is under your jurisdiction, and belonging to the said *vakıf*, are *serbest* (independent from non-*vakıf* taxes)—[when it comes

to] freedom from taxation, the people of the sub-district governor (*mirliva*) and other people, do not intervene, but [rather] the *vakıf* takes them, and besides, the village is under your judicial jurisdiction, and the affairs of the people, falling within the matters of Shari'a, used to be dealt with by their *naib*. But while this was so, in a *kaza* near Biga, that is, the Kadi of the said *kaza* always meddles in their affairs without Sultanic order, bringing the citizens to his own *kaza*, and with no justice, decides their legal issues, thereby committing oppression and injustice. They asked for an order of mine [in this affair].
The decree was written to forbid meddling against the Shar' and the *Kanun*.[222]
6-15 May 1675

No. 39

114a-3
Order to the Kadi of Rodosçuk[223] and its yeniçeri commander
[You have sent a letter, saying]: yeniçeri named Mehmed, serviceman in the 26th yeniçeri regiment, living in the said *kaza*, formerly hit the yeniçeri Ahmet with a knife, near the dock...[x], and the matter was duly proven in the Shari'a court and a court document was given. The officers of the yeniçeris wrote a letter saying that: a messenger (*çavuş*) from among the messengers of the yeniçeris was nominated to carry out what is incumbent [on the killer] according to the court document. And since the said killer deserves the punishment of retaliation (*kisas*)[224] in accordance with the Shari'a, the said messenger should be allowed to execute the punishment.
An order was written so that what was written in the above letter should be implemented.[225]
26 May-4 June 1675

---

222 This complaint tells an unusual story, of a Kadi, who meddles in the affair of a neighboring *kaza* and goes to the extreme of forcing people to come to his own court to be judged by him. While this is not narrated specifically in the document, it seems rather clear that the origin of the complaint is the common people themselves, and their stand seems like a strong vote of confidence in their own Kadi.

223 Modern Tekirdağ, in European Turkey.

224 Murder in Islamic law, if not part of highway robbery, was treated as a private affair—the next of kin of the slain person had the right to decide whether the killer would be put to death in retaliation (*kisas*), made to pay blood money (*diyet*), or even pardoned altogether (but execution was made conditional on premeditated killing, made evident solely by the tool used for killing. See Joseph Schacht, *An Introduction to Islamic Law*, Oxford: The Clarendon Press, 1966, Chapter 24.

225 This document is one of several cases in the Book of Complaints that relate negatively to an old historical theory, thereby the slaves, or *kuls*, of the sultan had their own laws and their own courts of law under the Ottomans. In this document, we observe that a *yeniçeri* who fatally wounded another *yeniçeri* with a knife, was tried simply by the Shari'a court, according to the same Shari'a applicable to the rest of the population, and by the same judge.

No. 40

76a-3

Order to the *naibs* of Dimetoka and Dagardi

Yusuf, who is the head of the Imperial Harem, has presented a petition, saying: Sayyid Murad from Dagardi (?), and Elmagöz-oğlu Osman, and Terzi Mehmed, and Kucuk Ahmed, of the citizens of Dagardi, that are situated in your *kazas*, forming part of the endowment of Şah Sultan, buried in Eyyub el-Ansari, under my supervision, are not behaving properly. They constantly interfere in the affairs of the *voyvoda* and the subjects of the endowment, so that one is obstructing the other (*bir birlerine düşer*), thus causing mayhem in the affairs of the *vakıf*, and besides, these things are sure to bring about dispersal and death of the subjects, what will also lead to a major fall in the income of the *vakıf*. He asked for an order to prevent interference in the affairs of the *voyvodas* and the subjects, and to warn the [aforementioned] by the Shari'a court to be concerned with their own affairs [only], so that if after the warning, they do not heed this [warning], then the oppression, the social mayhem (*fitna*), and the confusion that will befall the subjects of the said *vakıf* will be registered in the *sicill*, and a court order concerning them will be issued.

Now, the order was written so that behavior proceeds according to what was detailed.[226]

7-16 April 1675

No. 41

3b-5

Order to the kadis in the *sancaks* of Gelibolu and Biga

Holders of *ziamets* and *timars* in the said *sancaks*, along with their children,

226 In this complaint we find a story about a number of people who live in the region where there was a large Sultanic *vakıf*. These people meddle in the affairs of the *vakıf* officials in such a way that the management is seriously obstructed. There are no specific details on what these people do, besides the fact that they create social mayhem (*fitna*—the ultimate Islamic theology term for social mayhem). Thus, two points are important in this document. One is the elusive nature of the charge against those meddling in other people's affairs to the point of obstructing life in the area. Things like this, at that time, were clearly treated by the new law or rule of *siyasa shar'iyya*, that is, the right, or even obligation, incumbent on the ruler to run his state smoothly, even if that means resorting to unwritten and non-shar'ia laws. See Frank Vogel, *Islamic Law and Legal System: Studies of Saudi Arabia*, Leiden: Brill, 2000, Chapter 5 and passim. The second interesting point in this document is the reference to the Kadi's *sicill*. This wording goes to show, as several documents in this collection do, that the Ottomans related to their *sicills* extremely seriously, and rather than copying the record of the departing Kadi by the incoming one, as apparently was done in classical Islam, They preferred to preserve the original bound volumes as closely as possible—probably one reason why so much more *sicills* from this period survived. On classical Islam in this regard, see: Wael B. Hallq, "The Qadi's Diwan (*sijill*) before the Ottomans", *Bulletin of the School of Oriental and African Studies*, 61 (1998), pp. 415-436.

have sent a petition to My Porte, along with a messenger, saying: it has been the old law that when one of them needed to be taken and arrested in order to be brought to the Shari'a court to have a legal violation proven against him, in accordance with the Shar', such arrest and incarceration should be effected by their commanding officer (*alay bey*).[227] A noble order of mine to that effect has formerly been issued. Since such an order has not been carried out, they have asked for another order to that effect.
My order has been written to prevent any transgression against the old [custom].[228]
7-16 April 1675

No. 42

179b-5
Order to the *kaimakam* of Istanbul and its Kadi
Someone named Mustafa came [and presented a petition, saying]: he is one of the retired persons of the Corps of Gardeners of the Palace. His uncle, someone name Yusuf, died in the year 1080 and something. The things left behind by him, and the rest of his property and his money, invested in loans to other people, [all of this] passed to him [the complainant]. But he was all this time in another region, and *hassa Bostancı başı*[229] Osman, captured all the money and the things, then sold the house, the garden and properties for much less than the appropriate price. Doing this, he caused him a great harm, and in this regard a *fetva* was given in order to retrieve [the lost property]. He asked for an order of mine to bring the natter for treatment by the Shari'a court, so that justice is done.
An order was written to bring the matter for treatment by the Shari'a court.[230]
3-12 August 1675

227 The *alay bey* was the head of the *sipahi* corps in a province.

228 In this document holders of *timars* and *ziamets*, even they, we might add, complain that while in the past their commanding officer used to bring offenders from among them to court, the Shari'a court, state officials (*ehl-i örf*) had recently broken that custom and treated them personally, with unpleasant results, as it turns out. Thus, even *ziamet* owners, members of what might be called the real elite, were not in full solidarity with their fellow elite members.

229 The *Bostancı başı* of the seventeenth century was the official responsible for policing the shore neighborhoods of the Bosporus.

230 This document nicely shows how the Shar'ia court played a central role inside the state system. In this case, the complainant was a member of the corps of gardeners, who inherited an estate from his brother, who served on the same corps. The estate was sold by a substantial margin below the fair price, and by Islamic law the heir has the right to retrieve the properties. The interesting point is, however, that while all of this took place within the Ottoman administration itself, the solution did not lie with anybody in that administration, but with the kadi court alone.

No. 43

22a-3

Order to the Kadi of Megri[231]

The *naib* in the Shari'a court in the said *kaza*, Ali, sent a letter, saying: the citizens of the village of Budeme [?] appended to the same *kaza*, came to the Shari`a court and said: the citizens of this village used to go to the pasture area (*kuru*) of their village since olden times, and while they were going to their pasture, situated in place x...[empty], nobody else had any connection to this affair; but now, their *voyvoda* , somebody named ...[empty], brought Turkmens from the outside to their pasture, settled them in the area of their pasture, and these people let their sheep and cattle loose to graze among the gardens, the orchards, and the fields, and they were not free from causing harm. The people of this village came to the court and spoke of major oppression (*izhar-i tezalum*), and asked for an Imperial order of mine that would put a stop and push aside [such oppression].

Now, my decree has been written to order that this issue be dealt with by the Shari'a court; if they indeed cause any legal harm, what is incumbent on them by law should be implemented. Their harm to the [the local] people should be prevented.[232]

6-15 February 1675

No. 44

117b-7

Order to the Kadi of Mengen[233]

You have sent a letter to My Sublime Porte and said: the citizens of the said *kaza* came to the Shari'a court and said: every three months a *subaşı* is sent on the part of the *sancak* of Bolu, who extracts 1,500 *akce* from every village whose *maktu* is 500 *akçe*, and 3,000 *akçe* from every village whose *maktu* is 1,000 *akçe*. And in addition, every year they demand 600 *kile* (Istanbul measure) of barley, that is, its price, according to the calculation of 2 *piastres* per *kile*. Then when the taxes come through an Imperial order, we have no ability left to pay them. The extreme illegality of the *sancakbey*, [narrated] in this way, has caused most of the citizens to disperse. If the *subaşıs* will come and will exact *subaşılık* tax, and tour (*devriye*) tax, and additions to the *maktu*—all of this is nothing but a vi-

231 There were two places by this name—the modern Fethiye in South-Western Anatolia and one in modern Greece.

232 We shall see below that the *naib* was the black horse of the Ottoman legal system, taking much of the blame for its problems and difficulties. Probably most *naibs* were fair and dependable, however, and this document is one example to prove this line of thought. What is also distinct here, is the fact that the *naib* earns the legitimacy of those served by him.

233 A place name in the area of Bolu.

olation of legal rights,[234] and to exact every year 2 *asadi piastres* for a *kile* of barley [is also a major violation]. If they go on with these violations and transgressions, it is definite that we shall all disperse and die. We present our case to the state,[235] they said with emphasis (*ilhah*).
Now, an Imperial writing (*hatt-i hümayun*) and a lofty firman have been issued, to secure that these transgressors' acts, standing against the Shar', the *Kanun*, and the extant custom be stopped.[236]
5-14 June 1675

No. 45

117b-4
Order to the *naib* of Viran Şehri[237]
Naib Zulfikar sent a letter and said: the citizens of the *kaza* came to the Shari'a court and said: they have a tax regime of *maktu*, [fixed] by their *mirliva* but now the *subaşıs* come once every two months with many mounted men, settle on their backs and charge a village whose *maktu* is 5 *piastres*, 20 *piastres*; and from a village whose *maktu* is 10 *piastres*, 40 *piastres*. And besides, they also charge taxes of provision (*zahira*), *sursat*,[238] 4 and 5 *piastres* from each village... and this is how they presented the situation.
My noble order has been issued to prevent them from transgressing against the Shar', the *Kanun*, and the old custom.[239]
5-14 June 1675

No. 46

163b-7
Order to the *mufti* [sic!] of Selanika
A Jew named Halil presented a petition in which he claimed: his father, a Jew named...[x], was en route to Selanika when he died, and while he had no debt to anyone, the Jews of Selanika chose an evil path and said to him: "Your father owed some money to us." Saying this, at night they captured the properties,

234 The inconsistent grammar in this sentence—as in many others—is in the original, and I have tried of course to preserve it as much as possible.

235 The original term is *der-devletmedara*, literally, the state, the center of greatness.

236 In this document, which is a regular oppression document, although a bit extreme, the citizens narrate their plight and add that they ask justice from the state itself (a sole case of such exceptional use of terminology). Yet, even in such a case, they do not entertain the possibility of approaching the main state's representative, but instead, approach the Kadi.

237 A place name in the *sancak* of Bolu.

238 *Sursat* was an irregular tax levied in the form of actual goods and provisions.

239 In this document, again, various state officials abuse the villagers by overloading them with illegal taxes. The *naib*, however, seems to stand by them, accepting them in court, giving them a voice, and then passing their complaint on to Istanbul.

money and things that passed to him from his father, and the kadi of Selanika, too, took their side. Aside from the fact that this was a violation of his rights, the said kadi also took 1,650 *piastres* from him as a tax for the division of the estates, thereby causing him major oppression. He asked for a decree of mine that would order to deal with this matter in the Shari'a court and attain justice.
An order was written to bring the matter for discussion in the Shari'a court.[240]
24 July-2 August 1675

No. 47

28a-8
Order to the Kadi of Bosnia and to its *mütesellim*
Yeniçeri Mehmed, of the *yeniçeris* of My Porte and citizen of Gradcanica, came [and presented a petition, saying:] he is interested solely in his own affairs, and nothing was proven against him in a Shari'a court by just witnesses (*şuhud udul*), but now, the Kadi Mustafa, their Kadi (Gradcanica's) beat him up severely, and besides, also took from him 100 *piastres* unjustly, causing a violation of his rights. He asked for an order that directs him to return the money. The order was written so that you, who are the *mevlana* mentioned above [the Kadi of Bosnia]; you have been nominated *molla* for the said affair; check the situation of the said ones in the Shari'a court. If the sums extracted by the aforementioned from the said one are true, he has to be made to return them, and care should be taken not to allow a situation, giving rise to such a complaint again.[241]
16-25 June 1674

240 Among the few documents in the Book of Complaint that are not addressed to a Kadi is this complaint, addressed to the *mufti* of Selanika. The reason for this is obvious—the Kadi of the city is among those accused of wrong doing. The story revolves around a Selanika Jew who inherited an estate from his father, and the community all of a sudden claiming that his father owed money to them. The complainant also accuses the Kadi of taking the side of the Jewish community. In any case, the exceptional point is that the *mufti* is called upon to deal with the issue, probably as a compromise rather than anything else.

241 In most other cases in the Book of Complaints where a Kadi is nominated for *molla* (top-kadi) and sent for an ad-hoc legal mission, the reference is to a mission performed together with a *mübaşir*, and they are both seen as compromise seekers. This is the only case where we observe the type of cases alluded to by Rossitsa Gradeva, where the Kadi receives the nomination of *molla* to be more senior than the local Kadi and to be able to judge the behavior of that lower Kadi. This is still a far cry from an appeal, and is only a wrongdoing judge being judged by a superior judge. See: Rossitsa Gradeva, "On Judicial Hierarchy in the Ottoman Empire: The Case of Sofia from the Seventeenth to the Beginning of the Eighteenth Century", in M. Kh. Masud, R. Peters and D.S. Powers, eds., *Dispensing Justice in Islam*, Leiden: Brill, 2006, Chapter 11.

No. 48

224a-1

Order to the *naib* of the *kaza* of Mihaliç,[242] and to the *mütesellim* of Balikesir

Someone named Hasan presented a petition, saying: his brother, called Huseyin, went from Mihaliç to the *kaza* of Manyas. [Some] inhabitants of the villages lying between the two *kazas*, Çörekli, Burc Tayı, and Bulgarlar eliminated the absentee, thereby committing a major deprivation of rights and injustice. He asked that the Shari'a court check (*tefahhus*) the matter, and that justice be done.

The order was written so that the matter will be investigated by the Shari'a court.[243]

19-28 November 1675

No. 49

22b-5

Order to the kadi of Pertek[244]

The citizens of the *kaza* of Pertek have sent a man and a petition saying that: they paid in toto the taxes imposed on them for the years 1083, 1084, and 1085, like *ispence* and other taxes, [they paid them] to the hands of their officers, Cafer and Yusuf—[all this] according to the *Kanun* and the land register, and there was no fault with their payment. But the above officers were not content with what is legal and took from them much more than is allowed by the tax-order and the land register, thus violating their rights in a major way. Formerly an Imperial order came several times to prevent such activity, but [these officers] did not obey any orders, or the Shar' and the *Kanun*, and went on behaving in an oppressive way and illegally, with no end. They asked for a decree that would order to bring the matter to the Shari'a court, so that what they have taken more than the order and the register will be returned [to the complainants].

Now, an order was written so that the matter be brought for decision to the Shari'a court. What is proven as having been extracted against the *Kanun* and the register, they must be made to return.

15-24 June 1674[245]

242 Modern Karaca Bey, in Western Anatolia.

243 As this document shows, the kadi court received orders to send people to actively investigate crimes committed in the area of jurisdiction of the Kadi. It is not at all clear how this could be done in practice with the limited office-holders of the Shari'a court. Cooperation with the police force might be a solution, though what was done in practice is not yet known.

244 In Tunceli Province, central Anatolia.

245 This document is a regular case of tax extortion by officials, which is a good example showing how a group of citizens that complains straight to the central government and then for some inexplicable reason demands that the complaint be processed by the Shari'a court. Did they realize the case would have to be sent back to some sort of authority in the province and wished to make sure that it did not go to Governors and their aids?

No. 50

33a-6

Order to the Kadi of Balia,[246] held by *arpalik*[247]

Balia's *naib*, Abdallah, sent a letter, saying: the rich (*ayan*) and poor of Balia came to the Shari'a court and reported that the *mütesellim* of the Governor of Biga sub-province, Ali, came to the said *liva* in the year 1085, together with 130 mounted, armed men; pulled the inhabitants out of their houses with their families; settled in 16 villages in the said *kaza*; cooked 5-6 sheep in every one of them; and extracted from them 1,262.5 *piastres* more than their lump-sum due as tax (*maktu*) as registered in the land register. With this, he committed a major violation of rights.

My order was written so that the matter be brought to the Shari'a court. If it is true that he extracted from them so much money against [the Shar'] and the custom, he is to be made to return the sum in full. In the future, care must be taken to avoid molestation of the poor, against the noble Shari'a.[248]

16-25 February 1675

No. 51

73a-3

Order to the Kadi of Bolvan[249]

The guards of the Bolvan fortress sent a man and presented a petition to My Porte, saying: when someone among them used to be sued in the Shari'a court and it was necessary to cause him to be present in court, and when a shar'i violation was proven against him, and [the need arose] to capture and arrest him, it was customary that such a person would be fetched and made present through the Shar' and through the fortress commanders, others not having any basis to intervene in the affair. But lately, there has occurred an intervention by general governors, *sancak* governors, chiefs of police, and other state officials. Against the Shar', they commit captures and arrests, and extract a great deal of money, thereby committing a great deal of oppression and injustice. They asked for an exulted decree of mine that would order them to refrain from violating the old custom.

246 In *sancak* Biga, south of the Marmara.

247 *Arpalik* is a kind of apanage given to a non-military officer.

248 This is a regular tax extortion complaint, one special point in it is that it was organized and launched not just by the poor, but also by the rich notables (*ayan*) of the area. The term *ayan* refers to a socially strong man, on an informal basis. In almost no other complaint of tax extortion did the *ayan* come together and work with the poor people, in a situation where it is clear that those who suffered from the extortion were only the poor. How and why did the *ayan* join forces with the subaltern elements of the province in this case, is hard to know at present.

249 In modern Serbia.

Now, my order was written so that behavior will continue according to the *Kanun.*[250]
7-16 April 1675

No. 52

22b-2
Order to the General Governor of Bosnia and to the Kadi of Taşlica[251]
The citizens of the village of Derbayan (?) presented a petition and said: a brigand named Haci Umar Aga, a citizen of Raste (?) Fortress collected [around him] 70-80 people belonging to his state of mind. These people came with a flag, and settled in the *nahiye* [of the complainants], assaulted them, and robed [them of] their money and property, thereby causing dispersal and death of the citizens, without a doubt. In this way, they cause them oppression, tyranny, and anarchy. They asked for my noble decree that will order to bring the case to the Shari'a court so that justice may be done.
Now, the order is that the matter be brought [for resolution] to the Shari'a court.[252]
6-15 February 1675

No. 53

54a-5
Order to the Kadi of Osmancik[253]
The *naib* of the said *kaza*, Mehmed, sent a letter, saying: the people of the said *kaza* came to the Shari'a court and notified with enhanced emphasis (*ilhah*): to prevent the [possibility] of the *mütesellims* of Çorum and Sivas [sending people] with drafts [of taxation orders], demanding winter pasture money and "tour" money, [thus] molesting [the citizens] against the Shar' and the *Kanun*, for-

250 This is a complaint by fortress guards in the Balkans, who complained that traditionally, when someone among them made an offence justifying criminal treatment, the court in charge was always the Shari'a court, and the Shari'a court personnel, never regular state officials, including governors and down the ladder to police officers. Indeed, this group of complaints by fortress guards (of which this complaint is only one sample) makes an explicit comparison between state officials and legal officials, and is the best available proof of the prestige of the Shari'a court in Ottoman society at this time.

251 In *sancak* Hersek, an area of Bosnia.

252 This complaint tells the story of the attack of a group of brigands on a village, extortion of money, and the like. The interesting thing, however, is that the citizens demand that the issue be treated by the Shari'a court—a strange sort of demand keeping in mind that this is not a complaint against an official institution but against highway robbers, the classic stuff of the job of provincial governors in the Ottoman Empire. Actually, the order is addressed to a governor as well, but in practical terms, the governor does not seem to have anything practical to do in the affair.

253 In *sancak* Çorum, Central Anatolia.

merly an imperial order of mine was handed to the citizens, containing a Noble Rescript of mine. But yet again, at this time, 40-50 mounted, armed men come as representative of the chief of police, not heeding the Imperial order and, visiting village after village, taking large amounts of money from the poor citizens by force and without justice. Additionally, they [the accused] take their [the citizens'] sons as simple workers to another administrative areas, then charge each of them with paying a [penal] fine (*tacrim*). In this way, they commit major oppression and a violation of rights against the complainants. [Doing all this,] they are causing the citizens to disperse, and their ability to endure all of this has come to an end. Thus, if all this oppression is not stopped, we shall all die. Now, [my] order has been written so that their acts towards the poor citizens that are against the Shar' and the *Kanun* must be stopped.[254]
18-27 March 1675

No. 54

83a-5
Order to the Kadi of Olendorik and the *mütesellim* of Morea *sancak*
A man named Mehmed, an inhabitant of the town of Arkadia, situated in the Morea *sancak*, presented a petition and said: he has a debt to somebody in Edirne. He sent two people with 800 *piastres* [to this man]. These two people were subject to an attack by a group of 15 brigands, between two *derbend* villages belonging to the said *kaza*, [x and y], one man was killed and the other wounded, and their money [was] robed. They, thus, committed a major injustice. He asked for an imperial order that would take care of the problem.
An order was written so as to investigate the matter in situ via the Shari'a court. Those who have committed such a crime are to be found, and you are to see to it that those who have committed this deed will be punished according to the Shar'. But under this pretext, care should be taken not to molest or cross the line in relation to the poor. Special care should be used here.[255]
17-26 April 1675

254 Death and dispersal brought on the poor citizens by the extortions of state officials star in the content of this complaint as well, and even if an element of exaggeration in is probable, it is still impressive, not to say distressing. Despite the gravity of the situation, the case is effectively addressed by the local *naib* of the Shari'a court, who presents the story to the central government and seems to do a good job.

255 This document was presented to add a piece of flavor to the grave situation of brigandage in many areas of the empire at this time, but also to further show that the kadi court was often expected to do more than just to sit in the courthouse and wait for cases to arrive.

No. 55

29a-5

Order to the Kadis of Bosna Sarai and Bana Luqa

The citizens of the *kazas* of Bana Luqa and Grandcanica presented a petition and said: while these people have no quarrel with the state's treasury, contrary to my Imperial orders issued before, the *mütesellims* of Bosna and Bana Luqa, took more than 100,000 *akçe* from them in the year 1080 and something, with a draft [of tax order] and without an order, against the Shar', thereby causing them a great deal of oppression and a deprivation of [their] rights. They asked for an imperial decree that would order to bring the matter to the Shari'a court. Now, my order is that whatever he has taken contrary to the Shar' and the *Kanun*, he has to return.[256]

6-15 February 1675

No. 56

212b-2

Order to the acting supervisor of endowments in Istanbul, ...[empty].

The spouse of a [former] harem woman (*saraylı* [*kadın*]), a man named ... [empty], presented a petition saying: no one besides [the couple] has any say concerning a house, private property, situated in the neighborhood of Kandilli, and while from time immemorial it was the case that shar'i cases of such palace people used to be dealt with by the said supervisor, now a man named Ibrahim, the guardian of an underage boy named Ahmed, claimed that: "The said house was put up as a collateral (*rehn vez olmuştur*). I have now paid the loan and took possession of the house." [Saying this], he presented false witnesses, and tried to present the claim in a fringe area court (*kenar mahkeme*). This is injustice. He asked for a decree of mine that will order [such behavior] to stop and be repudiated.

My order is to deal with the case in the Shari'a court, in accordance with the *Kanun* [sic].[257]

11-20 September 1675

256 In this complaint document we find state officials exacting large sums from the citizens using the pernicious trick of presenting the draft order of taxation (probably phrased by provincial authorities then sent to Istanbul) as the final order, tantamount to pure and simple falsification. Though dealing with this unsavory ploy would call for the expertise of the Kadi in the intricacies of the Ottoman administration, it is the Kadi, not any other authority, that the citizens preferred to deal with the affair.

257 This document, not addressed to a kadi at all, though involving interesting information on how a Shari'a court at this time functioned, was brought into this collection as an extremely rare example of a complaint in the Book of Complaints that was not addressed to the Kadi.

No. 57

83b-6

Order to the kadi of Tirhala[258] and to the deputy-governor (*müteselllim*) of the sub-district of Tirhala.

The citizens of the Rarik (?) village, belonging to the said judicial area, presented a petition, declaring: while they pay their *ispence*[259] and the other taxes and liabilities to their superiors according to the Shar' and *Kanun*, there being no fault in [their payments] and no reason to intervene [in their affairs], the Chief of Police (*subaşı*) of the said judicial area, a person named Ali, extracted 38,000 *akçe* from them for the year 1080 and ...[empty], contrary to the Shar', *Kanun*, and land registry book, [thus causing them] excessive repression and a violation of [their] rights. They asked for an order of mine that would direct [everyone] to deal [with the matter] in the Shari'a court and that [the *subaşı*] would be ordered to return what he has taken contrary to the Shar', *Kanun*, and the land registry book, thus implementing justice.

My order is to proceed with the matter in the Shari'a court.[260]

7-16 April 1675

No. 58

104a-4

Order to the Kadi Kara Ferya

The people of the *kaza* of Kara Ferye came [with a petition] and said: they feel entirely satisfied with the taxation load imposed on them through the *avariz* tax [on real estate], and the rest of the impositions handed down by [Sultanic] order, but some holders of *ziamets*, or *timar*, and strong people who live in the said *kaza*, when they impose taxes on villages with which they have personal ties, they impose them in a way harmful to some villages and they impose an elevated load [than what is just] on some and a lower on [others]. In this way, they create injustice. They asked for an order that would recognize that village people and craftsmen, all have their assessment of taxes (*tevzi'*) made by the Kadi.

My order is that, as to those who have properties which pay *avariz* and other kinds of properties and lands, the taxes imposed on them by order will be paid

---

258 The sub-province of Tirhala, located in modern Greece.

259 *Ispence* was a pre-Ottoman poll-tax current in the Balkans, that remained in that area under the Ottomans.

260 This document is another fine example where we find the people of a village in a rural area of the empire being squeezed for taxes by state officials, who then ask the Sultan and the *Divan* to let the Kadi deal with their situation.

according to their relative load, and care should be taken not to defend special interests, or to offend existing rights.[261]
16-25 May 1675

No. 59

131 a-5
Order to the *paşa* of Diarbekir and the Kadi of ... [empty]
The people of *cemaat-i* x [empty], from the Kurdish *taife*, have written a petition saying: when the said ones went to graze in a summer pasture, and when they have been in stop-over in the village of Bulat, belonging to the *kaza* of Malatya, as is the custom with them for a long time, while they were minding their own affairs, the current *mütesellim* of Malatya, Mehmed, together with the village people belonging to his own state of mind, attacked their houses and plundered all their money and provisions, thus, causing them a major injustice, and in this affair they have a court document attesting to their orderly nature. They asked for an Imperial order.
The order was written so that their affair will be checked by the Shari'a court, and everything belonging to them and taken from them contrary to the Shar' and the *Kanun*, will be returned in its entirety.[262]
15-24 June 1675

No. 60

212b-5
Order to the Inspector (*Teftişçi Paşa*) and the Kadi of...[empty] and the deputy governor (*mütesellim*) of...[empty]
The *mütesellim* of Bozok *sancak*[263] sent a letter to My Porte and said: Sari, son of Ahmed, his brother, Ahmed, Kurd b. Veled, and twelve more people from the Turkmen tribe, sub-tribe of Küçüklü, community (*cemaat*) of Hasli, got into a fight with tribe [members] near Kubakli [?] Saray, then shot Musli b. Sunallah

261 This complaint is directed against state officials and other people, all of them unauthorized and unqualified to deal with the question of personal assessment of wealth for the purposes of taxation; for example, the value of houses in the case of *avariz* tax. The complaint calls on them to stop meddling in these issues and leave them to the Kadi, the one authority qualified for the job. Indeed, city studies from the seventeenth century show that it was the kadi who was responsible for such assessments. See for example Haim Gerber, *Economy and Society in an Ottoman City: Bursa, 1600–1700*, Jerusalem: the Hebrew University, 1988, Chapter 1.

262 This is a great example of the relations, according to the Book of Complaints, between the general governor and the kadi—the governor is mentioned in the title of the document, but in actuality is assigned no role at all. The real investigation is assigned to the Kadi, and this is just a small example of the superior role of the Kadi.

263 In the Yozgat area, South Eastern Anatolia.

with an arrow. When they were asked to appear in the Shari'a court, they refused. But after ten days, the said Musli died in place ...[empty] in the *kaza* of Huseyin Abad, [following which] a court document was written that reported an investigation of a dead body, where it was found that the aforementioned have committed a [crime] of oppression, violation of rights, and social corruption. An order was given to capture the said ones wherever they may be found, bring the matter to a discussion in the Shari'a court, thereby attaining justice.[264]
11-20 September 1675

264 This document tells a simple story of tribal people, some of whom came into conflict and became violent, at the end of which one of them was found wounded by an arrow; a wound from which he died ten days later. This fact made the event a murder. The order was to find the culprits and bring them to justice. The point I find intriguing in the document is the fact that the order was addressed to the Kadi but also to the *mufettiş*, also called *teftişçi*, a highly placed man of state responsible for fighting crime in the provinces. This is a classic officeholder to be found practicing law, but no, even he is ordered to bring the case to the Kadi for a trial and decision.

Chapter 6: (In)justice by State Officials

Preliminary Remarks

There is an old statement in Ottoman historical literature that provincial governors doubled as judges in every respect. Uriel Heyd was one major scholar who held this view as matter of course.[265] Abraham Marcus was one scholar who actually found empirical evidence that showed that state officials did actually meddle in judicial matters. It was usually considered disastrous for innocent and law abiding citizens to be summoned to the governor and come face to face with that "judicial" process.[266] Michael Ursinus adopted Heyd's view at the beginning of his book about complaints in Rumelia in the late eighteenth century,[267] but it seems to me that he relaxed his view considerably later in the book by showing that if a case sent to the offices of the province needed to be solved by trial, a kadi was called to the offices to conduct a regular shar'i encounter. Ursinus suggests that the site of this trial transformed this process from being a Shari'a trial into something else, but here, I disagree with him. Even the present collection shows that several trials took place in fields, for example, when agricultural matters were at issue. The place was not considered important at all, only the procedure was of importance.

Be that as it may, I want to repeat that while about 99 percent of the orders were addressed to a Kadi, calling on them to adjudicate or investigate, there is not a single case that calls upon a governor to adjudicate, and there are many examples where a governor was severely censured if a complaint showed that he meddled in any behavior that could be remotely portrayed as judicial. In this chapter of the collection, I made an effort to collect documents showing traces of judicial behavior by governors. Several such cases were in fact already encountered in Chapter 1.

Documents

No. 61

3b-1

Order to the Kadi of Lefkoşe

The pensioners of the *çorbacilar*[268] and the *yeniçeri* and guards of fortresses in the service of guarding the island of Cyprus sent a man with a petition, saying:

265 Uriel Heyd, *Studies in Old Ottoman Criminal Law*, Oxford: Oxford University Press, 1973, pp. 208 ff.

266 Abrahan Marcus, *The Middle East on the Eve of Modernity*, New York: Columbia University Press, 1989, pp. 107-108.

267 Michael Ursinus, *Grievance Administration (Şikayet) in an Ottoman Province*, London: RoutledgeCurzon, 2005, p. 6.

268 A term with several meanings, one being a high-ranking officer of the janissaries.

when someone of them was summoned to the Shar' and a penal violation (*curm*) concerning him was proven, [as a result of which] it was necessary to take hold of him and have him arrested, this capture and arrest used to be done by their officers, and their case used to be dealt with by the Shari'a court, [with] the *sancakbey* and other state officials not meddling at all. But now, the governors who come [to the island] capture some of them and incarcerate them, merely for the purpose of capturing and extracting resources, contrary to the Shar' and *Kanun,* and hold them for *tacrim*, when no crime has been proven on their part by just witnesses (*şuhud udul*). With this, they commit towards [the pensioner soldiers] a major violation of [their] rights. They asked for an order directing the governor and the other state officials not to transgress [their rights] and molest them in the aforementioned manner, and that their changing circumstances would be checked by their officers.
[My] order has been written down so that things will proceed according to what has been narrated.
8-17 January 1675

No. 62

15b-5
Order to the Kadi of Üsküdar
The inhabitants of the village of Kartal, belonging to the *nahiye* of Ada, forming part of the same *kaza*, have presented a petition, saying: since 40 or 50 years [ago] they have taken a family house, which they guard zealously, [in which to perform] their vane rites (*ayin-i batile*).[269] And while there is nothing in their behavior that is a molestation to anybody or contradictory to the Shar', the police officers (*subaşılar*) of the said village have now, for a year or two, extracted by force a "criminal" fine (*carima*) of 20 or 30 *piastres* from them, thereby committing against them a violation of [their] rights. They asked for an order of mine that would prevent and repudiate [this kind of illegal behavior].
[My] order has been given so that the matter will be dealt with by the Shari'a court in the place of origin, and justice will be done. What they have taken unjustly, they have to return.[270]
27 January-5 February 1675

269 On the whole, the *Divan* here is entirely in favor of the predicament of the Christians, but the secretary apparently could not hold himself back from making a negative remark, which was not of course the one uttered by the complainants.

270 Here, too, a group of citizens led quiet lives unmolested, but state officials created trouble in order to extort money from them, using the pretext that because of a suspicious crime they were owed a fine (*carima*), turning themselves into a form of self-styled judges. Neither the population or the central government bought into it.

No. 63

5a-6

Order to the Kadi of Ak Hisar

The inhabitants of the village of [?], of the villages of the deceased endowment of Iskender Paşa presented a petition in which they claimed: formerly, a body of a murdered person was found on the road between the village of the said persons and between village [?], within the summer pasture [in the area]. The killer of that slain person is unknown. Using wrong attribution (*isnad*) and the invention of wrong arguments, [those of the other villages] said to the complainants: "You are the ones who have killed him." The *kaimakam* of village [?] in the area sent a person who captured some of them and brought them to the Shari'a court [for trial], but in this [process] the issue of killing was not proven against them, but contrary to the Shar' these [the state officials] extracted 30,000 *akçes* from them, thereby causing them major injustice.

[My] order was written to ensure that [everybody] behaves according to the Shar' and the *Kanun*.[271]

18-27 January 1675

No. 64

21a-8

Order to the *naib* of Güzelhisar[272]

You have sent a person and a petition saying: in the villages of that *kaza*, some people freeze during winter and die because of the severity of the winter, and some fall off trees and die, and then the *sancakbey* and the *subaşı*, and the other state officials, only for the sake of capturing and extracting resources, say [to the citizens], under the name of blood money (*diyet*): "Give money", and in this way extract from them large sums of money. They always molest and bother them [on this account], against the Shar' and the *Kanun*. Now, an [order of mine] was written to make it clear that such types of death, which are caused by the person himself, such as falling off of a donkey, falling into water, falling off trees or a bridge, being burnt by fire or the collapse of a wall or dying via freezing—in all these things, the punishment of blood money (*uşr-i diyet*) has been cancelled.

27 January-5 February 1675[273]

271 The story in this document is about a dead body of a person found between two villages, where one village tried to ascribe the murder to the second village, a fact not proven when the case came to court. The officials of the first village, however, were unimpressed and continued to demand blood money from the other village, again behaving like judges, but in reality, distorting justice.

272 There are at this time two places with such a name in Western Anatolia.

273 From this document, we can understand that before that date, state officials went to extremes

No. 65

34a-2

Order to the *kaimakam* of Istanbul and its Kadi

Ibrahim, the leader [?] of the Turkmen [population], Danişmendlu [tribe], who are part of the *hass*[274] of Hasseki Sultan [Suleyman's wife], presented a petition, saying: he is a man interested in his own affairs [only], nothing had been proven against him in a court of law by the testimony of just witnesses (*şuhud udul*), [but now] supervisor[275] Mehmed Paşa, only in order to usurp and menace, said to him: "You have captured in some way the robber known as Alaca Murad, had taken some of his things, then let him escape." Then, against the Shar', he captured him, dragged and arrested him, and for three months molested him and subjected him to capital punishment (*siyaset*), and took from him, with no justice, 7 *kise akçe,*[276] 7 camels, 27 horses, 1 mare, 14 work horses, and... [a number of furs and weapons]. He thus caused him a great deal of injustice and oppression.

The order was written to say that you, who are the said vizier, the aforementioned *paşa*, all the items you have taken from this man, contrary to the Shar', must be recorded through the Shari'a court, then returned.

16-25 February 1675

No. 66

86a-2

Order to the kadi of Istrumca[277]

You have sent a letter, saying: the people (*ehali*) of the *kaza* came to the Shari'a court and said: the killer of [x], found dead in the mosque situated in that *kaza*, is not known, and in addition, it has been established by impartial witnesses (*şuhud udul*) that they [the complainants] have no connection to this murder, [yet] the people of the *sancak* governor have captured some of the citizens of that town, against the Shar', in violation of basic rights. [They also] let it be known that they have in their hands a *fetva* supporting their claim. They asked for an Imperial order of mine [in that matter].

---

in interpreting the criminal law and not only exacted blood money for every person who died in the *kaza*; they did so for every person who died from unnatural circumstances in the region. In this document, the central government announces that this "law" is null and void.

274 *Hass* was the top level of estates in the *timar* system, estates given as prebend to members of the royal household.

275 A military official assigned to stamp out brigandage in an area, who moved about in the countryside, with a substantial military retinue and extraordinary authority, though certainly not to overrule the Shari'a without good reason.

276 A sum that roughly amounts to 420,000 *akçe*.

277 Modern Struma, in Macedonia.

Now, an order was written so that the conduct will be according to the Shar' and the *Kanun.*[278]
(No date in the original; dates in neighboring documents: 17-26 April 1675)

No. 67

87a-5
Order to the Kadi of Istrumca
You have sent a letter to My Porte, saying: the citizens of the said *kaza* came to the Shari'a court and said: while there is nothing that has become clear or been proven concerning them, according to impartial witnesses, in 1080 and something, came from the office of the *mir-i miran* of Rumelia, Küçük Ahmed Ağa and ...[x, not specified by name], and from the *mütesellim*... [x—empty] and...[y, empty], and said to them: in your *kaza* a man has been killed [?], and with this pretext they captured kadi Osman and took him to another *kaza*, then imposed a *carima* of 11,000 *akçe* on him, against the Shar' and the *Kanun*. [They also exacted a *carima*] of 100 *piastres* from the citizens of village...[x], and 36 *piastres* from the citizens of the village of Balu, and 40 *piastres* from the citizens of village ...[z]. In addition, the said Ahmed took seven people and moved them to another *kaza*, using force[?]. Thus, there is no end to their acts of injustice. They asked for an order that would cause the return of the money extracted against the Shar', the implementation of justice, and to stop and abrogate all acts of oppression and violation of rights.
My order is that he is to return everything he has taken contrary to the Shar' and the *Kanun*.
17-26 April 1675

No. 68

76b-1
Order to the *Beylerbey* of Karaman and the Kadi of Akşehir
Mehmed, one of the gatekeepers (*kapıcı*) of My Porte, presented a petition, saying: while the said one dealt with his own business quietly, there not being anything in his behavior justifying any illegal action against him, the governor of Akşehir, together with some [kadi], captured and arrested the said one, then put him in chains, [finally] extorting 200 *piastres* from him, despite the fact that nothing was proven against him in a Shari'a court with the testimony of rightful witnesses (*şuhud udul*). They, thus, caused him an extreme injustice. He de-

278 In this document, a body was discovered in a mosque in a *kaza*. The matter ended up being discussed in the Shari'a court, where it was proven that the people of the town in question had no connection to the murder. However, the state officials thought they were better qualified as judges and captured some of the citizens, for whatever purpose. Here too, the officials acted as judges, but it was not accepted by anybody as a legitimate judgment.

manded that his money be returned through the Shari'a court, and that justice (*hak*) be done.

An order was written so that what was taken contrary to the Shar' be returned, and do not let a situation arise in which such a complaint is launched against you again.

7-16 April 1675

No. 69

114a-6

Order to the Kadi and *mütesellim* of Aleppo

A non-Muslim named Hanania came and said: there is nothing that can be said against him according to the Shar' by the testimony of rightful witnesses (*şuhud udul*), and, [further], Ovadis, of the non-Muslims of Aleppo, did not receive from me any position of agency (vekalet) to pay money to government officials (*ehl-i örf*), yet Ovadis, the said *zimmi*, made a claim [to my face]: "I have paid 900 *piastres* for you to the majordomo (*kethüda*) of Tutuzlu Mehmed Ağa, as *carima*." Then he took this sum from me, unjustly, causing a great deal of injustice. He also demanded this sum from Mehmed Ağa [the said *kethüda*], but that person took an oath that he had received no money at all to pay for [the complainant] from Ovadis. Thus, the debt remained in the hand of Ovadis, and I now sued for this sum, but he is causing problems in collecting it. I want an order.

An order was written, to bring the matter to a discussion of the Shari'a court in the place [where it all took place].[279]

26 May-4 June 1675

No. 70

75a-4

Order to the kadi of Sakiz

Memi Reis has presented a petition, saying: Before that, the officers (*zabits*) of Bozca Ada, known by the names of Mustafa and Ibrahim Efendi, captured and arrested the son [of the complainant], contrary to the Shar', who had died while in prison. Thus they caused a great deal of harm and injustice.

279 This document shows the devious ways in which the legal device of *carima* worked in practice, it being a major ploy by officials to extract money from unsuspecting citizens, in most cases for crimes they never knew about. The document, however, also shows that if a citizen was strong-minded enough, he could stop these exactions and maybe even get his money back. We also observe here, that in the final analysis, state officials had to come to the Shari'a court to settle their legal affairs (taking oaths and the like, things that are part of legal encounters), despite the claims that Aleppo was famous for the large-scale involvement of governors in judicial matters.

The order was written so that the affair be brought for treatment to the Shari'a court.[280]
7-16 April 1675

No. 71

95b-2
Order to the *paşa* of Erzerum and to the kadi of Ispir[281]
The guards of the fortress of Ispir sent a petition and said: they are the guards of the said fortress, by imperial nomination documents. They fulfill their assignments without any deficiency. And when it is proven in connection to one of them that he has committed a crime, and it becomes clear that he is to be summoned to the Shar', to capture him and to arrest him, it was the case from olden times that his case was dealt with by the Shari'a court, with the help (*marifetle*) of the fortress commander. But while this used to be the case, now *mütesellims* of *sancakbeys*, *voyvodas* [of *sancakbeys*], chiefs of police, intervene in this affair only to extract money [from the complainants], relying on baseless claims. Thus, they commit capture, arrest, oppression, and deprivation of rights. They asked for an order that would prevent and repudiate [all this behavior]. An order was written so that conduct goes by the *Kanun.*[282]
26 April-5 May 1675

No. 72

29a-7
Order to the kadi of Gradcanica
You have sent a letter, saying: the citizens of the *kaza* came to the Shari'a court and said: while they do not have a quarrel and conflict with anybody, the current *mütesellims* of Bosna and Bana Luka and the *sancakbey* of Izvornik, against [two different types] of Imperial orders of mine and against the Shari'a, with the help of draft [only], captured and arrested the [complainants]; took them to another *kaza*, where they took from them *carima*; and, under the cloak of tour (*devir*), took their money and property. Doing this, they brought on them a great deal of suffering and injustice. They asked for an order of mine that will prevent and eradicate [injustices of that nature.]

280 The distinct point of this document is that it shows that state officials (*ehl-i örf*) were not immune in their activities vis-à-vis regular citizens, but were liable even for potential criminal offences. What is more, the forum for the clarification of such claims was not some kind of a court reserved for state officials, but simply the Shari'a court, just as was the case for the rest of the community.

281 In the Erzerum area.

282 Again, we clearly see here that state officials think they have the right to exercise legal functions, though nobody else accepts this.

Now, my order is not to allow injustices against the Shari'a to stand, without an Imperial order of mine.
6-15 February 1675

No. 73

3b-4 eradicate
Order to the kadi of Beyşehir Fenar[283]
The citizens of the village of Zarik [?] situated in your *kaza*, and belonging to the villages of the *Hass* of the Grand Vizier, Ahmed Paşa, presented a petition, saying: formerly, a man known by the name of Momi Efendi Oğlu demanded from them an old debt, whereas, in truth, they do not have legal debt to anybody. He faced them, and there was a shar'i encounter, where the claim of the said one turned out to be baseless, and Momi Efendi was unable to sustain any of his demands. The court issued a court document to that effect. But the said one did not accept [that ending], and, contrary to the Shar', captured their old men, arrested them, and made them admit his claim by force, and brought about the issuance of a new court document [along these lines]. Doing this, he did not refrain from bothering them with illegal deeds. They asked for an order of mine that would direct to prevent and eradicate [such activities].
Now, my order has been given so that it be clarified that after a loan has been returned so that the loan base has been paid, no interest can be charged afterwards.[284]
8-17 January 1675

No. 74

219 b-3
Order to the kadi of Florina[285] and to Mehmed, in charge of supervision over *haydud* brigands in that area
Non-Muslims, inhabitants of the village of Nilai [?], of the villages of an independent *ziamet* [in the region] came and said: from olden times, these [villagers] used to catch fish in a lake which is free from any ownership and situated near their village, but when they came now to do this, [x], the officer of the village of Batram [?], situated in their vicinity, [prevented them from doing this,] claiming that: "Near the village of Batram [?] of which I am the officer, there is a mine of precious stones (*gevhere*), and you catch there fish", and this—despite

283 In *sancak* Mora (Morea).

284 This is indeed a breathtaking sort of oppression, carried out not by a state official, but by a private strong man. To arrest the old men of a community and frighten them into admitting to any charge is an exceptionally suspicious ploy, yet somebody had the entrepreneurship to do it.

285 In modern Northern Greece.

the fact that the lake is not registered in the new land register as yielding taxes for him, [and he is doing this] merely to take and extract [money]. And while there is nothing that can be proven against them in a Shari'a court, according to the testimony of reliable witnesses, he captured and incarcerated some of the *zimmis* living in the said village and unjustly extracted thirty *piastres* from them. A Shari'a court document attesting to his unjust behavior was issued. They asked for an order of mine.
An order was written so that if it is proven that what is claimed he has taken is true, he be made to return [the money].
21-30 September 1675

No. 75

89a-2
Order to the kadi of Aleppo and its *paşa*
Somebody named Haci Ahmed presented a petition and said: his son named Isa, came to the said protected city in the year 1080 and something in order to trade, to buy grape juice syrup (*pekmez*); and while nothing was ever proven against him by reliable witnesses in a Shari'a court, the said [*subaşı*], with no justice and against the Shar', put him to death by crucifixion. [Doing this,] he conducted instead a major violation of his rights.
The order is that, according to the *fetva* that he has in his hand, the case must be brought to the Shari'a court to be decided.[286]
17-26 April 1675

No. 76

30a-3
Order to the kadi of Aleppo and its *mütesellim*
Abu Bekir named person, presented a petition in which he claimed: he is a man interested in his own affairs [only], and although nothing had been proven against him in the Shari'a [court] by the testimony of reliable witnesses (*şuhud udul*), the former *mütesellim* of Aleppo, Şaban, arrested and incarcerated him contrary to the Shar' and extracted 700 *piastres* from him, thereby causing him a major injustice.
[An order] has been written so that the matter be brought to the Shari'a court and justice be done.
16-25 June 1675[287]

286 The chief of police of Aleppo is no doubt playing here the role of a judge and enforcement officer, and whether he had done this by authority from someone, we do not know. We also do not know his version of what happened here. We do know, however, that at least the case was transferred to the Shari'a court, that seems to stand here above the state officials (*ehl-i örf*).

287 This case is quite revealing about the relations between governors and the law in Aleppo,

No. 77

45b-4

Order to the kadi of Terkoz[288]

The citizens of the village of Turaghan have sent a petition to My Porte and said: they pay the taxes imposed on them by my Imperial order to those responsible for their collection and there is no justification for anybody to interfere and molest [them]. But now, the *mütesellim* of Silistre, [x], contrary to the Shar' and the *Kanun*, took 24 *piastres* from them and in addition arrested two people from among them, thereby causing a serious measure of oppression and injustice. They asked for an order that would make him return what he has taken against the Shar' and the *Kanun*, and to stop and prevent the injustice.

Now, the order was written so that what he has taken against the Shar' and the *Kanun* he has to return, [so that] no violation of rights is effected without shar'i justification.[289]

6-15 February 1675

No. 78

86a-6

Order to the *naib* of Balıkesir[290]

Someone named Ibrahim presented a petition saying: formerly, his brother, named Mustafa, strolled around the countryside of Izmir for the sake of trade, and was killed while doing this. His inheritance is strictly limited to him [the complainant]. He took hold of the remaining assets, and while nobody had any legitimate reason to interfere, Mehmed, who was formerly (for the year 1080 and something) holder of the *sancak* by way of *arpalik*, said to me: "Your brother was killed in the land of the said *sancak*, you owe me blood money [as compensation for the murder]." Saying this, he grabbed and arrested him, working in company with another Mustafa, and together they took 5-6 loads of textiles (*iplik*) and one rifle from the remaining estate. Doing this, they caused a severe measure of injustice. He asked for an order of mine.

An order was written so that what he has taken and is proven in the Shari'a

---

made famous by Marcus' study on that city. While in theory, the governor was independent and could interfere in legal affairs; here, we observe that if the governor crossed the line (as set by the Shari'a), he could be dragged into a legal encounter in front of the Kadi. See Abraham Marcus, *The Middle East on the Eve of Modernity: Aleppo in the Eighteenth Century*, New York: Columbia University Press, 1989, Chapter 3.

288 In the province of Silistre, modern Bulgaria.

289 Here, village people complained against a *mütesellim* who not only charged them sums against the law, but even arrested some of them with no justification. Again, these quasi-judicial measures were not accepted by the center or the people.

290 In Western Anatolia.

court as true, he has to return, and let there be no further [reason] for complaint.[291]
17-26 April 1675

No. 79

76b-2
Order to the Kadi of Istanbul
Osman, of the inhabitants of Qasim Paşa, presented a petition and said: there is no interference from his side in the affairs of anybody, and while no violation on his part has been proven by reliable witnesses (*şuhud udul*), the head of police (*subaşı*) of Istanbul, [x], extracted 74 *piastres* from him, against the Shar' and with injustice, thereby causing a violation of his rights. He asked for an order of mine that would direct him to return what he had taken contrary to the Shar', and that justice be done.
An order was written, so that the matter be brought for discussion in the Shari'a court.[292]
7-16 April 1675

No. 80

103a-6
Order to the Kadi of Lipova[293]
The citizens of the said *kaza* presented a petition saying: when a violation (*curm*) is proven in connection with someone from among them and a Shari'a court document (*huccet*) is given, and after a fine is taken from the culprits in accordance with the *Kanun*, they notified that the *mir-i miran*, the *mütesellim* of Temeşvar, and the *voyvoda* of [?], and the rest of the state officials, do not refrain from exacting [more] money under the name of *carima*, to harm and to molest, against the Shar' and *Kanun*. They asked for an order of mine [in this affair].

291 This document shows the limitless obstinacy of state officials in their exactions. The story is about a man whose brother was a merchant killed by brigands in the countryside of Izmir, yet some state officials claimed that because someone was killed in the area, he was liable for paying blood money (whereas, he was in fact entitled to receive blood money if such was paid because of the killing).

292 The *subaşı* was the head of police in cities and rural areas. According to Zarinebaf's valuable study, police officers in Istanbul oftentimes passed judgment on criminals on the spot, if caught red-handed. This complaint shows that there were limits to this hasty procedure, and that people could complain against such a police officer and even take him to court, the Shari'a court that is. See: Fariba Zarinebaf, *Crime and Punishment in Istanbul, 1700-1800*, Berkeley and Los Angeles: University of California Press, 2010, Chapter 7 and passim.

293 In the province of Temeshvar, in modern Romania.

The order was written so as to ensure behavior according to the Shar' and the *Kanun.*[294]
6-15 May 1675

No. 81

187b-2
Order to the Kadi of Menemen
The citizens of the *kaza* of Menemen came, and said: the son of ...[x] drowned in a body of water by his own action, and while there is no possibility that it could have been caused by somebody else, the *voyvoda* of Menemen, someone named ...[empty], claimed, without any justice: "In your *kaza*, blood has been spilt; you have to pay a tax (*uşr*) of blood money (*diyet*)." While formerly an order was issued to prevent such behavior, the said one did not obey the order and the Shar', and charged every villager 50 and even 100 *piastres*, thereby causing a major injustice.
Now, accidents that are an outcome of independent acts like this, such as drowning in water; burning in fire; falling from a cow or a donkey, from a cart or a shed or tree; or dying from old age [?], or remaining under a falling wall—on all these things, the payment of *diyet* tax has been cancelled. An order was issued so that no further molestation on this account takes place, contrary to the Shar' and the *Kanun.*[295]
13-22 August 1675

294 This complaint shows, again, how state officials went out of their way to charge the citizens with paying the fine of *carima*, after that fine had already been fixed by the Shar'ia court and duly paid. This is another case, however, where we observe that people resisted, and were supported in this by the central government.

295 This is a complaint against the *voyvoda* of Menemen, who came to the citizens and notified them that in their *kaza* blood had been spilled, hence they owed blood money for this crime. Here, too, there is no doubt that the pretext is some kind of right to judge.

Chapter 7: Complaints Against Kadis and *Naibs* (Assistant Judges)

Most of the complaints in the *Şikayet Defteri* revolve around the topic of abuses by state officials. In almost all the cases, those who are called to resolve the situation are kadis, whether local or neighboring. There were some rare cases, however, where the abuser is a kadi himself, or more often a *naib*. These cases were certainly unfortunate, at least from an Ottoman perspective, but not only were they rare, it is striking to see that even in these cases, those who were called upon to save the day were kadis. The kadis were, and remained even in 1675, the pinnacle of justice in the eyes of both the members of the *Divan* and of the population at large.

An extremely interesting point in the documents pertaining to local *naibs*, is that the abuse is connected with the fact that local *naibs* managed to hold on to their posts for long periods of time, thereby entrenching themselves in the area, solidifying personal relations that led to corruption in adjudication and exploiting suspicious economic avenues and connections. The situation became so bad that the central government forbade the hiring of local *naibs* altogether. This is another thread in a debate that runs throughout this study and documents, and connects the introductory studies and the documents into one meaningful whole. We have seen in the chapter on law that the Ottomans transferred judges and other personnel to maintain adherence to the law and prevent succumbing to personal connections and relations, and we have analyzed Peirce to show that even sixteenth century Ayntab remained within this general line of thought.

Documents

No. 82

86a-3

Order to the kadi of Ine Bahti (Morea)

The citizens of the *kaza* of Olendorik sent a petition in which they said: the *naib* of the said *kaza*, Ahmed, and some locals, in the names of Susmioglu (?) Mehmed, and Ali, all embarked on cooperation with one another, and besides the fact that they took, contrary to the Shar' and the *Kanun*, 190,000 *akçe* from the *avariz* and *sursat* taxes imposed by Sultanic order, the said *naib* also took much money from them under the rubric of tour (*devir*), and as to the tax of *avariz-hane*, he took 1.5 *yük akçe* from the revenues of this tax. From this oppression and injustice, the *reaya* have started to disperse and die. They asked for an order that would forbid all these [activities].

My order has been written to direct you, who are the Kadi of Ine Bahti, you have been nominated *molla* to deal with that affair; and you have to deal with this matter in the Shar'.[296]
17-26 April 1675

No. 83

39b-4
Order to the *naib* of Gelibolu[297]
The "people of the market" (*ehl-i suk*) from among the people of the town of Ipek, belonging to the said *kaza*, Salih the grocery man, Hasan the shoemaker, Hasan the copper smelter, Hatib Mustafa, Muezzin Yusuf, and x [unidentified], have presented a petition, saying: a Kadi named Ali, from the citizens of Gelibolu, was formerly their own kadi in the said *nahiye*, and [his behavior] towards the poor was one going against the Shar', and involving the violation of rights. Thus, he took 1200 *akçe* from Bakkal Salih, and 2 *piastres* from Hasan the shoemaker, ...[and some more sums from other artisans], and he took 350 *piastres* from the monks [of Gelibolu], then ran away [from the area]. In addition to that, he took from Nuh, citizen of the said town, eight *piastres*, but the said Nuh came and demanded the money he had taken from him contrary to the Shar'. The said Kadi captured the said Nuh, beat him strongly, injured him, [injuries from which] he eventually died. In addition, he cancelled many court documents in the hands of people, and tore [?] many of their *fetvas*, thus causing them a great deal of harm and violating their rights. They asked that the issue be checked by the Shari'a court, so that justice may be done.
Now, the order was written so that the issue will be dealt with by the Shari'a court in situ.[298]
27 January-5 February 1675

296 The citizens of Olendorik *kaza* complained in this document against their *naib* for extorting various sums of money from them illegally, under a variety of pretexts. Treatment of this affair was entrusted to the care of the Kadi of Ine Bahti, who was nominated to be a *molla*, a top-kadi, especially for this job, so that he had authority over the *naib* suspected of wrongdoing. A similar point was detected by Gradeva in Sofia, leading her to talk of an Ottoman hierarchy of kadis. At least here, it is only partially true, since we are talking about an emergency, rather than a normal situation, where every Kadi was independent of each other. See Rossitsa Gradeva, "On Judicial Hierarchy in the Ottoman Empire: the Case of Sofia from the Seventeenth to the Beginning of the Eighteenth Century", in Muhammad Kh. Masud, Ruud Peters and David S. Powers, eds., *Dispensing Justice in Islam*, Leiden: Brill, 2006, 271-298.

297 Town at the northern exit of the Dardanelles (Gallipoli).

298 This is an interesting document on the extortionist character of the *naib* of Ipek, apparently the *naib* of a small town in the vicinity. He extorted small sums from various artisans, but when someone dared complaining against him, he lost his temper and had that person beaten up, from which that person eventually died. Interestingly, and characteristically, we observe that the complaining citizens asked the *Divan* to deal with the situation via the shar'i system, and the *Divan* itself ordered that course as well.

No. 84

26b-3
Order to the Kadi of Florina
The imams, *hatibs*, *ulema* Sufis (*suleha*), the poor and the weak, and the *ayan* and *eşraf* of the *kaza* Cuma Pazarı sent a memorandum saying: when the taxes are handed down and when those that come carrying the [payment] orders, and the orders are read, it is not [ever] said concerning one kadi or one *akçe* —"Take, or nominate somebody else to take", and although warnings were made about all this in the past, the Kadi of Cuma Pazarı, collected, in 1085, 7,000 *akçe* from every shipment of sheep [sent to Istanbul]; and as *sursat* tax, he collected 9,000 *akçe;* as governor's expenses 3,000; as *nuzul* taxes and *avariz*—18,000 *akçe;* as *cizye*, 18,000 *akçe;* for... [certain type of] sheep, 6,000 *akçe;* and on producers of precious stones, 10,000. In all, he exceeded all bounds of oppression and tyranny.
My order has been written to [address] you who are the aforementioned *molla*; you have been nominated *molla* [for the said affair]; everything the said kadi has taken from the poor subjects, contrary to the Shar' and the *Kanun*, he must return and hand over to the rightful owners. What is revealed about this affair during the discussion is to be reported to the Imperial *Divan* in an exact way.[299]
16-25 June 1675

No. 85

48(II) b-4
Order to the Kadi of Siroz and... and the Kadis of ...[empty] and ...[empty]
Hac Huseyin, the Kadi of Manastir, sent a letter to My Sublime Porte saying: formerly, the citizens of the *kaza* of Yerliye have presented a petition complaining about their current Kadi, a Kadi named Abdulkerim. Before that, an order of mine was issued directing him to return sums of money taken [for himself] as part of the taxes collected from the Zaman [?] *kaza*. Mehmed Çavuş, of the messengers of My Porte, was nominated as agent (*mübaşir*), and you who are [the] agent, and you who are a Kadi, the *molla* mentioned above, you have been nominated *molla* for the said matter; and when the two reached the place, the said Kadi had escaped and has become absent. He [the petitioner] suggested enforcing the rights of the citizens.

299 This document narrates, yet again, the long list of abuses and extortions committed by the Kadi, and it is special because it details the social groups making the complaint, which included the elite and lower classes together. Here, too, a neighboring Kadi was nominated as an ad hoc *molla* to give him the authority to deal with the local Kadi.

The order was written so that the issue will be dealt with by the Shari'a court wherever this kadi will be found, and everything that he has taken contrary to the Shar' and the *Kanun*, he is to be made to return.[300]
13-22 August 1674

No. 86

71b-3
Order to the *naib* of Bolu and the *mütesellim* of *sancak* Bolu
The citizens of the *nahiye* of Sazak [?], appended to the said *kaza*, came [to the Shari'a court] and complained against Mehmed, living in the said *nahiye*, who has been *naib* there all these years. He has entered into cooperation with state officials, and these, relying on things lacking any basis [in law], led to the extraction of the money from them [the citizens], and the said one took money for himself as well, and he charged them 10 and even 15 *piastres* for a court document, against the Shar' and the *Kanun*, and also took from them money under the name of bribery (*rüşvet*); when two sides used to come with a mutual claim, he used to take the money of the side with the wrong claim, defending that side, thereby obstructing justice. Such acts of tyranny and injustice on his part are endless.
They asked for a decree of mine that would order to bring the case to the Shari'a court, and that the sums extracted against the Shar' and the *Kanun* be returned to their owners.[301]
7-16 April 1675

No. 87

100b-6
Order to the Kadi of Sinop[302]
The citizens of the *nahiye* of Balkol [?], appended to the said *kaza*, sent a petition in which they notified: while going out on a tour (*devir*) is forbidden, the person serving as *naib* of the said *nahiye* is going out [to visit] every village and

300 This is an interesting document on tax extortion by a Kadi, in all probability just a *naib*. It is difficult to visualize a real Kadi running away undetected. In this document, too, the coming Kadi receives the nomination of *molla*, specifically noted to be an ad hoc nomination.

301 This complaint really sums up the situation with *naibs* in the best way—this *naib* extorted money from the citizens under various rubrics, and went further than almost any other complaint that I have seen, by bending the law for bribes. Yet, the citizens are making this complaint to a Kadi, obviously expecting him to take their side and pursue the matter further. Then, at the end of their complaint, they specifically asked the *Divan* to decree giving judgment on the case over to the Shari'a court, as if saying, despite everything, we believe in the justice of the system.

302 Port at the middle of contemporary Turkey's Black Sea-coast, in 183 B.C. Sinope was capital of the Pontic Empire.

villager with many mounted, armed men, and takes from the citizens food, barley, straw, honey, oil, sheep, and lamb, and other things, without payment. And when somebody from among them dies and everybody [from the family] is present, underage boys and girls, nobody being absent, hence they do not want division of the estate [by the court], he forces such division on them, and after deduction of the debts of the deceased, charges them 136 *akçe* per 1,000 instead of 15, as is legal. And he charges them more for court documents, for signing, and for correspondence with other courts (*murasele*) and manumission than is allowed by the *Kanun*. And, basing himself on all sorts of things, he arrested [some of] them and took sums from them against the Shar', without any justice. Such acts of tyranny and injustice on his part have no end. They asked for an order of mine.
An order was written so that conduct will proceed according to the Shar' and the *Kanun*.
26 April-5 May 1675

No. 88

103a-5
Order to the Kadi of Tire,[303] who holds this position as *arpalik*
The citizens of the *nahiye* Barghus [?] Sarir in this *kaza* have presented a petition and said: while it was declared illegal for a local to be *naib*, a local man named Abdullah serves as *naib* in the courthouse of the said *nahiye*, while Hac Umar is the summoning officer. These cooperate with state officials and sneak and give away the poor, thereby causing the extraction of their money, with injustice. Similar transgressions of theirs are endless.
An order was written, with all its typical details, directing that the aforementioned not be hired into the offices of *naib* and the summoning officer.[304]
6-15 May 1675

No. 89

163a-2
Order to the Kadi of Valonia[305] and its *mütesellim*
You who are the Kadi, you sent a letter to My Sublime Porte saying: the commander and guards of the Tuzbay [?] fortress, situated in the said *kaza*, came to

303 In Western Anatolia.
304 We observe here, a problem that is further detailed in the next document—*naibs* that were local tended to keep their jobs for long periods of time. They would pair with various state officials and together would molest and abuse the citizens, particularly the peasants. This is why the Ottoman government often issued decrees forbidding the nomination of locals as *naibs*. How effective this prohibition really was, is hard to tell.
305 In modern Albania.

the Shari'a court and said: a person named Ilyas, the *naib* of the Karbash courthouse, citizen of the said fortress, is local (*yerli);* contrary to the Shar', he exacts 10 or 15 *piastres* [on each document given] as court expenses, and he is cooperating with state officials [of the region], and, as a consequence, takes a great deal of money from the poor, and he prevents every newly arriving *naib* from assuming his position, and as of 3-4 years, he occupies the position, with no justice. [In addition], he marries many of the poor without justice, taking from them many things, and [for] every two people coming with a *khulʿ* divorce matter, he takes the side of the unjust person, pushing aside justice in the process and obliterating the rights of those who have rights. And while it is illegal for locals to be *naibs*, and while four orders have been issued in the past to ban and disallow [such a possibility], he did not abide by the orders, and took money from the poor without any justice. There is nothing that can rival the oppression and injustice of these actions. They asked for an order to prevent these things.

Now, an order of mine was written, in order to prevent such a person from being a *naib* in the said *kaza.*[306]

24 July-2 August 1675

No. 90

197b-2

Order to the Kadi of Selanika and its *bey* (provincial governor)

The citizens of the *kaza* of Yenice-i Vardar sent a petition to My Porte [seat of the Ottoman government] in the year 1080 [and something], saying: their current Kadi, a Kadi named Ramadan, after they have paid for the winter pasture of the Janissaries, whose location was fixed by an order [of the center], also collected a "court tax" of forty thousand *akçe* from them, and also collected 22 thousand *akçe* from them as a tax on the transfer of cattle to Istanbul (*celep keşan*), and the price of drafting Sekban soldiers and *yava*, and in the court, for every decision given, when a tax is taken, one *akçe* is taken from every ten *akçe*, and if somebody from among them dies, the legal tax paid by the estate is 15 *akçe* per thousand, he charges 70 *akçe* per thousand. And also, while they have in their hands orders saying it is illegal to hire locals as *naibs*, locals are

306 In this document, we observe again the major problem with Kadis, which appears in many complaints—*naibs* tended to be people with little qualifications and commitments to the system, but worst of all, were prone to forge relationships with various officials, who swayed them into evil courses of behavior. They also tended to stay in their positions for a long time, subverting the golden rule of the Ottomans that short-termed officials prevented personal biases, and led Kadis to stick to the formal law more faithfully. Indeed, the material on Ottoman *naibs* is proof that the tendency among some historians to assume that Ottoman Kadis were very much inclined to informal dealings with their clientele is a mistake.

still serving in the service of the *niyabet*, and these things constitute oppression and violations of the rights of the poor. They asked for an order that would direct [him] to pay back the sums he had taken contrary to the Shar' to their owners.

Now, my order is that he be made to return the sums with the help of the Shar'. A rescript was written with all its attendant details.[307]

22-31 August 1675

307 In this document, we find an accusation of abuse by a Kadi, including all the usual details, but one of the points raised is that the Kadi is accused of hiring a local to serve as *naib*, whereas the people have in their hands several orders forbidding this altogether because of the damage and abuse it always leads to.

Chapter 8: Shari'a Court Decisions—Final?

Preliminary Remarks

The finality of the shar'i process is an important topic today in Islamic law. Baber Johansen was one of the first scholars to broach the topic with a discussion of Ibn Abidin, the last great Hanafi scholar. Ibn Abidin lived in Damascus in the first half of the nineteenth century. He suggested that there was no finality in Islamic law, and that one could raise an old issue again and again and take it to court at will, even after decades. The reference was not to an appeal, which is another matter that has to do with raising doubts about the validity of the judgment in a certain case because of reasons such as the discovery of new evidence relevant to the case. It is widely agreed that Islamic law lacked the appeal as well. David Powers conducted a study on this issue and mentioned the point of departure of no appeal, but went on to show that in practice quasi-appeal appeared, such as the accepted right of an incoming judge to review the decisions of the departing judge. For the Ottoman case, the issue was studied by Gradeva, who claimed that a quasi-review existed here too, in the form of *molla* kadis having more authority over the regular Kadis and, therefore, telling them how to handle cases. Obviously, any legal system should solve these issues in a definitive way, whatever that is, because as the case of Ibn Abidin shows, no legal system can exist with a chaos that lacks a finality of the legal process. These facts and thoughts are highly important to the present study, interested as it is in the position of the Kadi. Free appeals and, particularly never-ending court cases, were obviously devastating for the position of the kadi. Whatever the logical, or Islamic-law related observations relevant to these issues, however, it is important to note that so far no cases of never-ending recourse to the court for retrial or judicial reviews of the work of former Kadis' have been detected, though an ironic trace of Johansen's observations is to be found in the Book of Complaints itself, as discussed below.[308]

Several documents in the Book of Complaints make a contribution to this debate. The basic fact is that the Ottoman state decreed (exactly when, is entirely unclear) that hearing a court case for a second time is illegal. They also decreed that appeal was basically impossible, unless for a very good reason, and with the express approval of the Sultan. But this was far from the end of the story...

---

308 See: Baber Johansen, "Legal Change and the Problem of Change: The Case of the Land Rent", in Chibli Mallat, ed., *Islam and Public Law*, London: Graham and Trotman, 1993, pp. 33-34; David S. Powers, "On Judicial Review in Islamic Law", *Islamic Law and Society*, 2 (1992), 315-41; Rossitsa Gradeva, "On Judicial Hierarchy in the Ottoman Empire: The Case of Sofia from the Seventeenth to the Beginning of the Eighteenth Century", in M.Kh Masud, R. Peters and D.S. Powers, eds., *Dispensing Justice in Islam*, Leiden: Brill, 2006, Chapter 11.

Documents

No. 91

95b-3

Order to the *kaimakam* [of] Istanbul and its Kadi

Brothers named Receb and Mustafa presented a petition and said: formerly, a son of their aunt, Receb, died while living in a room (*oda*) in the Sultan Ahmet Han endowment, and his estate passed to them according to the division made by the Shari'a court. When they tried to possess it, the manager of the said endowment, Abdallah, intervened and said to them: "You are not the successor of the said deceased; he died while living in the courtyard of the endowment, and I therefore possess his estate for the benefit of the endowment." He went on to start a confrontation and when a shar'i encounter took place, in the presence of the endowment supervisor, they [the petitioners] proved that they are the rightful heirs of the [deceased], face-to-face with the said manager. The inheritance of the said deceased, the said *kapıkulu*, it was decided, belonged to them, and the court provided a court order [affirming this], while the kadi in charge of the division of estates (*kassam askeri*), divided the estate between them, and they took possession [of their parts of the estate]. In this way the confrontation and the quarrel came to an end. But while this was [seemingly so], the said manager, only for the purpose of capturing and molesting, said to them again: "You are not the heirs of the said deceased, and the estate was formerly given to you contrary to the true verdict of the court; I am suing you again." And so, against the court order given on this issue, and without an Imperial decree, he did not shrink from bothering the claimants, though they let it be known that they hold a *fetva* saying that court discussion of an issue already discussed in the Shar' once (and concerning which there is a court order) is forbidden. They asked for a decree that would stop and cut short such [a course of action].

The order was written so as to ensure behavior according to the Shar' and the *Kanun.*[309]

25 April-5 May 1675

309 The document is simply a conflict over the division of an estate and the wrangling among the heirs over their respective rights. Into this discussion, however, came a *vakıf* manager, who claimed that since the deceased was living in a *han* belonging to the endowment, the estate belonged to that endowment. While the court ruled against this argument, the manager did not let up and sued again. Here, the other heirs raised the basic Ottoman law, saying that the hearing of a question in a court of law is illegal if that question has already been discussed there—unless allowed by a Sultanic order. This was also backed by a *fetva* of the *şeyhülislam*. So this was certainly the basic Ottoman perception, but as we shall see shortly, it was quite a loose rule, more often overlooked than implemented, for reasons we shall try to sort out below.

No. 92

71b-6

Order to the *kaimakam* of Istanbul and its Kadi

The inhabitants of the *nahiye* of Etranos[310] sent a man and a petition saying: Mustafa, citizen of Istanbul, who was formerly, for the year 1085, responsible for the collection of the taxes of *sursat* and *bedel-i nuzul*[311] from this *nahiye*, charged 1,320 *piastres* more than the register and the order, thus causing them a major injustice. When he was summoned to the Shari'a court, he refused to obey, and when the said ones came [after him] to Istanbul, he ran away to Edirne, and when the [complainants] demanded, with the help of a Sultanic order, that he come to have an encounter in the Shari'a court, he did not leave [the house,] and attaining justice was impossible, while their money remained in his hands. The situation remained one of injustice. They asked for an order.

Now, my order is that he has to be summoned to the Shari'a court. If he refuses to obey the Shar', his house is to be sealed (*memhur*), attaining justice in this way.

7-16 April 1675[312]

No. 93

99a-4

Order to the *paşa* [sic] of Istanbul and its Kadi

Ahmed presented a petition, saying: when his step-father, Mehmed, wanted to go on the pilgrimage (*hajj*) in the year 1082, he took 800 *altun* from him [the complainant] as a loan, but died before repaying it. When he demanded the [money] from those holding the estate, the ladies ...[x], his wife, and his daughter, Hadice, they created trouble [and did not pay]. When the affair was brought to an encounter in the Shari'a court by their legal representative, Ahmed, there was a court decision, and a court order was issued [in his favor], but they again made problems [and did not pay]. He asked for a decree that would order to bring the issue to the Shari'a court and ensure conduct according to the court order, thereby achieving justice.

My order is to bring the matter to be decided in the Shari'a court.

26 April-5 May 1675[313]

---

310 Modern Orhaneli, in *sancak* Hüdavendigar, poetic Ottoman name for the city of Bursa, Westanatolia.

311 Two irregular taxes collected in kind.

312 This document shows the case of a tax collector who extorted illegal sums from his region of collection, and the people were chasing him after that, whereas he kept avoiding them. Finally, the Divan ordered his house be closed and sealed if he kept on like that. This is an exceptionally harsh punishment in comparison to extortion that looked much more serious. Could it be that the central government was more lenient on extortionists that were closer to the center?

313 The question of the finality of cases discussed by the Ottoman court is really a surprising roller coaster with no end to it, and we can join the circle at any point. Here, we read about a

No. 94

22b-4

Order to the *kaimakam* of Istanbul and its Kadi

Kapıcı Hasan, from the gatekeepers of My Sublime Porte, sent a petition, saying: a lady named Saliha, previously deceased, gave him [the complainant] a house of hers as a present, [a house] situated in the quarter of Mustafa Çelebi, that was in her possession, and which is known by borders, a legal present, including handing over, and he [on his part] paid her 2000 *akçe* as compensation, and took possession of the house, living in it for more than 20 years, in which time he held it as completely private property. And while no one had any right to intervene in this affair, [and, by the way—] the house was not a *vakıf* house, and it had no endowment document, and when the *sicill* was examined, no record of it was found either. And formerly, a man named Ismail got the house by rent, but he turned towards an evil course and sold the house to a lady named Saliha Memi, who [soon] claimed that the house was [always] a *vakıf* for *suleha* [pious Sufis] and claimed: "I am one of the *suleha*, hence I live in it by right." Her lonely voice and her overconfidence [?] go to discredit her testimony. But [by] some way or other a court document was also procured, and this is [nothing less] than usurpation and injustice. Many *fetvas* were [in fact] issued on this matter, and he let them know that he has many (*muteaddid*) court documents that related to the property as private property (*mulk*) for 70-80 years. He asked for a decree directing to bring the matter to be discussed in the Shari'a court. A decree was written, ordering to manage the affair as narrated above.[314]

6-15 February 1675

No. 95

67b-1

Order to the *kaimakam* of Istanbul and its Kadi

Someone named...[empty] presented a petition and claimed: formerly he had a loan in the form of a shar'i loan in the hand of Mehmed, for the sum of 17,000 *akçe*. He [Mehmed] died before the loan was repaid. His estate was seized by his son Mustafa. When the complainant [then] demanded repayment of the loan from the estate, [Mustafa] refused and the outcome was a shar'i en-

---

conflict over an estate between heirs, where the losing parties kept on bothering the winning side, until he became fed up and sued them again in a court of law. So what happened finally?

314 A man, in this document, got a house as present from a lady, then let it to renters, one of whom sold it (illegally of course). Then the house was given to rent to a lady who claimed it was a *vakıf* and she was entitled to receive it as such. In short, an entangled story that went on for scores of years, and the true owner now claims that he has numerous *fetvas* and numerous court documents attesting that the house is his. So obviously, the house was the subject of the court several times, a situation to which no one objected. So again, one wonders what happened to finality.

counter, in which the fact that Mustafa's father, the said deceased [person] owed the claimant a sum as detailed, was proven, and Mustafa was warned by the Shari'a court to pay. The court was on the brink of issuing a court order [to that effect], when the said Mustafa went down an evil path, and while a claim on the back of an unfinished one is not legal in Shari'a law, the said one managed to prove the [second claim] without [the claimant] receiving his rights from the Shari'a court, the heir [Mustafa] telling him: "I paid you the debt before." This was an evil claim, using false witnesses. Thus, his [Mehmed's] debt remained unpaid in the hand of Mustafa. He let it be known that he had a *fetva* in this matter, and asked for an order of mine.
The order was written for the issue to be brought for discussion in the Shari'a court.
28 March-6 April 1675[315]

No. 96

10b-1
Order to the *mufettiş* of Istanbul
The ladies Rabia and Aişe, daughters of former Rumeli Kazasker Abdulrahman, presented a petition, saying: ...[a *çiftlik*, a pasture, a winter pasture, and a further small winter pasture] known in terms of their borders, belonging to the endowment of the mosque and imaret of Bayazid Han Veli, and situated in the *kaza* of Hasslar, in the tax collection area [*cibayet*] of ...[so and so] and in the village of Ilyas Aga are in their possession by inheritance, passing from grandfather to father are [now] in their hands. They are well demarcated lands, pastures, and winter pastures, with independent documents; and while there has not been any reason for anybody to intervene, Sinan, of the said village, went to the Shari'a court suing three or four times, but they [Rabia and Aişe] turned out to be in the right, and the claim of the people of that village and the said Sinan was proven baseless, as made clear by the court, and [Sinan] was restrained from [further] objection and those land and pastures were declared by the court for them and a court order was given. [In this way], the conflict was decided and the conflict cut short, but now, Sinan is not satisfied and again intervenes and bothers [them], against the court order, and [against] the possession documents which they have in their hands.
An order was written so that [things go according] to the court order and the possession documents, and in order to stop and repudiate the [objection to them].
18-27 January 1675[316]

315 In this document, we find a debate about the return of a loan, where the borrower had passed away, and his heir refused to pay the money. He lost one case, but managed to sue again, possibly using false witnesses, probably in another court. When this exercise was discovered, the law reiterated that such a procedure is not legal.

316 In this document we find a quarrel between two women who inherited land in a village area

No. 97

78a-4

Order to the *Beylerbey* of Anatolia and the Kadi of ...[empty]

Sayyids (descendants of the Prophet) named *Sayyid* Yusuf and *Sayyid* Muhi al-Din, together with other *sayyids* that are citizens of the village of Sayidalar [?], in the *kaza* of Çaka (?), together with the other citizens of the village, presented a petition saying: these [people] discovered a free source of water in a mountain that is not possessed (*mubah dağ*) by anyone, named Kaya Binarı. They brought the water to their village and used it [for their purposes]. And while the waters are not entered in the land register as belonging to them, a neighboring village... [x] confronted them and made a claim against them: "These are waters that belong to our summer pasture (*yaylak*), and they are registered as such in our version of the register." Before that, the issue had already been raised and village [x] sued the petitioners in the Shari'a court, and when the issue was discussed, it transpired that the waters in question are not registered as the waters of the *yaylak* of the aforementioned [village x], but are free waters available for the use of anybody, and as [has been] done in the ten years the [petitioners] bring them to their village and enjoy them. Hence it was found that the connection of the other village does not exist, and they were warned not to bother the village with their objections. But while this was so, the said village sued, yet again, and at this stage two *fetvas* were issued [confirming the encounter above]. They asked for an order that would direct them to observe the two *fetvas* that are in their hand [and proceed] according to the court order that is also in their hand, and according to my orders, given before and now.[317] The order was written for the case to be brought to the Shari'a court to be decided.

7-16 April 1675

and the people of the village who sued the women again and again, despite the obvious fact that those women had all of the necessary documents to prove their ownership. What is more, no one raised their eyebrows at the supposed pertinence of suing again and again. This is not a very convincing case for the finality of the court process. It is time to try and figure out what went on here. My feeling is that much depended on the theoretical awareness of those involved in the process. When the parties did not know or care about finality, the Divan did not see it as appropriate to sound the alarm. The bottom line is that the law of finality was difficult to enforce, despite the fact that it existed on paper.

317 This document deals with a debate between two villages over an unknown source of water on top of a mountain in the area. The second village tried to "prove" that the source was actually in its area. The Shari'a court rejected this claim after a trial. The other village did not accept this, and went on to demand further legal encounters. In all of these discussions, however, no one raised the point that the later discussions were actually illegal, and once again, one gets the feeling that since the interested party were not aware of their rights, no one else—not even the Divan—was interested in mentioning them.

No. 98

57a-2
Order to the *kaimakam* of Istanbul and to its Kadi
Rali [?] the *zimmi*, came and claimed [in a petition]: he had an encounter with Hasan, a citizen of Istanbul, then there was a mutual exoneration from debts. To obtain an end to the confrontation a court order (*huccet*) was issued, but Hasan was not satisfied with this and went back to the road of confrontation.
The order was written to make it clear that according to a *fetva* by the *şeyhül-islam*, dealing with a court claim [for the second time] is forbidden.[318]
23 August-1 September 1674

No. 99

167b-6
Order to the *kaimakam* and Kadi of Istanbul
Two women citizens of Istanbul, known as ...[?] have presented a petition saying: formerly, their father, Solak Mustafa, bought a house in Istanbul and an estate outside of Istanbul; he obtained a confirmation document from the "land owner" [the *sipahi*, holder of the *timar*], a complete sale took place, [including] severance of relations [with the seller], but afterwards, the seller took an evil path, and did nor refrain from interference and conflict, and as a court document was being issued, their father died. They [his daughters] took possession of the estate, but [the accused] challenged them again, and again made a claim in court. Again, there was a mutual clearing of obligation with a court order issued, and while in cases like this, where a case has been decided by the Shari'a court, and a court order has been given, a second hearing of the claim is forbidden, the [accused] was not satisfied, and is again not free from [the spirit of] challenge. They drew attention to the fact that they have a court order and appropriate documents from the *timar* holder. They asked for an order that would direct all involved to proceed according to those documents.
Now, the order was written to draw attention to the need to behave according to the Shar' and the *Kanun*.
24 July-2 August 1675[319]

---

318 Then we come to this short and cryptic case, and we observe that both the *şeyhülislam* and the Divan are fully aware of the law forbidding a second hearing of a case, and proceed strictly according to it.

319 In this document, there is a discussion over the possession of land and again, the winning party is faced with a stubborn adversary who is determined to sue again and again. The complainants are fully aware of the law, however, and do not fail to mention it to the Divan, and seem to get positive cooperation with their position. So again, if any party was aware of the law and insisted on its implementation, it seemed to work.

No. 100

207b-1

Order to the Kadi of Ladiq[320]

The citizens of the said town have presented a petition, saying: the said town is part of the endowment of the mother of Prince Ahmed Han, Bulbul Hatun. And from the time of the Imperial conquest [of the area], the *malikane* tax of the said town belongs to the Sufi lodge [*zaviye*] of Sayyid Ahmed Kebir, the philanthropist, while its *divaniye* tax goes to the said endowment.[321] Taxes [usual in other places] like *tapu-i zemin* and *icare-i arazi* are not registered as belonging to the endowment, and the citizens of the said *kaza* have in their hands court documents and an Imperial freehold grant (*mulkname*), *fetva,* and Imperial orders, all passing from grandson to father now for more than 300 years, [attesting to their rights] in the said manner. In this way, while no one has the right to interfere in the matter, as of two years, the manager of the endowment, Ebu Bekir, went on an evil path and demanded *tapu* and *icare-i arazi* taxes, against the Shar' and the *Kanun*, against the Imperial order, and contrary to justice. This matter was already dealt with formerly by the Shari'a court, and a court order was given, directing the manager not to interfere. However, while the hearing of such a court case in a matter which has already been dealt with by the court is forbidden, the aforementioned Ebu Bekir, relying on some kadi, got a court document in some way, proceeded again to challenge the original *huccet.*

A signed document was given by Yusuf Ağa, the supervisor (*nazir*) of the said endowment, [also] the acting manager of the Imperial *harem*, affirming that one has to proceed legally according to the freehold grant held in their hands, as well as according to the [original] court document, the *fetva,* and the land register. [He also affirmed] that the way these people were possessing their properties should continue in the same way in the future, without any license being given to managers to bother with demands of *tapu* and *icare-i arazi* taxes, which are against the Shar', the *Kanun,* and contrary to the Imperial order.

My order has been given to proceed according to what was narrated above.

1-10 September 1675[322]

---

320 In *sancak* Amasya, Eastern Anatolia.

321 These taxes were related to forms of land possession that were outside of the dominant *çift-timar* system, characterized by *tapu-i Zemin.* See Halil Inalcık, *Economic and Social History,* pp. 120-131.

322 In this document, there was a quarrel over the rights connected to old award documents by the Sultanate, which the endowment manager was in fact trying to challenge. The court decided in favor of the holders of the old documents, and the complainants duly mentioned at this point the law forbidding a second hearing of a case, but the endowment manager was able to find "some Kadi" who was willing to go along with his claim. As the discussion over this case would have dragged a little further, somebody would have to check the nature of the second hearing, and in any case, the end of this case remains unknown to us.

No. 101

101b-2

Order to the Kadi of Istanbul

Aişe, a woman from Istanbul came and said against Halil, also from the people of Istanbul: [Formerly] she had a court case against the aforementioned, and the case was dealt with in the Shari'a court, and decided in her favor in every respect. The aforementioned was restrained from bothering [her]. As a token of finality of any further confrontation, a court decision (*huccet*) was issued by the court. But contrary to this document, and against the Shar' and the *Kanun*, the aforementioned does not refrain from further encounters, against all justice. She asked for an order of mine that would see to it that [his] behavior proceed according to the court verdict and contrary behavior be stopped and pushed back.

My order is that this matter has to be brought for decision to the Shari'a court.[323]

6-15 May 1675

No. 102

224a-1

Order to the Kadi of neighborhood ...[x] in Istanbul

A man named Ahmed, with his sister, have presented an order saying: while nobody else besides them had any connection to a house in their possession, which is situated near Khavaca Paşa Mosque in the quarter of Karali Huseyin Çelebi, the prayer leader (imam) of the said quarter's mosque and his brother Halil, interfered [in the matter] against the Shar', and sued the complainants in court a number of times. [But] the claims of the said persons were found worthless and evil, and their objection was rejected, and in order to decide the issues in a decisive way, a court document was issued. And though a repeated hearing of such a claim is illegal, the said ones did not shrink from disputing [it] once more. They [the complainants] also notified them that they have in their hand a *fetva* supporting their case. They asked for an order directing to act in accordance with the *fetva* and the court document.

My order is to check in the Shari'a court and decide.[324]

19-28 November 1675

323 In this document, we read a story of a conflict between a man and woman, with the court having decided in favor of the woman. The man decided to sue again. The lady asked the Sultan to enforce the court verdict, not mentioning that this was actually the law. Surprisingly or not, the *Divan* decided to transfer the issue to the Shari'a court—yet again, though this is not a review, but seemingly a new case. So again, the theory of finality is not corroborated.

324 In this document, we find a legal encounter between two siblings who own a house in Istanbul and a number of people who challenged their ownership. These challengers sued again and again, but the complainants were fully aware of their legal right concerning the finality of the process and the *Divan* supported them.

Chapter 9: The Agent (*mübaşir*)

Preliminary Remarks

Michael Ursinus may have been the first to discover the use of the office holder of the agent (*mübaşir*), as a multi-task official specially dispatched by high authority to sort out legal entanglements between individuals before, or instead of, taking the issue to court. He showed that most of the complaints that were presented to the governor of Rumelia in the late eighteenth century, were entrusted to *mübaşirs*, with orders to solve them. Ursinus seems to think that the *mübaşir* did this as a legal official of some sort. However, was this right? In any case, careful inspection of the Book of Complaints shows that a small number of documents contain references to *mübaşirs* that were, here too, nominated by the *Divan* to take care of various problems of a legal nature. My interest here is to try and find out whether the *mübaşir* really enter into the legal orbit, thereby detracting from the authority of the kadi. My conclusion is that on the whole, this was not the case. The wording of the documents is very careful to preserve the fact that the role of the agent was to give assistance to the Shari'a court, but by no means to meddle in judicial decisions.[325]

Documents

No. 103

186b-6

Order to the Kadi of Izmir and the *naib* of Menemen

The citizens of the *kaza* of Menemen presented a petition saying: people called Serdar Haci Suleyman, Sazi [?], Feyzullah, and Hamze Kadi-oğlu Ali Efendi, all of them also citizens of the said *kaza*, are not behaving properly, but are rather evil, and informers: they always are on the side of the kadis, *voyvodas, subaşıs,* and other state officials (*ehl-i örf*), as well as nominated tax collectors; and contrary to what is right, pass on many pieces of information, take money, and cause others to take [money from people]. They also meddle in the affairs of tax collection and oppression, and denial of rights of the type that know no bounds. They ask for a decree, that would order to check [this affair] via the agent [*mübaşir*], nominated to go to that place to take care of a number of things via the Shari'a court. Owners of rights that will be disclosed during this investigation must be given their rights; let them not interfere in the affairs of the owners of rights and the affairs of the *reaya*, thereby attaining justice.

Now, my order is that this matter be dealt with by the Shari'a court; sums of

325 See: Michael Ursinus, *Grievance Administration (Şikayet) in an Ottoman Province*, London and New York: RoutledgeCurzon, 2005.

money they have taken contrary to the Shar', whatever they are, are to be returned via the *mübaşir*, and justice must be attained.[326]
13-22 August 1675

No. 104

76b-5
Order to the *paşa* and Kadi of Diyarbekir
Haci Mehmed presented a petition saying: I have a shar'i loan of 500 *piastres* in the hands of the former governor of the *sancak* of Kultuk [?], situated in the province of Diyarbekir, with the surety of his brother, Mustafa. When he came to ask for the repayment, [the borrower] raised problems, [and failed to pay]. He asked for an order in the matter of [collecting] the said sum from the former governor or his surety, through the intervention [*mübaşeretile*] of Kaptan Ibrahim, chief gate-keeper in My Sublime Porte, who was nominated to go to the said location.
The order was written to direct that the matter be brought for decision in the Shari'a court.[327]
7-16 April 1675

No. 105

155a-2
Order to the *monla* of Filibe
The citizens of the village of Nasuh Fakih, belonging to the said *kaza* [sic], and forming also part of the endowment of Mihrimah Sultan, presented a petition saying: between the said village and the village of Koz Uzunlu, otherwise known as Koz Bağlı, current name Kara Mustafalar, there is an area of some 500 *dönüm*, well known as to its [topographic] borders, which is an old pasture [free for all]; [but while this was so] Yusuf Çavuş [came] and said: "This village, Kara Mustafalar, is a village in my *ziamet*, and as of two years I allow the villagers to do agriculture there." Before that, an order was issued, and a *mübaşir* was nom-

326 Among the types of criminals that we encounter in the countryside of seventeenth century Anatolia, we find people who were not content with living their own life, but wished to run the lives of all those living around them. They often did this by getting close to state officials socially, proximity that too often ended in the extraction of resources from the poor citizens. This activity was certainly suspicious, but whether it was also criminal remains questionable. Certainly, the whole affair was worthy of investigation by an able *mübaşir*, who was here nominated to investigate whether violations of the law were involved as well.

327 In this document, we find a discussion of a loan of a large sum of money, where the borrower was a provincial governor who made problems regarding returning the money. It was a problem that naturally attracted the interest of the Ottoman center, and its mode of treatment for this issue was to send an agent, or *mübaşir*, who tried to reconcile the parties, find a compromise, and finally bring the matter to the Shari'a court. In this document, it is quite clearly seen that the *mübaşir* is not doing anything more than this.

inated who came there and there a [shar'i] encounter (*murafaa*) took place, to which were summoned Hasan and objective people, and there it was ruled that the land is a pasture, and the said Yusuf was restrained from further bothering the [villagers]. A court document was given by the Shari'a court, attesting that the land is in the possession of them [complainants], and they [for their part] asked for an Imperial order to be given that would prevent intervention and molestation.

Now, the order was written so that there be conduct according to the court document.[328]

15-24 July, 1675

No. 106

156b-4

Order to the *paşa* of Yenişehir Fenar and to its Kadi, and to Şahin, nominated to be agent

Merchants came and claimed: we bought silk in Mizistire in Morea and brought it to the market in Mashkulor. When we paid the tax of the silk weighing scales to the managers of the scales, no one had any reason to meddle in the affair; but you who are the aforementioned Kadi, [you] took 200 *piastres* from them, against the Shar', and doing this you acted unjustly. You, who are *mübaşir*, an order was issued that the money will be returned with your help (*marifetenle*) and via the Shari'a court.[329]

15-24 July 1675

No. 107

28a-7

Order to the Kadis of ... [empty] and ...[empty]

The people of the *kaza* of Kalacik Keskini, belonging to the *kaza* [sic] of Kangari, presented a petition saying: formerly, two Imperial orders have been issued that

328 This document deals with a conflict between villagers and a *ziamet* holder, over the status of a 500 *dönüm* piece of land, claimed by the villagers as a piece of pasture, providing free grazing for everyone, not subject to any taxation. The *zaim* claimed it is part and parcel of his estate as regular agricultural land, liable to taxation. The problem for the *zaim* was that agricultural experts testified that the land was easily recognizable as an old pasture. From our point of view, it is important that a shar'i encounter took place on the land itself, in which a *mübaşir* (sent from Istanbul) also took part, but it was legally a regular shar'i trial, and a court document was issued, so the role of the *mübaşir* was one of technical help, no more. Here too, by the way, the location of the court was not considered as something very important, if at all.

329 This is again an exceptional document that crosses the line of the cool (even cold) tone usually associated with Ottoman documents, and becomes personal. Here, a Kadi is squarely blamed by the *Divan* for being unjust to merchants, by illegally exacting unwarranted taxes from them. He is called upon to return the money to the nominated *mübaşir* sent thither, who would then pass it on to its rightful owners.

directed that the *mütesellim* of Kangari, someone named...[empty] of the inhabitants of the said *kaza*, return immediately sums taken against the Shar' and the *Kanun* to their owners. But the said *mütesellim* is not [now] in the *kaza* of Kalacik Keskini, [so] they asked for an order that his case will be heard wherever he may be found through the [work] of Bekir Çavuş, nominated as *mübaşir* [for this matter].
Now, the order was written so that wherever he may be found, this case must be checked by the Shari'a court. Everything he has taken contrary to the Shar', the *Kanun*, and the custom, he has to return.[330]
6-15 February 1675

No. 108

105a-2
Order to the Kadi of Muzakye and...[empty] and to the *mütesellims* of Avlona and Ilbasan
The *naib* of the *kaza* of Muzakye sent a letter saying: the brigands Omer and Mehmed, citizens of the said *kaza*, killed...[331] [x, probably a woman], of the people of Aslan Village in the said *kaza*, plundered her property and things, and denied her daughter the right of *hidana*.[332] Doing this, they committed a major violation of rights. And the head (*muhtar*) of the said village, Musa, was notified before that when the aforementioned were invited to the Shari'a court, they did not obey the Shar' [and did not come]. Then a *mübaşir* was nominated, and an order was given to bring the matter to the Shari'a court, but again they did not comply with the order and it was not possible to achieve obedience and attain justice at all.
Now, an order was issued so that their condition be checked in situ by the Shari'a court and by means (*marifet*) of the *mübaşir* nominated. Then, the matter should be brought to a legal encounter (*murafaa*) in the Shari'a court, and if proof is found against anyone, what is incumbent according to the Shar' should be done.
16-25 May 1675[333]

---

330 This document is a regular tax extortion, but it is exceptional since the whereabouts of the culprit were not known. He has to be looked for in various administrative areas, and for this, a special agent was nominated. It is indicated specifically, however, that his role was to bring issues and people into the Shari'a court, where the legal resolutions were made.

331 Three words were smeared in the original at this point.

332 *Hidana* the right of a divorced wife to raise her child in the first years of his life.

333 This is an exceptionally lucid document about the role of the agent. Here, a lady was killed and her properties robbed, and no one was able to bring the criminals to justice. The job was given to a *mübaşir*, and here it was said specifically that the investigation should be done by the *mübaşir* and the court together, while the adjudication should be done exclusively by the Shari'a court.

No. 109

105a-1

Order to the Kadi of Arnavud Belgrad[334] and to the *mütesellim* of Avlona *sancak*

Musa [bearing several stately titles] came and claimed that: he had in his hand the tax-farm for collecting the real estate tax (*avariz*) for the year 1083. But the inhabitants of the village of Haikal, belonging to the *kaza* of Arnaud Belgrad, in cooperation with brigands from [another] village [in the area] assaulted his relative who was occupied with the work of collection of the *miri* taxes for him, shot him with a rifle and killed him. The matter was investigated legally on site and a court document (*huccet*) was issued. The [complainant] asked an order to direct, in accordance with the court document, to nominate an agent (*mübaşir*) that will be sent to that area and that an order will be given to investigate the matter through him, and that the perpetrators must be arrested at all cost and brought to the Shari'a court for justice to be done.

My order has been that the matter must be brought to the Shari'a court for resolution.

16-25 May 1675

334 In modern Albania.

Chapter 10: The Role of the *Divan* in the Legal Process

Preliminary Remarks

A small number of documents in the Book of Complaints end with an order to notify the Imperial Council of what went on in certain investigations ordered before or an order to summon complainants and suspected violators to the *Divan* to have the case clarified further. These documents raise anew the interesting question of the role of the *Divan* in the Ottoman legal process, an old question, with many theories and few facts to support any of them. There are those who claim that the *Divan* was a review forum, to which people simply came to appeal against a certain kadi. In all the relevant cases that went to the *Divan* that I have seen in the Book of Complaints, no such case ever surfaced. What many of these documents show, is the complete opposite, viz., that appeal was considered illegal and strictly forbidden. This does not rule out the possibility that in rare cases some sort of appeal did take place there, but it required the support of a Sultanic decree. An entirely unexpected phenomenon was that part of the documents revealed a situation in which people were invited to the *Divan* simply to have a regular shar'i encounter there. However, the bulk of the issues that were brought before the *Divan* were probably the difficult matters of brigandage and oppression that nobody else could solve. What we have here, is only the summoning to the *Divan*, not any indication of what actually took place in these processes; for that, we are left with no more than guesses.

Documents

No. 110

10b-3

Order to the Kadi of Silivri[335]

You have sent a letter, saying: the *reaya* living in the town of Silivri, who are connected to a road station (*menzil)*, came to the Shari'a court and said: in this year, their *menzil* is 3 *yuk* and 18,000 *akçe*, and the *zimmi* Avram is their *menzilci*. But he served as *menzilci* for a month then left the *menzil* and ran away. Again, a man was nominated to the post by Ibrahim Paşa, the *kaimakam* of Istanbul, and the said *menzil* was rented to the said Avram, for the sum of 4 *yuk akçe*. The said *reaya* said: we have no possibility to procure the addition of 82,000 *akçe*, and they protested the oppression. Also, the agent sent thither claimed that there is no possibility to run the post of *menzilci* for less than 4 *yuk akçe*. Saying this, he was not free from molestation [towards them]. They asked for an order that will summon the parties to the *Divan-i Hümayun*, for the sake of having a [legal] encounter (*murafaa*) there.

335 In *sancak* Vize, European Turkey.

The order was written so that the two parties will be summoned to the *Divan* for the sake of conducting a shar'i encounter.
18-27 January 1675

No. 111

40b-5
Order to the *naib* of Hezargrad[336]
Someone named Karaca, living in the town of Hezargrad, came and said: two years before, a Latin-z*immi* was found dead in his house. [Now] his brother, who lives in another country, came with an Imperial order, and said: "You are my suspect, you," the Kadi of Shumni being [at the same time] nominated as *molla*.[337] [With his above mentioned statement], he went on to sue the [complainant] in the Shari'a court, but [in the shar'i trial] no connection was established through impartial witnesses between him [the complainant] and the killing, and the accuser was restrained, a court document being issued in the matter.[338] But now, using false witnesses, he demanded from the [complainant] 5,500 *piastres*, thereby committing a large-scale oppression against him. He asked for an order that will summon the parties to the Imperial *Divan* to deal with the matter in a shar'i way there.[339]
The order was written to summon both sides to the *Divan-i Hümayun*.
3-12 August 1674[340]

336 In sancak Niğbolu, modern Bulgaria.

337 Though there seems to be no secondary literature on this, it should be evident by now that the administrative Ottoman system used to nominate Kadis as agents dealing with complicated legal matters, who were upgraded for the task at hand to the degree of *molla*, or top grade Kadi.

338 This point is somewhat elusive, something is probably missing: according to Islamic law, a man in whose house a murder had been committed is liable for the blood money, provided he is formally exonerated from the actual killing, and the identity of the killer is unknown. Here the man is acquitted of having killed, but is nevertheless responsible for the blood money. I would guess that there was a mistake in the wording of the text, and in reality the actual killing was not proven; to revert to Islamic law, if no active killing was involved in the death, no one is liable for anything, as the death could be interpreted as natural.

339 The summoning to the *Divan* here is highly important to understand the role of the *Divan* in the Ottoman legal process. What we see here, is that the intention of all parties was to discuss the issues anew. This was not a sort of appeal through the officials of the *Divan*, but a new shar'i discussion, probably conducted by one of the Kadis of Istanbul. It may be considered a sort of half-hearted appeal, but no more than this.

340 What we have here, is at base a claim against one person of killing another man found dead in his house, apparently that of the accused. Obviously, the body should have carried marks of being killed, otherwise no one was liable for anything. Possibly also, the house was rented, so according to Ebu Suʿud's law from the sixteenth century, the renter, rather than the owner, was liable for a body found in the house (this was Ebu Suʿud's innovation, forming part of his famous *Maruzat*, suggested to Sultan Suleyman and authorized by him in Imperial rescript. Ebu Suʿud's innovation here was in fact a return to an old opinion by Abu Yusuf, one of Abu Hanifa's disciples, after centuries in which the master's opinion held sway, whereby only the

No. 112

205b-7

Order to the Kadi of ...[empty]

The Kadi of Yanya sent a letter saying: Osman, possessor of a *ziamet*, came to the Shari'a court and said: his father was in the position of taking and holding all the produce and taxes of the said *ziamet*, which he holds by [Imperial] nomination document (*berat*), for a number of years and up to the end of the period of tax farm. [The father] then died; and when he [the complainant] asked [for] the proceeds from the other heirs, Ali and his sisters, they made problems in [regard to] payment. Before that, an order was issued [concerning this affair] and an agent [*mübaşir*] was sent thither, but they did not obey either the order or the Shar'. He now asks for an Imperial order [yet again].

An order was written to summon the aforementioned to the *Divan* in Edirne.[341]

1-10 September 1675

No. 113

99a-5

Order to the Kadis and *mütesellims* of Kangari, Canik, ...[empty] and ...[empty]

Osman, who holds the sub-province of Kangari by way of *arpalik*, sent a petition saying: while I was formerly in charge of collecting the taxes due to the governor from the citizens of the sub-province of Kangari, a man named Ali appeared and said: "I am an agent (*mübaşir*)." Saying this, he started to incite and rouse the people, made a club and an assembly (*dernek* and *cemiyet*), things contributing to anarchy and social unrest (*fitna*), then ran away in the direction

owner of the house was liable for criminal responsibility. See: Paul Horster, *Zur Anwendung des Islamischen Rechts im 16. Jahrhundert*, Stuttgart: Kohlhammer, 1935, pp. 58-59). If this was the case, we can understand why the owner was acquitted every time the matter was pursued in the Shari'a court. The other side went on bothering him endlessly, so in the end the complainant demanded a hearing in the *Divan*. Possibly it was going to be one final shar'i encounter, or maybe another kind of trial; it certainly does not seem to be an appeal, but rather, a new kind of trial.

341 The story of this complaint is a *ziamet* owner who nominated his father to be the tax collector for him in the villages of the estate. When the father died in the middle of the year, large sums fell to other heirs, his brother (?) and sisters, who refused to part with this money. Since the Kadi is the one passing the complaint to Istanbul, it is clear that the matter was already decided by the Kadi's court, but the money was nevertheless not paid. It was then that a *mübaşir* was sent thither to convince the heirs to abide by the Kadi's verdict. It is only then that the *Divan* summoned the parties to that council. Again, it was not going to be an appeal, since nobody seems to suspect any fault with the Kadi's decision. It is also interesting to observe that the internal structure of the Ottoman family was much less cohesive than might be thought, and much more "modern", in fact, I found as much in another study. See: Haim Gerber, "Anthropology and Family History: The Ottoman and Turkish Families", in Gerber, *State and Society in the Ottoman Empire*, Ashgate [Variorum Reprints]: Farnham, 2010, Chapter 5.

of Canik. He asked for a decree that would order the capture of the said Ali and bring him [to the *Divan-i Hümayun*].
My order is that he is to be brought to the said place.[342]
26 September-5 May 1675

No. 114

49b-6
Order to the *naib* of the island of Kos and the *yeniçeri* commander of the place
Haci Mehmed, citizen of the said *kaza*, presented a petition and said: the said person has a loan of 2,280 *piastres* in the hands of the *yeniçeri,* Daud, from unit 94, living in the same *kaza*, and the named person is presenting problems with repayment. For the claim to be heard by means of the Shari'a court in my *Divan-i Hümayun* and justice (*haq*) be achieved, Mehmed Çavuş, officer of the six [*yeniçeri*] regiment was nominated as the agent (*mübaşir*), and the said agent was annexed to the court that dealt with the shar'i trial within the *Divan-i Hümayun*. Also, the acting commander of the *yeniçeris*, Mustafa Aga, sent a signed letter to achieve justice and bring the sides [together].
An order was written so that things proceed according to what was detailed.[343]
16-25 June 1674

No. 115

102a-4
Order to the kadi of Vizen[344]
The citizens of the village... [x] in the said *kaza* presented a petition saying: the above [people] have no debt to a certain...[y] known as *deveci* [camel owner and driver], and nothing has been proven against them or made clear about them in the Shari'a court; but the said camel driver has decided to take an evil path and said: "You owe me 1,100 *piastres*." Saying this, he interfered in their affairs, and [further], sent an agent (*mübaşir*), committing a transgression.

342 This document returns to a topic seen already earlier in this collection: the effort of some people to incite rural populations against the government, especially in the context of tax paying. Like in all the other documents of this nature, it is not made clear what these people really wanted, and how they thought they could force the hand of the government. In any case, the government did relate to this pattern seriously, and tried to summon these people to the *Divan*—for what exactly, is never made clear.

343 In this document, two *yeniçeris* have a conflict over a shar'i loan, but here we find an interesting surprise in that the two parties are summoned to the *Divan-i Hümayun* to have a shar'i encounter in the full sense, though in the presence of a *mübaşir*, and also a *yeniçeri* officer. It is a surprise to realize that summoning to the *Divan* did not in fact rule out the possibility that what took place in the *Divan* was more or less a shar'i trial.

344 In European Turkey.

Now, my order is that if he has an answer valid by shar'i terms, let him come, and let them have a shar'i trial within the *Divan-i Hümayun.*[345]
17-26 May 1674

No. 116

56a-6
Order to the *Bostanci başı* in Edirne and to the Kadi of Şumni[346]
Someone named Dhu al-Fiqar came and claimed: formerly, in the year 1080 and something, his brother Abdulkadir was beaten by a war tool (*alet-i harb*)[347] without justice, and died. He was beaten by Ahmet, the servant of Yahşi oğlu Amr ...[and six more people, their names given]. Doing this, they committed a great oppression and injustice. He asked for an Imperial order of mine in this regard.
Now, my order was given that you, who are the said *Bostanci başı*, nominate a faithful expert (*usta*) and let the situation of the above people be checked by the Shari'a court. If indeed the said persons have committed the oppression of the said nature, as becomes clear and duly proven in the Shari'a court, then the matter should be presented to my *Divan-i Hümayun.*[348]
18-27 March 1675

No. 117

154a-3
Order to the *naib* of Islimye[349]
Huseyin came and complained that: another Huseyin, of the citizens of the

345 This document features a conflict between village people and a camel owner and driver, usually a wealthy figure in Anatolia at that time. The camel driver claimed that he had made a loan to the people of the village, which they denied. It is not clear why the parties to this conflict were invited to the *Divan*, but the important point of the document is the statement that the purpose of the invitation was to conduct a shar'i trial between the parties in the *Divan*, and this is said in the clearest possible terms. One can only wonder how many invitations to the *Divan* were made exactly for this simple purpose.

346 In European Turkey. The *Bostanci başı*, originally chief gardener, was in the seventeenth century chief of police around the Bosporus villages, and probably around Edirne, when the Ottoman court resided in Edirne, like in this period.

347 Making the whole affair a pre-meditated murder in Islamic law.

348 This document deals with a case of the killing of a person with a war-tool (*alet-i harb*), considered to be a tool used for premeditated killing, or murder, making the killer liable for the death penalty or blood money. It is quite clear from the documents that the Ottoman government related to such an offence as a very grave one. Hence, the *Divan* directs that the *Bostanci başı* should nominate an expert (*usta*—a sort of *mübaşir*), to help investigate the matter together with the Shari'a court. Then, if it would be proven in the Shar' that these people really committed the crime, the *Divan* should be notified. The story is a grave one, hence the *Divan* is drawn into the story.

349 In the province of Silistre, modern Bulgaria.

kaza of Islimye, is not behaving properly, but is a man of corruption. He produces petitions and court orders by himself; he takes the endowment allocations of some and nominates guardians for underage children. He takes as much money as he wants. Acts of oppression similar to this have no end. It is necessary to invite the said one [to the *Divan*].
My order is to invite the said Huseyin to the *Divan-i [Hümayun]* in Edirne.[350]
15-24 July 1675

No. 118

210a-5
Order to the Kadi of...[empty][351]
Somebody named Ahmed presented a petition and said: somebody named Ivaz, of the inhabitants of the *kaza* of Karacik, said in relation to a six year old girl called Imhani, of whom I am the guardian: "Formerly, and without the permission of her mother, I married [that child] to my son Ismail." He did this in concert with the Kadi of Karacik... and took a court order, against the Shar'. Formerly, the said Ivaz and the guardian conducted a shar'i trial on the issue before the *kazasker* of Rumelia in Edirne, and when the matter was checked, the court order presented by Ivaz was found untrue [forged?]. The Shari'a court told Ivaz: "Bring forward the said underage girl." And although warned [in the said way], he did not obey the Shar' and his claims were not an expression of justice at all. He [Ahmed] asked for an order that will bring the said Ivaz and the said underage girl to the *Divan* of Edirne.
The decree that was written ordered them to be brought [there] and that they should have a shar'i encounter (*murafaa*) in the *Divan-i Hümayun*.[352]
1-10 September 1675

---

350 This is a fascinating little story on a man who "worked" as a forger of documents, helping people obtain nominations for various jobs, firing other people, extracting sums of money from people and the like—breathtakingly modern. It reminds us again of the extent in which Ottoman society used such documents. Of course, such a crime had to end up with the *Divan* —it was a crime that goes to the very foundation of civilization in Ottoman society.

351 Possibly a small place in the Kastamonu region.

352 In this document, a man married a six year-old girl to his son—without any authorization from a parent or a guardian, and without explanation of how this was at all possible. He then refused to bring the girl to the court. This looked like kidnapping, and small wander that the *Divan* ordered the parties to come to the *Divan*, probably to have a formal shar'i encounter. Again, the *Divan* does not look like a court itself; it probably summoned people to it for important issues, then conducted proper shar'i trials where the locations of the cases was within the bounds of the Shari'a, or decided administratively (in terms of *siyasa shar'iyya*) when it was not.

No. 119

98b-2
Order to the Kadi of Vize, held by *arapalik*, and to its *mütesellim*
Hasan presented a petition saying: the *zimmis* Yazici..., [x], Kara oğlan, Ak Bıyık, and Sarı oğlan, and some other *zimmis* from a village named Sucuk, forming part of the said *kaza* (sic), are indebted [to him] by shar'i loan of 1,100 *piastres* they had formerly taken. Formerly, two Sultanic orders have been issued on this matter, and at one time an agent and a messenger (*çokadar*) have come from the aforementioned kadi and sued the said ones in the Shari'a court, but together with people belonging to their same mental state, the said *zimmis* claimed that the said agent took the money [from them] but did not obey the Sultanic order [and did not pass the money on to its owner]. In claiming this, they make a major injustice. He also let it be known that there is a court order in the matter. He asked for a Sultanic order of mine.
The order was written to bring the said parties to the *Divan-i Hümayun* in order to check their cases via a Shari'a court [process].[353]
26 April-5 May 1675

No. 120

6a-2
Order to the *Beylerbey* of Rumelia and the Kadi of ... [empty]
A man named Ahmed presented a petition and said: he has a loan of 3,800 *piastres* in the hands of Mehmed, son of the brother of the governor of Eger [?], Ali Paşa. The said one runs away sometimes to Rumelia and sometimes to Anatolia, and now he is said to be in the second location. He did not pay his debt. Now, this debt of such and such a sum was proven in the Shar'.
The order is that when he is asked to: "Pay," and he creates problems, without legal justification, he is to be made to come to the *Divan-i Hümayun*.
18-27 July 1675

No. 121

156b-2
Order to the Kadi of Ergiri–Kasri
A Christian named Nizalhu veled Navli presented a petition saying: formerly, a person named Qasim, known as Hasan Aga Oğlu, of the village of...[?] in the said *kaza*, was in charge of collecting the *cizye* tax in the province of Ergiri

353 This document is a further example that whenever possible, the *Divan* provided the stage for parties to conduct a proper shar'i encounter, rather than decide cases administratively. Here, the story is about a loan that became entangled because the borrower created problems in returning the loan, but the idea was the same in other cases as well.

Kasri. [At one point,] he captured his [the complainant's] son in one of the villages [in the region], and arrested him in a matter connected with the *cizye*. Later, he put him [the son] in chains, and later killed him. He thus committed a major oppression. When invited to appear before the Shar', he did not obey the call to appear, and made [another] major transgression. He [the complainant] let it be known that he has in his hand a court order (*huccet*) in this matter. He asked for an order of mine in this matter.

My order is to make the aforementioned [Qasim] appear before the *Divan-i Hümayun*.[354]

15-24 July 1675

No. 122

87a-2

Order to the Kadi of Güzelhisar[355]

The *naib* in the town of Güzelhisar, Mehmed, presented a petition saying: the citizens of the said town came to the Shari'a court and claimed: Nuh Ebu Bekir Efendi, citizen of the said town, together with the current *mufti*, Küçük Mehmed Efendi, have not been behaving as befitting their positions; while it is illegal for a local to be a *naib*, the aforementioned [Ebu Bekir] was *naib* many times, and they [the two subjects of complaint] said to some: "We reduce your assessment of *hane*", and they were in cooperation [with each other], and took from the citizens a large amount of money, and besides, they defended some villages and abandoned some other, and those they chose, they elevated [in *hane* assessment], the others [they] lowered; all of the affairs of *hane* [assessment] became confused and disrupted and created a great deal of social unrest (*fitna*). And they failed to acknowledge the rights of those who had rights, also capturing sums of money and lands of citizens, against the Shar'. Also, they interfered in legal claims of people with whom they had no connection, and doing this, obliterated the rights of people from whom they demanded things using false witnesses. Doing all this, they created a great deal of violation of rights and major corruption, dispersal, and death among the subjects. They [the citizens] asked for an order [to stop all this].

Now, my order is that the situation must be checked by the Shari'a court. If there is proof of such oppression done by the [subjects of complaint], these

354 In this document we find a grave situation, where the collector of *cizye* taxes in Albania got in some obscure quarrel with a citizen, whom he arrested and later killed. We do not know whether this was done directly or indirectly. What is more, the collector then refused to come to the Shari'a court. His summoning to the *Divan* was thus inevitable.

355 There are two places of this name in Western Turkey.

things are to be recorded in the kadi record (*sicill*) and in a court order (*huccet*), then the two sides must be brought before the Imperial *Divan.*[356]
17-26 April 1675

No. 123

2b-2
Order to the Kadi of...[empty]
A man named ...[?] presented a petition saying: Abdulmumin, the manager (*voyvoda*) of the affairs of the Turkmen of the Boz Ulus, sub-tribe Iz el-Din, arrested his father, somebody named Husam, for a year and half, with injustice, and against the Shar', saying to him: "You are going to launch a complaint against me." In addition, he took two horses and 120 *piastres* from him, thus causing a great deal of oppression and injustice.
My order has been to nominate Şahin Mustafa, the chief messenger of the palace, to go to that area to check the situation of the [suspect] with the help of the Shari'a court. Afterwards, the situation must be reported with precision to the *Divan-i Hümayun.*[357]
8-17 January 1675

---

356 In this complaint, which is presented to the center by citizens who come to do it in the Shari'a court itself, the former *naib* of a town and the current *mufti*, are accused of conspiring to wrong the citizens by extracting resources contrary to the law. The *naib* is accused of serving as *naib* many times, despite being a local, a strictly forbidden concept. Furthermore, these two created mayhem by meddling in the affairs of the most important urban tax of the time in Ottoman society, the *avariz* tax on individual real estate, assessed both individually and collectively in terms of quarters and villages. These assessments, for *hane* imposed on the collective and the individual assessment within the *hane*, are often laid bare in documents in the Ottoman *sicills*, and were strictly within the contours of the Kadi's job, working together with citizens of quarters and villages (See: Gerber, *Economy and Society in an Ottoman City*, Chapter 3). Any intervention in this process from the outside was tantamount to causing mayhem. A less than totally just *naib* or Kadi could really create havoc. Yet, amazingly, hope was not lost, and the citizens came to the same court of law to launch the complaint in front of the new *naib*, believing they would obtain a better deal this time. Not surprisingly, because of the importance of the *avariz* tax at the time, the *Divan* ordered that if the chaos around the assessments were not cleared by the court, the issue was to be passed on to the *Divan.*

357 In this document we find a strange story, told in a characteristically skeletal manner, about a Turkmen chief who arrested someone for a year and a half, claiming he was on his way to launch a complaint against the chief. The most important piece of information here is really the aforementioned one, showing again that the complaining process was effective in restraining people in their behavior. Be that as it may, the arrest of a person for a year and a half was a very serious affair, and we can readily understand why a special agent was nominated to investigate the case and why the order was also to report everything found to the *Divan.*

No. 124

34a-4

Order to the Kadi of Kayseri [Kaysariyye][358]

The citizens of the said *kaza* came [to the court and said:] three former governors of the province (*sancak*) extracted 22 *kise akçe,*[359] from the aforementioned [the citizens of Kayseri], against the Shar', and this sum was taken from them back [i.e. returned], and put in the fortress [of Kayseri] for safekeeping. But now, the "head of the city" (*şehir kethüdası*)[360] who was saved from service on the galleys [as major punishment] by his friend, Mahmud, and heads of the villages of Arab Oğlu and Ali Kalayci, together with their kadi, "ate" and did away with this sum, and in addition demanded the payment of an additional sum of 18 *kise akçe* from the poor, assigned to and imposed [on the poor], thus causing a major injustice. They asked for an order that would summon the [culprits] to the *Divan.*

Now, the order was written so that the said ones will be summoned to the *Divan-i Hümayun.*[361]

16-25 February 1675

No. 125

34a-5

Order to the Kadi of Kayseri

The citizens of Kayseri and the people of its villages came to the court [and said]: three people who were city heads and village heads, together with quarter heads, collected [certain] sums per *hane* (household) from the villagers for seven years. The matter was investigated in various ways and their incomes have been documented in a Shari'a court document and in a copybook, and they asked to do justice in all this.

Now, the order was given so that the matter would be investigated in place, questions would be asked and the matter be written down in a copybook as it happened, which will be sent to the *Divan.*

16-25 February 1675

358 In Central Anatolia, the ancient Caesarea.

359 About 1.5 million *akçe.*

360 Jennings, who studied the Kayseri region up close, was at a loss to find a good account of this term, and I find myself in the same position. See Ronald Jennings, "Kadi, Court, and Legal Procedure in 17 C. Ottoman Kayseri", *Studia Islamica*, 48 (1978), p. 150 and note.

361 This document and the one after it tell the story of tax abuse in the form of over taxation in the region of Kayseri. The main value of these documents is that they show that state pressure on provincial officials could sometimes work and force abusers to desist (though here only temporarily). These documents also reveal the existence of little known terms in the local politics and society of contemporary Anatolia.

Chapter 11: Miscellaneous

Preliminary Remarks

In this chapter, I have collected some documents that are highly important for this study, but do not fit into the classifications of the other chapters. Such was the document on the existence (or lack thereof) of a specialized place for the courthouse in Ottoman cities and towns, and the case for the transfer of a legal case from Ayntab to Maraş because "sticky" social relations prevented the possibility of attaining justice in Ayntab. Such documents, however, were rare, and most documents translated in this chapter were not intended to make a historiographical point.

These documents are ones that I came across in the Book of Complaints and that seemed to me to make an interesting point, which sometimes may mean use of direct talk, so rare in documents of this nature. More generally, the reference is to documents relating to topics of general and long-standing interests of mine. One such topic relates to the status of women. I have always maintained that on the whole, Ottoman women were much more forceful and powerful than is allowed by the literature of the older generation. I was glad to find some documents supporting this thesis in the Book of Complaints, and I have translated some of these documents. Another topic of long-term interest to me is the status of religious minorities in Ottoman society, and I have translated some documents relating to this issue. Other documents in this chapter are of general interest, such as a document showing that a fifteenth century Sultanic endowment devoted some of its revenue to supply daily food rations to 60 poor, blind people living in Istanbul. (The endowment survived to 1670!).

Documents

No. 126

75b-3

Order to the *kaimakam* of Istanbul and its Kadi

Someone named Mehmed sent a petition and said: before that, Katib Mehmed, living in Istanbul, who was in possession of a *timar*, farmed out the taxes of that [estate] to that Mehmed [the complainant], effective to the year 1675, according to his letter of appointment—so that the tax farmer, will take and capture the tax-produce occurring until the end-date of the tax farm. The complainant then came and said: he occupied the legal incomes relating to the said year, and brought and handed his collected tax to the said [*timarci*], but the said one, just for the sake of giving trouble, said: "I gave you a contract on 600 *piastres*, and exactly 600 *piastres* is what I demand." In this matter, a *fetva* was asked from the *şeyhülislam*, which said: after the tax-farmer has handed over what he had col-

lected legally, which is also what he has collected practically, and he takes an oath that the estate did not yield more taxes, the other side cannot tell him: "I heard [that you have collected more]", and cannot under this pretext, take more from him. And a Sultanic order was given in accordance with that. When the order arrived, the aforementioned Mehmed was safe [in his legal position], and no one else had any rights in the matter, but he [the complainant] let it be known that the *timar* possessor raised problems again, and therefore he asks for a [new] order, to make sure that everyone behaves according to the *fetva* in his hand and the order given formerly, and that the efforts of the *sipahi* be stopped and pushed aside.
The order was written so that no one bothers [others] against the Shar'.[362]
7-16 April 1675

No. 127

163a-1
Order to the Kadi of Nif[363] and the *mütesellim* of Saruhan
Mevlana Ali presented a petition and said: the *abdallar* (wandering dervishes) living in the sufi lodge (*zaviye*) of... [?] drink wine on a regular basis, and cause corruption, as is well attested to by the testimony of reliable people. The said Mevlana [lives] inside the said *zaviye*, but he nevertheless asked for an order to stop [this corruption].
The order was written to say that you who are the said *mütesellim*, if the corruption of the said *abdallar* living in the said *zaviye* is true and proven, as reported above, then what they deserve according to the Shar' should be implemented.[364]
16-25 August 1675

No. 128

34b-6
Order to the Kadi of Benefşe[365]
The unbelievers living in the suburb (*varoş*) of this town presented a petition, saying: these ones are occupied with pursuing their own affairs, and do not

362 This document is a legal conflict between a *sipahi* and a tax farmer regarding the taxes of the estate. The *sipahi* lost, because he did not prove that he deserved the bigger sum supposedly collected by the tax farmer. I have translated the document because of the use of personal language, and for the use of a *fetva* in a case unrelated to Shari'a law.

363 In *sancak* Saruhan, Western Anatolia.

364 This is an example of a document of general interest only—the wandering dervishes of Anatolia is an obscure topic of some interest, so a tiny addition to their history may be of some interest. See in more detail, Colin Imber, "The Wandering Dervishes", in his *Studies in Ottoman History and Law*, Istanbul: The Isis Press, 1996, pp. 129-145.

365 In Morea.

pose any transgression to anyone. And yet the guards in the fortress [of the said *kaza*] are not satisfied with their own affairs, but constantly meddle in the life of the said *zimmis* and members of their families, and once or twice they have been the cause for the death of people; they also harass their wives and commit various acts of corruption and molestation, as well as [make] attempts to rape. In the past, their officers were several times approached and complaints were launched, but the said criminals did not desist, and commit moral crimes and illegality even more than before. The subjects (*reaya*) now fear molestation and the possibility that they [the guards] will reach their homes. Acts of oppression and injury like these are endless. They asked for an order that would prevent and repudiate [such acts].

Now, the order has been written so that, if there are, among what they [the guards] do, acts that are against the Shar' and the *Kanun*, these are to be stopped and repudiated; and those who are not impressed by warnings, their case must be presented [to the Divan].[366]

16-25 February 1675

No. 129

86b-3

Order to the Kadi of Sakiz [Chios]

The poor citizens of Sakiz sent a petition, saying: before that, the ambassador of France (Franca *elçisi*) came to Sakiz to live in his house [on the island]. During the evening prayer, three brigands assaulted him and robbed from him...[a number of clothing items] and a rifle. The people of the ambassador shot at the brigands, one of them was injured and captured, the other two escaped. The injured fellow admitted to his crime, and was incarcerated in the fortress, with the approval of the kadi. While in prison, he died. The father of the said brigand, someone named ...[empty] took an evil path, saying to the ambassador: "You are the reason for the death of my son; I demand from you his blood money (*dam diyeti*)." [Saying this,] he molested him unjustly. The ambassador also had in his hand a *fetva* of the *şeyhülislam* [speaking in his favor]. We ask that an order be issued to reject and prevent [this claim].

---

366 In this document, we are presented with what amounts to the oppression of the Christian population living adjacent to a fortress in the Balkans, the abusers being the guards themselves. This was not really a systematic molestation of the people coming from authority, but disruption of regular life on the initiative of the guards. This molestation included killing people and some attempted rapes, two items that were rare even among the usual cases of oppression surveyed in this collection. This is probably why the central government seemed to be somewhat alarmed, and called on the Kadi to notify the Divan if the situation did not improve shortly.

My order has been written so that the matter be brought for discussion in the Shari'a court.[367]
17-26 April 1675

No. 130

32b-3
Order to the Kadi of Maraş and its *müteselim*
Huseyin, citizen of Ayntab, came and said against another citizen of Ayntab, Sayyid Mehmed: the [complainant's] brother, Sayyid Ali, was occupied entirely with his own affairs, posing no threat or molestation to anybody; but [acting] against the Shari'a, he [Sayyid Mehmed] killed him [the brother, Sayyid Ali]. Doing this, he committed a major injustice. The said killer is from the usurper (*mutegalliba*) people, and those with social power (*zi kudret*), and was even working in concert with the *naib* of Ayntab, so that there is no possibility of ever achieving justice in the said place. He also said that he has a *fetva* on this matter supporting his case, as well as a court document [supporting him]. My order was written so that the case be brought to the kadi court [in Maraş] and that justice be done.[368]
16-25 February 1675

367 This document is of interest, first of all, because it deals with the French ambassador to the Ottoman state, who came to stay in a house of his on the island of Sakiz (Chios). The document itself is quite legal in nature: the party of the ambassador was subject to an assault and robbery one day, where the ambassador's guards, previously shot at, returned fire, and wounded one of the assailants, who later died in prison. His father sued the ambassador for blood money, as if he was the murderer. The people of Sakiz had a good reason to be concerned, because it was a common distortion of the law of killing to demand blood money from a large area, when the law really only allowed this from one village or one street. In this case, the killing was in self-defense any way, a well-accepted concept in criminal Islamic law.

368 This is an exceptionally important document for this study. It deals with a legal encounter that should have been (or was about to) take place in Ayntab between a person whose son was killed at the order of a socially strong person. The complainant was afraid that the influence of this strong man on Kadis and others in Ayntab would affect the fairness of the court, and that a more objective and impersonal process would be more likely to create a fair trial. This draws attention to the discussion, still raging, of whether the Ottoman Kadi was preconditioned to conduct his legal affairs with as little personal involvement as possible, as I claim, or whether he was inclined to work on the basis of personal relations, as in many other legal systems in the world. It is interesting, though no more than pure chance (though I detect some irony) that much of this discussion is conducted around the study of Leslie Peirce on sixteenth century Ayntab, the very site of "our" document, which seems to be a serious blow to the theories of Ottoman informal legal system. In our document, relations that were seen as too friendly were reason enough to approve the transfer of a legal case from Ayntab to Maraş. See Leslie Peirce, *Morality Tales*, Berkeley and Los Angeles, University of California Press, 2003.

No. 131

78b-1

Order to the *kaimakam* of Istanbul and its Kadi

The poor, blind people of Istanbul have presented a petition and said: as part of the conditions of the public kitchen endowment (*imaret-i amire*) of Şehzade Sultan Mehmed endowment in Istanbul, sixty feeding positions were allotted by the founder to the poor among the blind people [in the city]. Until today, they have held this right according to the conditions of the founder. But now blind *şeyhs* of the said community, *şeyhs* Isa and Dilaver, and Mehmed and Mustafa and Zulfikar, and... and ... said: one of us is *şeyh,*[369] and one of us is *yiğit başı,*[370] and one of us is *kethüda;*[371] and, saying this, they did not give [newly] available spots (*duşen mahlulu*) to the poor, contrary to the condition of the founder. And only to molest and harm [them], said [to the holders of positions]: "If you give [us] such and such amount of money, fine (*fiha*); and if not—there is no bread for you." Formerly, there was a legal encounter on this in the Shar'ia court, where the transgression of the [said *şeyhs*] was prevented and repudiated and they themselves received numerous court documents, but the accused were still not satisfied, and again did not refrain from overstepping the rights of [the poor]. They [the poor, blind people of Istanbul] asked for a decree that would order them [the accused] to behave according to the court document, and that the illegal transgressions of the said ones against the condition of the founder be stopped and cut short.

An order was written to say that the new survey [of endowments?] kept in the treasury was checked, and it was registered [there] that sixty meals a day were allotted to the poor, blind people, while there was no writing concerning *yiğit başı* and *kethüda;* the order is not to allow transgressions contrary to the Shar', the *Kanun*, and the condition of the founder.[372]

7-16 April 1675

369 Leader in some guilds in Ottoman Istanbul. Obviously, the ploy of the *şeyhs* here was to look at the poor, blind people in question as a sort of guild.

370 This was the technical term to denote the deputy head in most Ottoman Turkish guilds. See Haim Gerber, *Economy and Society in an Ottoman City: Bursa, 1600–1700,* Jerusalem, the Hebrew University, 1988, Chapter 3.

371 This was the usual term for heads of guilds in Ottoman society. See Gerber, *Bursa*, Chapter 3.

372 In this document, we find an interesting and little known story—one of the Sultanic *vakıfs* of Istanbul set aside in its founding deed 60 meals a day for the poor, blind citizens of Istanbul. This condition was applied until some leading *şeyhs* of these blind people hit upon the idea of nominating themselves as guild-like jobs of *kethüda* and *yiğit başı,* demanding special salaries. A short inspection of the founding deed of the endowment, however, exposed the bluff.

No. 132

40a-2

Order to the *kaimakam* and Kadi of Istanbul

A monk named Gregory veled-i Nikula, one of the monks of the monastery situated in the island of [?], have sent a petition saying: formerly, Şahin Ağa, the manager of affairs (*kethüda*) of my commander of the Mediterranean [fleet], Mehmed Paşa, captured the [complainant], and arrested him within the monastery, then took 750 *esedi piastres* from him, thereby causing him a great deal of violation of his rights. Formerly, in an encounter in the Shari'a court, [what was done by the *kethüda* was declared] oppression (*zülüm*), and a court document (*huccet*) was given, but the [accused] went on making trouble. He asked for a decree that would order to bring the matter to the Shari'a court and attain justice. My order has been that the matter is to be dealt with by the Shari'a court, in accordance with the court document.[373]

26 April-7 March 1675

No. 133

81a-5

Order to the Kadi of Viran[374]

The citizens of the village of Çeltuk Kirlar, of the villages of the *hass* of Musahib Mustafa Paşa, presented a petition saying: the said people are rice cultivators (*çeltükçü*), and while no one has a reason to interfere in their affairs, the former officer of theirs, Mustafa, said to them: "An order has arrived, directing to conduct a new survey of you, and here I come to survey you." Saying this, he collected 300 *akçe* from each person. They, on their part, arrived to my seat of power, and [heard the news] that there was no basis to the news of a new survey of the place. Now, when the said one was required to return, through the Shari'a court, the money he has taken with no justice, he created problems. They asked for an order in this regard.

An order was written so that the issue be brought for discussion in the Shari'a court, and the money that he has taken contrary to the Shar' and the *Kanun* be returned.

17-26 April 1675[375]

---

373 This document is also of relevance to the situation of non-Muslims in the Ottoman Empire. We do not receive a clue as to why the high-placed official molested and incarcerated the poor monk, but at least it is striking that this high official was summoned to the Shari'a court and had to defend himself, just as the low class individuals did, with no special treatment what-so-ever.

374 In Eyalet Rumelia.

375 The great land and population surveys carried out by the Ottomans in the fifteenth and sixteenth century were the main hallmark of that state's administrative greatness. The meaning of the disappearance of these surveys after the sixteenth century is a question that still haunts

No. 134

68a-6

Order to the Kadi of Florina

You who are the kadi, you sent a letter and reported on a non-Muslim [*zimmi*] named [?] from village of [?] in the said *kaza*, who came to the Shar'ia court and made a claim against a brigand named Ahmed, known as Topcu-oğlu, living in the village of Nevgrad, situated in the said *kaza*, who is a man of corruption (*fasad*). [This man] captured his [the complainant's] daughter ... [x] by force, a non-Muslim [girl], and raped her, thereby causing an act of oppression, violation of rights (*taaddi*), and corruption. When the said criminal was summoned to the Shari'a court, he did not obey [the call], and instead—disappeared. He [the complainant] asked for a decree that would order this case be brought to the Shari'a court, and to see to it that justice is done.

Now, the order was written so that wherever [the suspect] may be found, the case is to be dealt with in the Shari'a court in that place, so that justice is done.[376]

28 March-6 April 1675

No. 135

213b-4

Order to the governor and Kadi of Maraş

The community of *zimmis* of Maraş sent a man and let it be known in a petition they presented: Genç Hasan, who was in the year ... [empty] *mütesellim* of Maraş and supervisor nominated by an Imperial order of mine to prevent the activity of oppressors (*zalama*), captured and arrested [some of the complainants] then took 525 *piastres* from them, thereby causing a major injustice. They asked for an order of mine demanding conduct according to an imperial order of mine [already] in their hands, and that the said Hasan will return the sum of money he has taken from their hands, and that after today such injustice will cease to exist.

My order was written so that if there is proof of the sum of money he has taken from them contrary to the Shar' and the *Kanun*, he is to be made to return it.

17-26 April 1675[377]

---

historians, and is likely to continue doing so for quite some time. It is, therefore, quite amazing to find the official in this complaint coming to a village announcing that he was given the assignment to conduct a new survey. A short investigation in Istanbul revealed, of course, that it was just another trick to extract money from the poor peasants.

376 This document deals with the predicament of a man (a *zimmi*) whose daughter was assaulted by a highway robber and raped, who then disappeared; a quite serious crime concerning public safety and other aspects, but one that was entrusted solely to the Shari'a court.

377 The official who seems to have committed the abuse in this document is a provincial governor nominated especially to curb those committing oppression committed by either brigands or

No. 136

220a-3

Order to the Kadi of Aleppo

The Jew, Salmon, of the Jews of Aleppo, sent a petition to My Porte saying: formerly, the Jew, [x], also of the Jews of Aleppo, died, being poor [and] needing help, so that his estate did not need [formal] distribution (*qismet*). But while this was so, the former kadi of Aleppo, a kadi named Ebu Saud, arrested him [the complainant, the sole heir of the deceased] for thirty days then took from him 1,200 *piastres* for himself, giving also 400 *piastres* to his manager (*çokadar*). Doing this, they committed a great injustice and oppression. He asked for a decree ordering to bring the matter to the Shari'a court and do justice.

My order has been written to find out that: if what he has taken against the Shari'a and the *Kanun* is proven legally, he has to return everything in total, and you have to be careful not to let any similar complaint against you [from] being launched again.[378]

25 June-2 July 1675

No. 137

212a-5

Order to the Kadi of Kastamonu

[x] and [y], *zimmi* citizens of Kastamonu, sent a letter to My Sublime Porte and reported that: these people engage solely in their own affairs, and present no violation to anyone's rights or at all. They engage in teaching the children of the Christians according to the customs of their religion, and constitute no transgression against anybody. But some state officials, just for extracting money, with no justification and no reason, captured some of the Christians, and took large sums of money from them, contrary to the Shar'. Oppression and tyranny of this nature knew no bounds. They also let it be known that they have in this matter a *fetva* from the *şeyhülislam*. They asked for an Imperial decree to stop and repudiate the said oppression and tyranny.

My order is to prevent an illegal act which is also against the Shari'a.

11-20 September 1675[379]

---

officials. It is a great irony, therefore, that it was exactly this official who should be captured red-handed committing the same sort of abuse.

378 I had put this document in this chapter as an example of the treatment of minorities, though it is also classifiable as a case against Kadis. The most interesting aspect of this document is the fact that despite the complaint being directed to a kadi, no despair is raised against the system as a whole, and the new kadi is suggested as the right person to deal with the situation, by the complainant himself. This is an impressive vote of confidence in the legal system and in the impartiality of the kadis, since even if inclined to be just, the new Kadi might realistically be suspected of defending the decisions of a colleague.

379 This is a clear case of a molestation of a Christian community in Anatolia just because that

No. 138

166b-4

Order to the Kadi of Sultaniye[380]

The Jews... [space for three names] presented a petition, saying: these people behave properly, and now, for more than 30 years, they live in the suburb (*varoş*) of the said fortress [sic]. Payment of the *cizye* [of these Jews] is tied to the [salary of] the guards of the said fortress. They pay the *cizye* due from them without any deficiency, but [now], the kadis serving in this place have said to them, merely for the sake of dragging and incarcerating: "In your houses you teach your kids and pray according to your vain ceremonies." And, saying this, they take from them sums of money under the name of *carima*, doing against them a wrong. They asked for an order of mine that would stop and repudiate such behavior.

An order was written so that the money of the said [complainants] will not be taken from them contrary to the Shar'.[381]

24 July-2 August 1675

No. 139

29a-3

Order to the Governor of Rumelia and the Kadi of Bihlişte[382]

The citizens of the *kaza* of Guzelce have presented a petition saying: before, Mehmed, citizen of the said *kaza*, was in charge of collecting the *cizye* tax [in the area] for the year 1080 and something. We have paid the *cizye* imposed on us according to the *Kanun* and the land register without any deficiency, but the said Mehmed was not satisfied with this, but extracted 634,000 *akçe* from us, with injustice, causing a major transgression. They asked for an order directing that the issue be brought for resolution in the Shari'a court.

My order is that the matter be dealt with in the Shari'a court, and that if it is proven that he had taken from them more than the *Kanun* and the land register, he has to return the difference to its owners.

6-15 February 1675[383]

---

community was engaged in teaching their religion in their houses. At least the central Ottoman government was not amused, and took the necessary measures to prevent the intransigence.

380 In Eyalet Karaman, modern Karapınar.

381 According to this complaint, Jews, no less than Christians, were liable to denigration and even be targets of monetary extortion by local tax officials, only because they pursued in their houses the religious teaching of their children. Here, too, the central government was not impressed by the behavior of the local authorities, and called upon them to retract.

382 Modern Bihlishte, Albania.

383 It is noteworthy that while these *zimmis* suffer exactions from one official in the system, they still expect justice from other sections of the administration, and particularly the judicial system.

No. 140

166b-5

Order to the Kadi of Zagra-i Atik

The citizens of the Imaret quarter of the quarters of the *kaza* of Zagra-i Atik presented a petition saying: citizens of the said quarter, Ahmed b. Mehmed, Mehmed b. Ahmed, and Huseyin b. Ahmed, did not behave in a way proper to their position—they do not keep their wives from forming ties with unrelated male [*na-mahram*—not forbidden from marriage], and besides, many times their obscene language (*fuhş*) is apparent. Their corruption against the Shar' is endless. The case was formerly dealt with by the Shar'ia court and their immorality was clarified and proven. [The possibility] of their banishment from the quarter was made clear by the court, but they were not convinced and not satisfied, and contrary to the given court order, do not shy away from conflict. They asked for an order directing to act in accordance with the court order in their hands.

The order was written so that if the contents of the order will be proven in the Shar', the matter will be written down in the kadi record (*sicill*).[384]

24 July-2 August 1675

No. 141

28a-4

Order to the *paşa* of Erzerum and its *monla* [Kadi]

The citizens of the *kaza* of Kara Hisar-i Şarki presented a petition and said: those who are kadis in Kara Hisar-i Şarki occupy rented houses in the said town and live in them. And while the kadis have no specific [*muteayyan*] house that is a courthouse, as of few years, the kadis pile the rent of their houses on the [shoulders] of the citizens. And in addition, they add to those houses additions such as rooms, whose costs and their rent they take from the poor, thereby causing a great harm.

The order was written directing that conduct should be according to the Shar' and the *Kanun*.

6-15 February 1675[385]

---

384 This is an exceptional document in any respect, in which the men of Zagra-i Atik are accused of allowing their wives laxity in following social codes bordering on the sexually scandalous. The reference is to talking freely with unrelated men and the use of foul language, probably also with some sexual overtones. The *Divan* warns that continued behavior of this nature could lead to expulsion from the neighborhood, but in the meantime the affair is recorded in the *sicill*, something obviously seen as a warning.

385 This document is particularly interesting because of the light it sheds on the issue of the existence of a particular, formal location of the Ottoman court in any Ottoman town. One hears sometimes the opinion that such a location was obligatory, but this is not corroborated by this case, taken from a town in the region of Erzerum. In this town, there was no special courthouse, and nobody in the *Divan* thought this was something terrible or illegal. The thing

No. 142

114b-1
Order to the Kadi of Istanbul
Musa the barber presented a petition, saying: he [never] divorced his wife Saliha Hatun, [who he was] married to for more than ten years. And while he was away in another region of the country, much of his stuff had disappeared and been destroyed, and [his wife], getting together with a shoe maker (*hafaf*) Veli, degrading him in this, went on an evil path and claimed against me: "You have divorced me three times." And in agreement with some butchers belonging to her own mental situation, against justice and law, using false witnesses, without [proper] shar'i process of checking the suitability of the witnesses (*tadil* and *tazkiya*), got into her hand by some way a divorce certificate, then married the said shoe maker Veli. As to himself [the claimant], when he demanded to be joined by his wife, she made all sorts of avoidance exercises, with no justice. Before that, a *fetva* of the *şeyhülislam* was issued, as well as a court order, but these were not carried out, what was for him a great transgression and injustice. He [repeated] that he has in this matter a *fetva* supporting his point of view. He asked for an Imperial order of mine.
The order was written to bring the matter for discussion in the Shari'a court.[386]
26 May-4 June 1675

No. 143

32a-1
Order to the Kadi of Burgos[387]
Mehmed came and presented a petition, saying: a lady named ... [x], his wife, living in the said *kaza*, died in the year 1080, and her mother, Fatima, is in possession of all of her estate. When the said Fatima was sued for the portion she had to part with when the court made a calculation, she raised problems and persisted in avoiding paying. The claimant also pointed out that he has a *fetva* supporting his case. He asked for an Imperial order of mine.
The order was written to see to it that the issue be dealt with in situ by the Shar'.
16-25 February 1675[388]

---

that was captured here as illegal was the effort of the Kadi to place the costs of their housing on the community as a whole.

386 This document again brings the story of an exceptionally strong woman in Ottoman society, a woman who did not follow the narrow path allotted to her, thereby breaking many historic myths about women in Islam in general. The woman in this document went to extremes to dump an unwanted husband, violating even *fetvas* and court orders along the way. This is no doubt a very impressive document.

387 In *sancak* Vize, modern Lüleburgas in European Turkey.

388 This is another case of a lady who refused to passively accept what was imposed on her by

No. 144

95a-6

Order to the Kadi of Galata

The *naib* of the *nahiye* of Su Dağı sent a letter in which he reported: the non-Muslims living in the town of Bandırma, situated in the *nahiye* of Kapı Dağı, one of the places belonging to the said *Kaza* (of Galata), came to the Shari'a court and said: they are satisfied to pay the *cizye* tax as fixed via an Imperial order and the new Imperial register, relating to the year 1083, but their *cizye* collector, a person called Mehmed, known as Nicelu, was not satisfied with this, and just for the sake of extortion of money, told them: "I am collecting solely according to the old register." And contrary to the Shar', arrested all of them, gave them severe beatings, and besides, contrary to the order and the register, took 2,500 *piastres* from them, thereby causing them a serious violation of their rights. Thus, they presented this case, emphasizing my order.

Now, an order was written so that he must be made to return what he has taken beyond the *Kanun* and the register, and you must take care in the future not to let a complaint like this be heard [against you] again.[389]

26 April-5 May 1675

No. 145

41b-2

Order to the Kadi of Yanya[390] and its *mütesellim*

Formerly, an exalted order of mine was issued to the effect that no one was to sell and buy wine and *arak* and to destroy all drinking houses in the cities, towns, and in mosques and in villages of the people of Islam. According to the Imperial rescript (*hatt-i hümayun*), an Imperial order (*emr*) was issued as well as a severe warning [banning the above]. But now, some people were not satisfied with this, and bought wine and *arak* in the said *kaza*, in front of all the people to see, thereby causing corruption of proper behavior. In this matter, the issuance of a [new] order was asked for.

My exalted order was issued to direct them to act according to the *fetva* issued following my [former decrees] and according to my former order (*firman*).

26 February-7 March 1675

---

men around her, but took care of her own interests, even when this meant breaking some laws, at least for the time being.

389 It is a bit surprising that such a severe abuse, including the severe beating of citizens, was taking place so close to the political center of the empire, with nobody to stop it in real time. Maybe it was indicative of the real weakness of the empire in controlling its rural areas. But it was also surprising that these *zimmis* did not simply write to the far away Sultan, but played local politics by going through the Shari'a court.

390 In modern Albania.

Glossary

Akçe—the basic Ottoman silver coin

Alay bey—commander of the sipahis in a sancak

Asker—belonging to the military class-member of the military, administrative or religious establishment of the empire

Avariz—important tax on real estate introduced in the seventeenth century

Bey—title of a middling military man or provincial administrator

Beylerbey—title of a general governor of a province. Synonym of mir-i miran

Bidaa—illegal innovation

Boz Ulus Turcoman—tribal confederation in East Anatolia

Carima, also curm, tacrim (Arabic jarima, jurm, tacrim)—crime, offence, and sometimes an alleged crime, used by state officials with bad intentions as "legitimate" excuse to extract resources from villagers, illegally

Celali rebellions—large scale social mayhem created by unemployed soldiers between 1596 and 1610

Cihad—Islamic Holy War

Cizye—Islamic poll-tax imposed on non-Muslim populations

Curm—see carima

Divan—a council of the major officials of the Ottoman state, functioning very similar to a government in other pre-modern states

Diyet—part of the law of homicide. Blood money, payment of which is incumbent on a person or group that did not commit the crime, but considered responsible for not preventing it, hence their liability for payment. Liability fell to the village or street, by no means an area larger than those two, as so often claimed by abusers in the Book of Complaints. Diyet also referred to the situation where a killer was captured and tried. It was then the right of the next of kin to decide whether to demand putting the culprit to death in "retaliation" (kisas) or whether to commute the punishment to payment of blood money (diyet).

Fetva—a legal opinion supplied by a scholar versed in Islamic law

Hadith—is one of various reports describing the words, actions, or habits of the Islamic prophet Muhammad.

Hane—a house, a family, and by extension, taxation unit defining the size and wealth of villages and town quarters. While in the sixteenth century it was basically a family, in the seventeenth it became a unit of assessment, decided upon by bargaining between the citizens and the Kadi. From here to the Book of Complaints it was a short road, because little objectivity remained in the process.

Hass—prebend, feudal estate belonging to members of the state's elite or even the sultan

Hayduk, or *haydud*—originally a Hungarian foot soldier; later a brigand

Imam—Prayer leader. After Muhammad the leader of the Muslim community

Kadi—the Ottoman judge

Kaimakam—deputy grand vizier when the last one was away on campaign or en route to one.

Kanun—state law, enacted by the Ottoman Empire in the fifteenth and sixteenth century. There are no signs that the kanun was enacted in the spirit of siyasa sharʿiyya (see below), as no kanun preamble mentions the siyasa sharʿiyya which probably came to exert its main influence after most kanuns were in place. And while in practical terms Heyd showed that the penal Kanun was already in decline by the late sixteenth century, and while studies by Gerber and Jennings from the seventeenth century show almost no reference to penal kanun, there are in the Book of Complaints, hundreds, if not thousands of references to the kanun, together with the Shar' as the legal principle that was violated by what was narrated in the complaints. At least ideologically the kanun remained an important document.

Kaza—area of authority of a kadi. But as the role of the kadi was mainly judicial, who really administered the kaza on a daily basis remains a mystery.

Kazasker—literally judge of the army; it is not known that either of the two kazaskers ever fulfilled that function. In the official hierarchy they came straight after the şeyhülislam, and were in charge of nominations of kadis and teachers in medreses. But as members of the Divan they were from time to time involved in adjudication of complex issues.

Kethüda—head of an Ottoman guild, mainly in the Turkish speaking areas. Also—manager of private affairs of an important man of state

Kisas—retaliation, in the law relating to homicide. See Diyet above.

Kise—500 (usually of piasters, the bigger coin in daily use)

Kul—slave of the sultan, soldiers and bureaucrats recruited by the sultans, taught to serve the sultan even after ending their formal slavery. Some dispute if such a stage ever existed.

Liva, also sancak—sub-province

Martolos, martelos—Pre-Ottoman militia that under the Ottomans became really a gang of brigands

Mir liva, also sancakbey—governor of a sub-province

Mirror of Princes—a literary genre in the Ottoman society and the Middle East generally in the centuries around the date of this collection of documents. This genre revolved around writing advice to princes and rulers, advising them about the hidden wisdom of milking their citizens to the utmost possible extent.

Molla, also *monla*—a regular low grade kadi who is nominated as ad hoc molla (top grade kadi) to sort out a mess and disorder created by a corrupt kadi

Mütesellim—a deputy governor of a sancak bey, and the record shows that most sancak beys had recourse to the services of these shady figures. If the kadis were the heroes of the Book of Complaints, the mütesellim was clearly the black horse: He was responsible for ninety percent of the troubles brought on the heads of the poor people of the time, and the reason for this is not far to seek—the Şikayet Defteri overflows with examples of encounters between mütesellims and sancak beys over mütesellims' violating their contract of hire, which was always for a very short period of time, probably half a year for the most part. Clearly, mütesellims were guys with little prospects of success, hence with very little commitment to the Ottoman system.

Nuzul—irregular, then regular tax meant to feed the Ottoman army

Piastre, kuruş—the basic Ottoman silver money

Reaya—all population below the asker class

Sancak—sub-province, governed by sancak bey or mir liva

Serbest—"independent", having freedom from regular taxes enjoyed by peasants, such as villagers of endowments who owed taxes only to their endowment

Şeyhülislam—in the seventeenth century, head of the religious-legal institution in the Ottoman Empire

Shia—the second great branch of Islam after the majority of the Sunna. For most of classical Islam, the Shia was an underground movement having its own laws, but enjoying little influence in the actual world of Islam. In 1501 a basically Shiite movement called the Safavides took control of Iran and turned the Shia into state religion. In the coming years, no one in Iran could remain Sunni without risking his life. What was worse for the Ottomans was that many of the supporters of the new Iran were actually Turks living in Anatolia, members of an underground society called kizilbaş, or readheaded. The ideological challenge to the Ottomans, which was initially quite serious, continued for centuries.

Sipahi—holder of a prebend estate in the timar system

Siyasa sharʿiyya—literally, state administration under the aegis of the Shari'a, a legal idea that became widespread in the early days of the Ottoman Empire, and suggested that as long as the ruler had no intention of harming the Shar', he could devise policies that were free from Shari'a restrictions. See further Kanun.

Siyaset—capital punishment, a historical development from Siyasa sharʿiyya.

Subaşi—chief of police in any Ottoman city. In the Şikayet the subaşi was for the most part appearing as an evil figure, in fairness to him it may be added that in seventeenth century Bursa I found him performing a much more positive role.

Tazkiye—screening of witnesses, one of the major jobs of a traditional Muslim judge, making sure that only people of probity and integrity would be allowed to take the stand.

Timar—"feudal" estate, the basic Ottoman land regime in the classical period, offering estate revenue in lieu for fully equipped mounted soldiers in time of war

Vakıf, vakf, from Arabic waqf—an endowment, an institution of major size and importance in the Ottoman Empire, where endowments by sultans, their wives, daughters and high men of state controlled much of the urban landscape

Voyvoda—a low grade officer fulfilling administrative and economic jobs for high men of state in the provincial service

Yeniçeri, janissary—elite soldier in the Ottoman army

Yuk—100,000 (usually akçe)

Zaviye—sufi lodge, lodging people devoting their lives to religious worship

Ziamet—a prebend, an estate supposed to grant to its holder a revenue of up to 100,000 akçe, a year

Bibliography

Abaci, Nurcan, *The Ottoman Judges and their Registers: the Bursa Court Register B90/295 (dated A.H. 1081/A.D. 1670)*, 2 vols., Harvard, Mass.: Harvard University Department of Near Eastern Languages and Civilizations, 2007.

Abou-El-Haj, Rifaat A., "The Ottoman Vezir and Paşa Households 1683–1703: A Preliminary Report", *Journal of the American Oriental Society*, vol. 94 (1974), pp. 438-447.

Abou-El-Haj, Rifaat Ali, *The 1703 Rebellion and the Structure of Ottoman Politics*, Istanbul: Nederlands Historisch-Archaeologisch Instituut te Istanbul, 1984.

Abou-El-Haj, Rifaat A., *Formation of the Modern State*, Albany: State University of New York, 1991.

Agmon, Iris, "Review" of Leslie Peirce, Morality Tales, <www.h-net.org/reviews/showrev.php?id=13539>

Altunsu, Abdülkadir, *Osmanli Şeyhülislamlari*, Ankara: Ayyildiz Matbaasi, 1972.

Amitai-Preiss, Reuven and David O. Morgan, eds., *The Mongol Empire and its Legacy*, Leiden, Brill, 1999.

Arnold, Thomas, W., *The Caliphate*, London: Routledge and Kegan Paul, 1967.

Axworthy, Michael, Iran: Empire of the Mind, London: Penguin Books, 2008.

Bang, P.F., "Rome and the Comparative Study of Tributary Empires", in The Medieval History Journal (Special Issue on Tributary Empires), vol. 6 (2003), pp. 169-306.

Barbir, Karl, K., *Ottoman Rule in Damascus*, Princeton: Princeton University Press, 1980.

Barbir, Karl K., "One Marker of Ottomanism: Confiscation of Ottoman Officials' Estates", in Baki Tezcan and Karl K. Barbir, eds., *Identity and Identity Formation in the Ottoman World*, Madison: The Center for Turkish Studies at the University of Wisconsin and the University of Wisconsin Press, 2007.

Barkan, Ömer L., "Edirne Askeri Kassamina Aid Tereke Defterler", *Belgeler* vol. 3, Ankara: Turk Tarih Kurumu, 1968, 1-end.

Barkan, Ömer,L., *Istanbul Vakiflari Tahrir Defteri, 953 (1546) Tarihli, Istanbul*: Baha Matbaasi, 1970.

Barkey, Karen, *An Empire of Difference*, Cambridge: Cambridge University Press, 2008

Bayly, C.A. and Bang, P.F., "Introduction: Comparing Pre-Modern Empires", *in: The Medieval History Journal*, vol. 6 (2003), pp. 169-188.

Birnbaum, Eleazar, ed., *Kai Kaus Ibn Iskandar, The Book of Advice: The Earliest Old Ottoman Turkish Version of his Kabusname*, Duxbury, Mass.: Harvard University Printing Office, 1981.

Blake, Stephen P., "The Patrimonial-Bureaucratic Empire of the Mughals", *Journal of Asian Studies*, 39 (1979), 77-94.

Boyle, J.A., *The Cambridge History of Iran*, vol. 5 (the Seljuq and Mongol Periods), Cambridge: Cambridge University Press, 1968.

Buzpınar, Tufan, Ş., "The Question of the Caliphate under the Last Ottoman Sultans", in: Itzhak Weismann and Fruma Zachs, eds., *Ottoman Reform and Muslim Regeneration*, London: Tauris, 2005, pp. 17-36.

Cahen, Claude, *The Formation of Turkey*, London: Longman, 2001.

Calder, Norman, *Islamic Jurisprudence in the Classical Era*, Cambridge: Cambridge University Press, 2010.

Canbakal, Hulya, *Society and Politics in an Ottoman Town: ʿAyntab in the Seventeenth Century*, Leiden: Brill, 2007.

Canfield, Robert, *Turko-Persia in Historical Perspective*, Cambridge: Cambridge: Cambridge University Press, 1991.

Cohen, Amnon, and Bernard Lewis, *Population and Revenue in the Towns of Palestine in the Sixteenth Century*, Princeton: Princeton University Press.

Cohen, Amnon, Palestine in the Eighteenth Century, Jerusalem: the Magnes Press, 1973.

Cohen, Amnon, "Le Rouge et le Noir Jerusalem Style", in idem, *Studies on Ottoman Palestine*, Farnham: Variorum Reprints, 2011, chapter VIII.

Crone, Patricia, *Medieval Islamic Political Thought*, Edinburgh: Edinburgh University Press, 2005

Danişmend, Ismail, H., *Izahli Osmanli Tarihi Kronolojisi*, vol. 5, Istanbul: Turkiye Yayinevi, 1971.

Darling Linda, T., *Revenue Raising and Legitimacy*, Leiden: Brill, 1996.

Darling, Linda, "The Development of Ottoman Governmental Institutions in the Fourteenth Century: A Reconstruction", in Vera Constantini and Markus Koller, eds., *Living in the Ottoman Ecumenical Community*, Leiden: Brill, 2008.

Darling, Linda, T., "Medieval Egyptian Society and the Concept of the Circle of Justice", *Mamluk Studies Review*, 10 (2006): 1-17

Ergene, Boğaç, *Local Court, Provincial Society and Justice in the Ottoman Empire*, Leiden: Brill, 2003.

Ergene, Boğaç, "Why Did Ümmü Gülsüm Go to Court? Ottoman Legal Practice between History and Anthropology", *Islamic Law and Society*, 17 (2010), 215-244.

Erimtan, Can, *Ottomans Looking West? The Origins of the Tulip Age and its Development in Modern Turkey*, London: Tauris 2008.

Faroqhi, Suraiya, "Political Activity among Ottoman Taxpayers and the Problem of Sultanic Legitimation, (1570–1650)", *Journal of the Economic and Social History of the Orient*, vol. 35 (1992), pp. 1-39.

Finkel, Caroline, *Osman's Dream*, New York: Basic Books, 2006.

Fleischer, Cornell, "Royal Authority, Dynastic Cyclism and "Ibn Khaldunism" in Sixteenth Century Ottoman Letters", in Bruce, B., Lawrence, ed., *Ibn Khaldun and Islamic Ideology*, Leiden: Brill, 1984, pp. 46-68. [circle of justice at pp. 48-50]

Gerber, Haim, *The Social Origins of the Modern Middle East*, Boulder: Lynne Rienner, 1987.

Gerber, Haim, *Economy and Society in an Ottoman City: Bursa, 1600–1700*, Jerusalem: the Hebrew University, 1988.

Gerber, Haim, *State, Society and Law in Islam: Ottoman Law in Comparative Perspective*, Albany: State University of New York Press, 1994.

Gerber, Haim, *State and Society in the Ottoman Empire*, Farnham: Variorum, 2010.

Gerber, Haim, *Islamic Law and Culture, 1600–1840*, Leiden: Brill, 1999.

Gibb, Hamilton, A.R., "Constitutional Organization", in Majid Khadduri and Herbert J.

Liebesny, eds., *Law in the Middle East*, Washington: Middle East Institute, Washington, 1955, pp. 3-27

Gibb, Hamilton, A.R., "Some Considerations on the Sunni Theory of the Caliphate", in idem, *Studies on the Civilization of Islam*, Boston: Beacon Press, 1962, pp. 141-50.

Gibb, Hamilton, A.R., "Lutfi Paşa on the Ottoman Caliphate", *Oriens*, vol. 15 (1962), pp. 287-295.

Gibb, Hamilton, A.R., "Al-Mawardi's Theory of the Caliphate", in idem, *Studies on the Civilization of Islam*, Boston: Beacon Press, pp. 151-165.

Gradeva, Rossitsa, "On Judicial Hierarchy in the Ottoman Empire: The Case of Sofia from the Seventeenth to the beginning of the Eighteenth Century", in Muhammad K. Masud, Rudolph Peters and David S. Powers, eds., *Dispensing Justice in Islam*, Leiden: Brill, 2006, pp. 271-298.

Hallaq, Wael B., *Shari'a*, Cambridge: Cambridge University Press, 2009.

Heyd, Uriel, *Ottoman Documents on Palestine*, Oxford: Oxford University Press, 1960.

Heyd, Uriel, *Studies in Old Ottoman Criminal Law*, Oxford: Oxford University Press, 1973.

Ibn Taimiya, Ahmad b. Abd al-Halim, *Majmuat Fatawa Ibn Taimiyya*, vol. 4, Cairo: Dar al-Rahma li'l-Nashr wa al-tawzi', 1980.

Ilmiye Salnamesi, Istanbul: Matbaa-i Amire, H. 1334.

Imber, Colin, "The Persecution of the Ottoman Shi'ites According to the Muhimme Defterleri, 1565–1585", *Der Islam*, vol. 56 (1979), pp. 245-273.

Imber, Colin, *Ebu's-Su'ud: The Islamic Legal Tradition*, Stanford: Stanford University Press, 1997.

Imber, Colin, *The Ottoman Empire*, Houndmills, Basingstoke: Pelgrave Mcmillan, 2002

Imber, Colin, "Fiqh for Beginners: An Anatolian Text on Jihad", *Journal of Semitic Studies*, Supplement 12 (Studies in Islamic and Middle Eastern Texts and Traditions, in Memory of Norman Calder, eds. G.R. Hawting, J.H. Mojaddedi and A. Samely), pp. 137-148.

Inalcık, Halil, "Turkish and Iranian Political Theories in *Kutadgu Bilig*", in idem, *The Middle East and the Balkans under the Ottoman Empire*, Bloomington: Indiana University Press, 1993.

Inalcık, Halil, *The Ottoman Empire: The Classical Age, 1300–1600*, London: Weidenfeld and Nicolson, 1973.

Inalcık, Halil, "The Ottoman Succession and its Relation to the Turkish Concept of Sovereignty", in *The Middle East and the Balkans under the Ottoman Empire*, Bloomington: Indiana University Press, 1993, pp. 37-94.

Inalcık, Halil, "Comments on 'Sultanism': Max Weber's Typification of the Ottoman Polity", in *Princeton Papers in Near Eastern Studies*, No. 1, 1992, pp.49-72.

Inalcık Halil and Quataert, Donald, eds., *An Economic and Social History of the Ottoman Empire*, Cambridge: Cambridge University Press, 1994.

Itzkowitz, Norman, "Eighteenth Century Ottoman Realities", *Studia Islamica*, vol. 16 (1962), pp. 73-94.

Itzkowitz, Norman, "Men and Ideas in the Eighteenth Century Ottoman Empire", in Thomas Naff and Roger Owen, eds., *Studies in Eighteenth Century Islamic History*, Carbondale and Edwardsville: Southern Illinois University Press, 1977, pp. 15-26.

Itzkowitz, Norman, "Health, Education and Welfare—Ottoman Style", *Midway*, vol. 8 (1968), 59-68.

Jansen, Johannes, J.G., *The Neglected Duty*, New York: Macmillan Press, 1986.

Jennings, Ronald, C., "Kadi, Court, and Legal Procedure in Seventeenth Century Ottoman Kayseri", *Studia* Islamica, No. 48, (1978), pp. 133-172.

Jennings, Ronald, C., "Limitations on the Judicial Powers of the Kadi in 17th Century Ottoman Kayseri", *Studia Islamica*, No. 50 (1979), pp. 151-184.

Jorgen S. Nielsen, *Secular Justice in an Islamic State: Mazalim under the Bahri Mamluks, 662/1264–789/1387*, Istanbul: Dutch Historical-Archeological Institute in Istanbul, 1985.

Joseph, Sabrina, *Islamic Law on Peasant Usufruct in Ottoman Syria*, Leiden: Brill, 2012.

Kafadar, Cemal, *Between Old and New*, Berkeley and Los Angeles: University of California Press, 1986.

Kafadar, Cemal, "Janissaries and Other Riffraff of Ottoman Istanbul: Rebels without a Cause?", in Baki Tezcan and Karl Barbir, eds., *Identity and Identity Formation in the Ottoman World* [see Tezcan].

Kafadar, Cemal, "On the Purity and Corruption of the Janissaries", *Turkish Studies Association Bulletin*, 15 (1991), 273-279.

Keddie, Nikki, R., *Scholars Saints and Sufis*, Berkeley and Los Angeles, University of California Press, 1972.

Köprülü, Fuad, *The Origins of the Ottoman Empire*, Albany: State University of New York Press, 1992.

Kunt, Metin, I., "Kullarin Kullari", *Boğaziçi Üniversitisi Dergisi*, vol. 3 (1975), pp. 27-42.

Kunt, Metin, I., "Sultan, Dynasty and State in the Ottoman Empire: Political Institutions in the Sixteenth Century", in *The Medieval History Journal*, vol. 6 (2003), pp. 217-230.

Lambton, Ann, K.S., "Justice in the Medieval Persian Theory of Kingship", *Studia Islamica*, vol. 17 (1962), pp. 91-119.

Lambton, Ann, K.S., "Changing Concepts of Authority in the Late Ninth/Fifteenth and Early Tenth /Sixteenth Centuries", in Alexander S. Cudsi and Ali E. Hillal Desssouki, eds., *Islam and Power*, London: Croom Helm, 1981, pp. 49-69.

Lambton, Ann, K.S., "The Dilemma of Government in Islamic Persia: the Siyasatnama of Nizam al-Mulk", *Iran*, vol. 22 (1984), pp. 55-66.

Lambton, Ann, K.S., "The Internal Structure of the Saljuk Empire", in J.A. Boyle, ed., *The Cambridge History of Iran*, vol. 5, Cambridge: Cambridge University Press, 1968, pp. 203-282

Lambton, Ann, K.S., "Islamic Mirror of Princes", in idem, *Theory and Practice in Medieval Persian Government*, London: Variorum, 1980, Chapter 6.

Lapidus, Ira M., "The Separation of State and Religion in the Development of Early Islamic Society", *International Journal of Middle East Studies*, 6 (1975), 363-385.

Lewis, Bernard, *The Emergence of Modern Turkey*, Oxford: Oxford University Press, 1968.

Lindner, Rudi, P., *Nomads and Ottomans in Medieval Anatolia*, Bloomington: Research Institute for Inner Asian Studies, Indiana University, 1983.

Lindner, Rudi, P., *Studies in Ottoman Pre-History*, Ann Arbor: University of Michigan Press, 2007.

Lindner, Rudi, P., "How Mongol were the Early Ottomans?" in Reuven Amitai-Preiss and David Morgan, eds., *The Mongol Empire and its Legacy*, Leiden: Brill,1999, pp. 282-289.

Lindner, Rudi, P., "Anatolia, 1300–1453", in Kate Fleet, ed., *The Cambridge History of Turkey*, vol. 1, Cambridge: Cambridge University Press, 2009, 102-137.

Lowry, Heath, *The Nature of the Early Ottoman State*, Albany: State University of New York Press, 2003.

Lowry, Heath, *Defterology Revisited*, Istanbul: Isis Press, 2008.

Majer, Hans, G., ed., *Das Osmanische „Registerbuch der Beschwerden" (Şikayet Defteri), vom Jahre 1675*, Band I, Verlag der Österreichischen Akademie der Wissenschaften, 1984.

Mandaville, Jon, E., "Usurious Piety: The cash Waqf Controversy in the Ottoman Empire", *International Journal of Middle East Studies*, vol. 10 (1979), pp. 289-308.

Manna', ʿAdel, *Liwa' al-Quds fi Awasit al-ʿAhd al-ʿUthmani*, Beirut: mu'assasat al-dirasat al-filistiniyya, 2008.

Marcus, Abraham, *The Middle East on the Eve of Modernity*, New York: Columbia University Press, 1989.

Mastres, Bruce, "Semi-Autonomous Forces in the Arab Provinces", in Suraiya Faroqhi, ed., *Cambridge History of Turkey*, vol. 3, Cambridge: Cambridge University Press, 2006, pp. 186-208.

Masud, Muhammad, K., Brinkley Messick and David S. Powers, "Muftis, Fatwas, and Islamic Legal Interpretation", in Masud, Messick and Powers, eds., *Islamic Legal Interpretation: Muftis and their Fatwas*, Cambridge, Mass.: Harvard University Press, 1996.

Matthee, Rudolph, *Persia in Crisis: Safavid Decline and the Fall of Isfahan*, London: Tauris, 2012.

Melville, Charles, "Anatolia under the Mongols", in Kate Fleet, ed., *The Cambridge History of Turkey*, vol. 1, Cambridge: Cambridge University Press, 2009, pp. 51-101.

Miller, Barnette, *The Palace School of Muhammad the Conqueror*, Cambridge, Mass.: Harvard University Press, 1941.

Morgan, David, *Medieval Persia, 1040–1797*, London and New York: Longman, 1968.

Morgan, David, *The Mongols*, Oxford: Basil Blackwell, 1986.

Morgan, David, and Reuven Amitai, eds., *The Mongol Empire and its Legacy*, Leiden: Brill 1999.

Nagata, Yuzo, "Ayan in Anatolia and the Balkans during the Eighteenth and Nineteenth Centuries", in Antonis Anastasopoulos, ed., *Provincial Elites in the Middle East*, Rethymnon: Crete University Press, 2003, pp. 269-294.

Newman, Andrew, J., *Safavid Iran*, London: Tauris, 2006.

Pamuk, Şevket, *The Ottoman Economy and its Institutions*, Farnham: Ashgate Variorum, 2009

Peirce, Leslie, *Morality Tales: Law and Gender in the Ottoman Court of Aintab*, Berkeley and Los Angeles: California University Press, 2003

Powers, David, S., "On Judicial Review in Islamic Law", in *Islamic Law and Society*, 2 (1992), pp. 315-341.

Raff, Thomas, D., *Remarks on an Anti-Mongol Fatwa by Ibn Taimiya*, Leiden: Brill, 1973.

Repp, Richard, C., *The Mufti of Istanbul*, Oxford, Ithaca Press, 1986.

Repp, Richard, C., "Some Observations on the Development of the Ottoman Learned Hierarchy", in Nikki Keddie, ed., *Scholars, Saints and Sufis*, Berkeley and Los Angeles: University of California Press, 1972, pp. 17-32.

Repp, Richard, C., "Qanun and Shari'a in the Ottoman Context", in Aziz el-Azmeh, ed., *Islamic Law: Social and Historical Contexts*, London: Routledge, 1988, pp.124-145.

Rosen, Lawrence, *The Anthropology of Justice: Law as Culture in Islamic Society*, Cambridge: Cambridge University Press, 1989.

Rubin, Avi, *Ottoman Nizamiye Courts*, Basingstoke: Pelgrave Macmillan, 2011.

Shaw, Stanford, *History of the Ottoman Empire and Modern Turkey*, 2 vols., Cambridge: Cambridge University Press, 1977.

Shinder, Joel, "Early Ottoman Administration in the Wilderness", *International Journal of Middle East Studies*, vol. 9 (1978), pp. 497-517.

Somel, Selçuk, A., *The Modernization of Public Education in the Ottoman Empire*, 1839–1908, Leiden: Brill, 2001.

Stavrides, Theoharis, *The Sultan of Vezirs: The Life and Times of the Ottoman Grand Vezir Mahmud Pasha Angelović*, Leiden: Brill, 2001.

Tezcan, Baki, *The Second Ottoman Empire*, Cambridge: Cambridge University Press, 2010.

Tezcan, Baki and Karl K. Barbir, eds., *Identity and Identity Formation in the Ottoman World*, Madison: The Center of Turkish Studies at the University of Wisconsin, and the University of Wisconsin Press, 2007.

Tezcan, Baki, "The Politics of Early Modern Ottoman Historiography", in Virginia H. Aksan and Daniel Goffman, eds., *The Early Modern Ottomans: Remapping the Empire*, Cambridge: Cambridge University Press, 2007, pp. 167-198.

Togan, Zeki, V., "Economic Conditions in Anatolia in the Mongol Period", *Annales Islamologiques*, vol.25 (1991), pp. 203-239.

Tsafrir, Nurit, "The Beginning of the Hanafi School in Isfahan", *Islamic Law and Society*, 5 (1998), 1-21.

Turner, Bryan, S., *Max Weber and Islam*, London: Routledge and Kegan Paul, 1974.

Ursinus, Michael, *Grievance Administration (Şikayet) in an Ottoman Province*, London: Royal Asiatic Society Books, 2005.

Veinstein, Gilles, "Les Ottomans", in Dominique Iogna-Prat and Gilles Veinstein, eds., *Histoire des Hommes de Dieu dans l'Islam et le Christianisme*, Paris: Flammarion, 2003, pp. 179-202.

Weber, Max, *Economy and Society*, New York: Bedminster Press, 1968.

Winter, Michael, "Ottoman Qadis in Damascus in the 16th–18th Centuries", in Ron Shaham, ed., *Law, Custom and Statute in the Muslim World*, Leiden: Brill, 2006, pp. 87-109.

Winter, Michael, "'Ulama between the State and the Society in Pre-Modern Sunni Islam", in Meir Hatina, ed., *Guardians of Faith in Modern Times: the Ulama in the Middle East*, Boston: Brill, 2008, pp. 21-45.

Winter, Michael, "Inter-Madhhab Competition in Mamluk Damascus: Al-Tarsusi's Counsel for the Turkish Sultans", *Jerusalem Studies in Arabic and Islam*, vol. 25 (2001), pp. 195-211.

Wittek, Paul, *The Rise of the Ottoman Empire*, London: Royal Asiatic Society of Great Britain and Ireland, 1938.

Zarinebaf-Shahr, Fariba, "Ottoman Women and the Tradition of Seeking Justice in the Eighteenth Century", in Madeline C. Zilfi, ed., *Women in the Ottoman Empire: Middle Eastern Women in the Early Modern Era*, Leiden: Brill, 1997, pp. 253-263.

Zilfi, Madeline, C., *The Ottoman Ulema*, Chicago: Bibliotheca Islamica, 1988.

Zilfi, Madeline, C., "'We don't get along': Women and Hul Divorce in the Eighteenth Century", in Zilfi, M.C., ed., *Women in the Ottoman Empire*, Leiden: Brill, 1997, pp. 264-296,

STUDIEN ZUR SPRACHE, GESCHICHTE UND KULTUR DER TÜRKVÖLKER

Barbara Kellner-Heinkele / Elena V. Boykova / Brigitte Heuer (eds.)
Man and Nature in the Altaic World
49th Permanent International Altaistic Conference, Berlin, July 30–August 4, 2006
SSGKT 12. Berlin 2012, Hc. 492 pp., ISBN 978-3-87997-408-5

Tatiana Pang / Simone-Christiane Raschmann / Gerd Winkelhane (eds.)
Unknown Treasures of the Altaic World
in Libraries, Archives and Museums
53rd Permanent International Altaistic Conference, St. Petersburg, July 2010
SSGKT 13. Berlin 2013, Hc. 440 pp., ISBN 978-3-87997-409-2

Barbara Kellner-Heinkele / Simone-Christiane Raschmann /
Claus Schönig / Gerd Winkelhane / Peter Zieme (eds.)
Monumenta et Studia Turcologica
Ausgewählte Schriften von György Hazai
SSGKT 14. Berlin 2013, Hc. 719 pp., ISBN 978-3-87997-412-2

Gundula Salk
Die Morphologie der Sarbagïš
Zur Pragmatik der Konstruktion eines kirgisischen Stammes
SSGKT 15. Berlin 2014, Hc. 333 pp., ISBN 978-3-87997-435-1

Tadeusz Majda
Turkish Religious Texts in Latin Script from 18th Century
South-Eastern Anatolia
Transcriptions, Translations, and a Study of the Language
SSGKT 16. Berlin 2013, Hc. 238 pp., ISBN 978-3-87997-428-3

Hartmut Walravens (ed.)
Giovanni Stary. Selected Manchu Studies
Contributions to History, Literature, and Shamanism of the Manchus
SSGKT 17. Berlin 2013, Hc. 352 pp., ISBN 978-3-87997-425-2

Julian Rentzsch
Modality in the Turkic Languages
Form and Meaning from a Historical and Comparative Perspective
SSGKT 18. Berlin 2015, Hc. 320 pp., ISBN 978-3-87997-447-4

Barbara Kellner-Heinkele / Simone-Christiane Raschmann (eds.)
Opuscula György Hazai Dicata
Beiträge zum Deutsch-Ungarischen Workshop
aus Anlass des 80. Geburtstages von György Hazai
SSGKT 19. Berlin 2015, Hc. 223 pp., Ill., 978-3-87997-434-4

STUDIEN ZUR SPRACHE, GESCHICHTE UND KULTUR DER TÜRKVÖLKER

Nur Sobers-Khan
Slaves Without Shackles
Forced Labour and Manumission in the Galata Court Registers, 1560–1572
SSGKT 20. Berlin 2015, Hc. 384 pp., 978-3-87997-436-8

Irina Nevskaya/Marcel Erdal (eds.)
Interpreting the Turkic Runiform Sources and the Position of the Altai Corpus
SSGKT 21. Berlin 2015, Hc. 224 pp., Ill., 978-3-87997-417-7

Ingeborg Hauenschild / Matthias Kappler / Barbara Kellner-Heinkele (eds.)
Eine hundertblättrige Tulpe – *Bir ṣadbarg lāla*
Festgabe für Claus Schönig
SSGKT 22. Berlin 2016, Hc. 507 pp., 978-3-87997-453-5

Pál Fodor / Pál Ács (eds.)
Identity and Culture in Ottoman Hungary
SSGKT 24. Berlin 2017, Hc. 386 pp., 978-3-87997-460-3

Klára Hegyi
The Ottoman Military Organization in Hungary
Fortresses, Fortress Garrisons and Finances
SSGKT 25. Berlin 2018, Hc. 620 pp., 978-3-87997-467-2

Oliver Corff
60 Years of the Permanent International Altaistic Conference (PIAC) A Bibliography
SSGKT 26. Berlin 2017, Hc. XI+ 130 pp., 978-3-87997-469-6

Elzbieta Swiecicka
The Turkish Dictionary of Giovanni Molino, Born Yovhannês from Ankara
Annotated Legal Documents from the Ottoman Book of Complaints of 1675
SSGKT 23. Berlin 2018, Hc. ca 380 pp., 978-3-87997-432-0

KS
Klaus Schwarz Verlag • Berlin
Klaus Schwarz Verlag GmbH • Fidicinstr. 29 • D–10965 Berlin
Tel +49-30-916 82 749 / 751 • Fax +49-30-322 51 83
www.klaus-schwarz-verlag.com eMail: info@klaus-schwarz-verlag.com

Bei Fragen zur Produktsicherheit wenden Sie sich bitte an:
If you have any questions regarding product safety,
please contact:

Walter de Gruyter GmbH
Genthiner Straße 13
10785 Berlin
productsafety@degruyterbrill.com